The

Book

Outpouring of the Soul

Collected and constituted addressing the old holy way, that every person, in all that transpires with him, and all that he is lacking, be it physical needs or in the service of Hashem, for all of them he should pour out his heart and his soul like water directly before the countenance of Hashem, mercifully and entreatingly, as is explained in the introduction and foreword of the book, from the Torah, Prophets, Scriptures, Talmud, Medrashim, and Holy Zohar, and inside the book, from the books **"Likutay Moharan"** (A Collection of Our Master and Leader Rabbi Nachman, two volumes), and the books **"Likutay Halachos"** (A Collection of Laws) from his holy disciple, the righteous of blessed memory, who (plural) renewed this old way. For he (Rabbi Nachman) imparted of his splendor upon him (Rabbi Nussun) to inoculate his holy *daas* (realization of knowledge) in all those that fall and descend, so that they strengthen themselves constantly with prayer and entreaty, as is explained in Likutay (Moharan) volume 2, teaching 7, regarding the disciple who is the aspect of Yehoashua (-Joshua) – acronym (Isaiah 26:18): **Yi**koomoon (they will rise) **Hu**keetzoo (they will awaken) **Vi**rahninoo (and they will sing praise; the Vuv in Hebrew can be used as a vowel, as in "oa") **Sh**oachnay (the dwellers of the) **U**far (earth; i.e. the dead), see there what is explained regarding the Rav and the disciple whom are the aspect of Moses and Joshua.

Na Nach Nachma Nachman MeUman

www.BreslovBooks.com
All of Rebbe Nachman's books
at non-profit prices and for free download
"MAL'E VEGADISH" Foundation +972-52-888-7039

All inquiries regarding this book or
Rabbi Nachman of Breslov can be directed to:
naanaach@gmail.com
naanaach.blogspot.com
youtube.com/ancientlyoung

2016   -   התשע"ו

Table of Contents

Outpouring of the Soul was compiled by Rabbi Moshe Yehoshua Bizshilianski, better known as Reb Alter Teplicker (-of Teplick), of blessed memory, may the Holy Merciful One avenge his blood. It was printed first in Jerusalem in the year 5664 by Rabbi Yisroel Karduner o.b.m., and subsequently in the year 5673 in the city of Pramful. It is a cornerstone of the holy ways of Breslov, and many great souls have drawn close to Breslov and to Hashem Yisburach thanks to this holy work.

Na Nach Nachma Nachman MeUman

This page is dedicated

in loving memory

of

my grandparents:

Yaakov Tzvi and Chasha Hochman

(24 Cheshvon, 5753; 11 Ellul, 5756)

Moshe Menachem Mendel and Shprintza Weinberg

(22 Tishray 5763; 23 Eyar 5752)

May Hashem Yisburach bless profusely their offspring,

my distinguished beloved parents

Rabbi Moshe and Chava Bracha Hochman

and all my siblings:

Rena, Chaya Leah, Ayala Hinda, Sara Atara, Yitzchok Matisyahu, Aviva Rochel, Devora, Bas Sheva Rosa, Yosef Noach, Rivka Rus, Yisroel Meir.

Na Nach Nachma Nachman MeUman!

Introduction

Who is the man who desires life (Psalms 34:13), who truly has pity on his soul, who desires to merit the devotion of prayer, through which one receives the primary vitality, as it says (Psalms 42:9), 'prayer to the G-d [of/is] my life', and through which life is expended to all the worlds, as brought down in Likutay Moharan (vol. 1, Torah 9), he will put his heart to the matters which have been collected and brought in this book. They will address the eminence of prayer and *hisbodidus* (being alone in communion with Hashem) in a designated place, to pour out his soul and heart like water there, before the face of Hashem, and to beseech of Him everything that may be deficient by a person, be it his physical needs, and be it regarding his service of Hashem, and only through this can he have deliverance in *every* matter. For this holy way is the old way in which our forefathers, and our prophets, and our holy rabbis o.b.m. traversed from time immemorial. As we find by Adam HuRishon (the first) of whom the verse says (Genesis 2:5), "And all the vegetation of the field had yet to be in the land, for rain was not forthcoming etc. and man was not etc.," and Rashi explains, "and on the third day, on which it is written, 'The land should produce', they did not come out – they only stood up to the entrance of the ground... [until] Adam HuRishon came ... and prayed for them (the rain), and they came down, and the trees and grasses burgeoned."

And so with Noah, it is brought in the Zohar Chadash (Torah Portion of Noah), "Our Rabbis learned; What did the Holy One Blessed He answer Noah when he left the ark

5

and saw the whole world destroyed and began to cry over it, and said, 'Master of the World, You are called Merciful, You should have had mercy on Your creations'? The Holy One Blessed He answered, 'Foolish shepherd! Now you say this?! And not at the time when I told you, 'for you I have seen righteous before me in this generation (Genesis 7:1), and I am hereby bringing a flood of water etc. (Genesis 6:17)', all that I told you, in order that you should request mercy on the world, and now that the world is destroyed you open your mouth to speak before me in supplication and entreaty.' When Noah saw this, he brought burnt (*oaloas*) offerings and (other) offerings, and he rose up and prayed before Him etc. 'And Hashem smelled the pleasant fragrance (Genesis 8:21)', this is the fragrance of his prayer etc.." see there.

And so we find by Abraham, when the Holy One Blessed He said to Abraham, "The screaming of Sodom and Gomorrah are great (Genesis 18:20)," immediately (verse 23), "And Abraham drew close and he said etc.," and he spoke at length opposite the Holy One Blessed He in his prayer (verses 24 & 28), "Perhaps there are fifty righteous etc., perhaps there is missing etc.." And also our Sages o.b.m. expounded (Talmud Tractate Brachos 26b) on the verse (Genesis 19:27), "And Abraham got up early in the morning to the place where he stood there," that he established the morning prayer (*shacharis*). And so the Holy One Blessed He said to Avimelech (Genesis 20:7), "Return the man's wife, for he is a prophet and he will pray for you etc. (verse 17) and Abraham prayed to G-d." And our Sages o.b.m. said in the Medrash Rabba there (Portion of Va'yaira 52:13), since our father Abraham prayed, this knot (that Hashem brought upon Avimelech and his household) was untied.

And so we find by Eliezer his slave; when he went to search for the soulmate of Isaac his son, he spoke out his words before Him Blessed He in his prayer (Genesis 24:12), "And he said, 'Hashem, G-d of my master Abraham, bring about before me today, and do kindness etc.'." And our Sages o.b.m. expounded in the Medrash Rabba there (Portion of Cha'yay Sura 60:2) that he said, "Master of the World, You began – finish." That is, Abraham accomplished with his prayer and his request, that You give him Isaac when he was one hundred years old, finish this kindness with him that he should find the soulmate for his son.

And so we find by Isaac (Genesis 24:63), "And Isaac went out to pray (/converse) in the field," and our Sages o.b.m. expounded (Talmud Tractate Brachos 26b), that he established the afternoon prayer (*mincha*). And they said there in the Medrash Rabba (Portion of Cha'yay Sura 60:15), Rebecca saw that his hand was outstretched in prayer, she said, "certainly he is a great man". Immediately she inquired about him (Genesis 24:65), "Who is this man who is going in the field towards us?" And afterwards, when he saw Rebecca barren, it is written (Genesis 25:21), "And Isaac beseeched Hashem opposite his wife," and our Sages o.b.m. expounded (Beraishis Rabba 63:5), that he poured out prayers with wealth (-abundance. The word for prayer here 'ettehr' is very similar to 'oashehr' – wealth); another approach expounded: that he reversed the decree (that Rebecca should be barren) with his prayers (asra – like the word for prayer - being a tool which turns things over).

And so we find by Jacob it is written (Genesis 28:11), "And he came to (*vayifga* - lit. hit, also one of the ten words for prayer) the place (Hashem is called the place, because all of space exists in Him)," and our Sages o.b.m. expounded (Talmud Tractate Brachos 26b), that he established the evening prayer (*arvis*), and he expressed his words before Hashem Yisburach, and said (Genesis 29:20), "If G-d will be with me, and protect me etc. and give me bread to eat and clothing to wear etc.." And our Sages o.b.m. said in Medrash Rabba there (70:6; Sefer Hameedos, hisbodidus 2:1), the Holy One Blessed He took the words of the forefathers and made them the key for the redemption of the children. And they said further in Medrash Rabba (Vayaitzay 74:11), all the fourteen years that Jacob was in the house of Lavan, he did not sleep at night, and what was he saying? The fifteen Songs of Ascent (*Shir LaMaaloas*) of the Psalms (Chapters 120-134). Because Jacob engaged overly in this, to express his words before Him Blessed He every night, as is brought down (see Beraishis Rabba 68:14). And also when he sent the messengers to Esau, he said before Him Blessed He (Genesis 32:12, and see Zohar vol. 1 pg. 168:), "Save me now (/please) from the hand of my brother etc.."

And so all the holy mothers engaged in prayer and entreaty. And they said in the Medrash (Beraishis Rabba 45:5): Why were the mothers barren? Because the Holy One Blessed He desires their prayer. And our Sages o.b.m. said (ibid 41:2) regarding Sara, when Sara was taken to the house of Avimelech, that whole night she was flat on her face

Introduction

saying, "Master of the World etc.." And by Rebecca it is written (Genesis 25:21), "opposite his wife," and our Sages o.b.m. expounded (Rashi), this (he) stood in this corner and prayed, and this (she) stood in this (other) corner and prayed. And by Rachel we find that she said (Genesis 30:6), "G-d has judged me and has also listened to my calling etc.. (verse 8) I have stubbornly persisted supplicating G-d etc.," and Rashi explains, 'requests that are dear before Him etc.'. And so it is written of her (verse 22), "And G-d listened to her, and He opened her womb." And further it is written of her (Jeremiah 31:14), "Rachel cries over her children etc.." And by Leah it is written (Genesis 29:17), "And Leah's eyes were tender," and our Sages o.b.m. expounded (Tractate Buva Basra 123a, Medrash Saichel Tov, Vayaitzay 29:47), that she would cry and pray so that she would not fall into the lot of Esau.

And so all the tribes (- sons of Jacob, all of them) went in this way, as is brought down (see Rabbainu Bachya, Portion of Vayaitzay on the verse, and the men are shepherds of sheep). And when Jacob sent Benjamin with them to Josef, our Sages o.b.m. said (Beraishis Rabba end of 91), Jacob said to them, 'Here is the money, and here is the gift, and here is your brother etc..' They said to him, 'we need your prayer.' He said to them, 'if you need my prayer: G-d Almighty (*E"l Shad"ai*) should give you mercy etc.. He who in the future is going to say, enough, to my suffering, He shall (already) say, enough, to my suffering.' And so too when Josef was in jail, he prayed profusely before Hashem Yisburach, as we say in the prayers (*Slichos* – penitential prayers), "He Who answered Josef in jail, He should (/will) answer us." And so when Josef took Benjamin, it is written (Genesis 44:18),

"And Judah drew close to him," and our Sages o.b.m. expounded (Beraishis Rabba 49:13), we find drawing close in reference to prayer.

And so our fathers, when they were in Egypt, it is written (Exodus 2:23), "And it was in those many days, and the Children of Israel sighed from the work, and they screamed, and their outcry went up to G-d." And so too on the sea, it is written (Exodus 14:10), "And the Children of Israel screamed to Hashem," and they said in Medrash Raba (Song of Songs 2:2), "My dove in the crevices of the boulder etc. let me hear your calling (Song of Songs 2:14)," it doesn't say 'let me hear a call', rather, 'let me hear your call' – that same call that I already heard in Egypt, for the Holy One Blessed He desires the prayers of Israel etc., see there.

And so Moshe Rabbainu (our Leader Moses) r.i.p., it is known in the words of our Sages o.b.m., how much he engaged all his life in prayer and entreaty, for himself and for Israel. They sinned with the calf – "And Moshe beseeched etc. (Exodus 32:11)," and it is written (Deuteronomy 9:18), "and I fell before Hashem forty days etc.." And in Medrash Rabba (Shemos – Portion of Ki Seesa 43:3) they expounded on the verse "And Moshe beseeched," that the Holy One Blessed He taught him how to pray before Him, and He said to him, "Say like this, 'make the bitter, sweet' etc.," Moshe said before the Holy One Blessed He, "Did You not say to me in Murra, to pray and say, 'make the bitter, sweet'? So even now sweeten (lighten – *chal*, same root as 'beseech') the bitterness of Israel and heal them," this is: "And Moshe *beseeched* [-sweetened]." And

10

it is written in Zohar Chadash (Portion of Noah), What is *'va'yichal'* (and he beseeched)? It teaches us that he prayed for them until he was seized with trepidation (*-chalchallu* – same root word as beseech). The Rabbis said, until he gave his soul for them, from this world and from the coming world, as it says (Exodus 32:32), "If not (-no pardon is granted to Israel), erase me now (/please)." [t.n. it should be noted that these words, when read from left to right, spell out, "I am Nachman," and the acronym is 'MeUman' – from Uman, "erase <*michainey*>"- the Arizal says can be rearranged to spell "waters of Noah" <may-Noach>, because Noach didn't save his generation, whereas Moses did, and now Rabbi Nachman is saving the entire world]. And also look in Tractate Brachos (pg. 32a) [That you have no one greater in good deeds than Moshe Rabbainu r.i.p., and he wasn't answered except through prayer (this is explained in Adir BaMurom pg. 167)]. [Rashi on Numbers 16:4] They sinned with the calf – "and Moshe beseeched (Exodus 32:11)," with the complainers (Numbers 11) – "And Moshe screamed etc. (ibid verse 2)," etc.. And so with Miriam when she got leprosy, it is written (Numbers 12:13), "And Moshe screamed to Hashem, 'G-d please heal her now'." And so when it was decreed on him that he won't enter the land (of Israel), it is written (Deuteronomy 4:23), "And I entreated Hashem," and our Sages o.b.m. said in Medrash Rabba (Devorim 11:9), that he prayed 515 prayers like the numerical value of the word *'vu-eschanan'* (and I beseeched). And it is brought down (see Nachal Kidumum, Vu'eschanan 25) that if he would have prayed one more prayer, he would have been answered. And see there in the Medrash how many prayers Moshe prayed on the day of his passing. And so he prayed for Joshua, "Y-ah (one of the Names of G-d) should save you from the scheme of the spies" (Tractate Sotah 34b).

And so Caleb, when he saw that Moshe didn't pray for him, he went and prostrated himself on the graves of the forefathers to pray, that he shouldn't be tested with the scheme of the spies (Zohar, Leviticus 158b).

And so Aaron, at the time of the plague with the story of Korach, "And he took the pan (Numbers 17:12)," And he prayed copiously then before Hashem Yisburach, as we mention in our prayers (*Slichos*), He Who answered Aaron with the pan etc..

And so Pinchus when he got up from the midst of the assembly (Numbers 25:7), it is written (Psalms 106:11), "And Pinchus stood and prayed."

And so Joshua, when the inhabitants of Eye smote Israel, "And Joshua tore his robes and he fell on his face on the ground etc. and he said, 'alas Hashem G-d etc. (Joshua 7:6)."

And so in the days of the Judges (*Shoaftim*), when Israel sinned, "And G-d was enraged with Israel, and gave them into the hand of their enemies (Judges 2:14 and other similar verses)," what did the Children of Israel do? "And they screamed to Hashem (Judges 3:9, 15 and other similar verses)," until He had mercy on them and empowered a Judge (*shoafait*) over them and saved them, and so it was with each and every Judge.

And so with Samson the *Geebor* (-mighty), when the Philistines gouged out his eyes, and bound him in copper chains, "And Samson called to Hashem, remember now

(/please) and give me strength just this time etc. (Judges 15:28)."

And so Chana, when Hashem closed her womb, "and she prayed to Hashem, and she would cry passionately etc. and it was when she had prayed copiously (Samuel I:1:10)," and our Sages o.b.m. expounded in the Medrash (Medrash Samuel 2:20), from here (it is learned), that whomsoever prays copiously, he is answered. And so they said in Tractate Yoomu (pg. 29a), tzaddikim, whenever they pray copiously, their prayers are answered. And so it is written by Chana (Samuel I·1·15), "and I poured out my soul before Hashem etc. (verse 27) regarding this boy I prayed etc. (ibid 2:1) and Chana prayed and she said etc.." And our Sages o.b.m. expounded (Medrash Samuel 4:1), she began expressing herself with her convictions (to Hashem).

And so in the days of the Prophet Samuel, when the Philistines were overpowering Israel, "And Samuel said, gather all of Israel to Mitzpah and I will pray for you to Hashem. And they gathered at Mitzpah and they drew water and they poured it before Hashem (Samuel 1:7:5)." And the commentaries (Rashi in the name of Targum Yonasun) explained that they poured our their hearts like water. "And Samuel screamed to Hashem on behalf of Israel, and Hashem answered him (ibid verse 9)."

And so all the prophets engaged abundantly in prayer, like we find by Elijah who said (Kings 1:17:1), "As G-d Lives, Whom I stood before Him," and the commentaries (Metzudas Duvid) explained, Whom I am accustomed to stand before Him in prayer. And so too when the son of the (woman of) Tzorfas died, it is written (Kings I:17:21-22), "And he called to Hashem and he said, 'Hashem my G-d, return now (/please) the soul of the child. And Hashem listened to Elijah's call." And so too at Mount Carmel, when he gathered all of Israel and the prophets of Baal, and he wanted to reveal to them that G-d's Presence is in Israel, it is written (Kings I:18:36-37), "And Elijah the Prophet drew near, and he said, 'Hashem, G-d of Abraham, Isaac, and Israel, today it will be known that You are G-d etc., answer me Hashem, answer me!" And so with all the miracles performed by Elisha, our Sages o.b.m. said (Tractate Megila 27a), and Elisha when he performed (miracles), he performed (them) with prayer. And so with the Prophet Jonah it is written (Jonah 2:2), "And Jonah prayed from the belly of the fish etc.." And so with Habakkuk it is written (Habakkuk 3:1; in the Book of Character, Rabbi Nachman says that someone who is confused should say this regularly), "A prayer of Habakkuk the Prophet on errors etc.." And so with all the prophets, our Sages o.b.m. expounded in Medrash Rabba (Yalkut, Vayairu 88), "and the prayers of the tzaddikim He listens (Proverbs 15:29)," these are the prophets of Israel. And look at Jeremiah (27:18), "And if they are prophets etc. they should pray to Hashem of Hosts."

And so with King David r.i.p., he overly engaged his whole life in prayer, and supplication, and screaming, and crying to the Holy One Blessed He, and to express his words before Hashem Yisburach, until he merited to compose from this, the holy Book of Psalms, which is completely full of screaming and crying out to Hashem Yisburach. And our Sages o.b.m. expounded in Zohar Chadash (Portion of Noah), "And he sent the raven (Genesis 8:7)," this is David

who comes from Judah, who said, "I will guarantee (*uraiv* –
same root at raven) him," who was always calling out to
Hashem Yisburach like a raven etc.." Another
interpretation: that he used to go about in the mountains (to
do hisbodidus there, and express his words before Him Blessed
He) like a raven, as it is written (Samuel II:15:30), "And
David was going up the ascent of Mount Olives, ascending
and crying, and his head wrapped up etc.."

And so too Solomon his son, when he built the Temple, it
is written (Kings I:8:22), "And Solomon stood before the
alter of Hashem, opposite the entire congregation of Israel,
and he spread out his hands to the sky," see there his whole
prayer at length.

And so Chizkiya King of Judah in his sickness, it is written
of him (Isaiah 38:2), "And Chizkiya turned his face to the
wall and he prayed etc.."

And so with Daniel, when he needed to tell
Nebuchadnezzar the interpretation of the dream, "Then
Daniel went to his house (to do hisbodidus and supplicate
Hashem – Metzudas Duvid), and told the matter to Chanania,
Mishu'el, and Azaria. To pray for mercy from before the G-
d of the Heavens regarding revealing this secret etc. (Daniel
2:17-18)." And when King Dar'yuvesh decreed that anyone
who supplicates any G-d or any man in the next thirty days,
will be thrown to the lions' den (Daniel 6:8), it is written
there (verse 11), "And Daniel went up to his house, and the
windows were open in his attic opposite Jerusalem, and
three times a day … and prayed and expressed gratitude
before his G-d." And also when he was thrown to the lions'
den, he prayed copiously to Hashem Yisburach, as we say

in our prayers (Slichos), "He Who answered Daniel in the lions' den etc.." And so he cried out and screamed before Hashem Yisburach on the destruction of Jerusalem, as it is written (Daniel 9:3), "And I put my face to Hashem the G-d, to ask, pray, and supplicate, with fasting, and sack, and ashes. (verse 4) And I prayed to Hashem my G-d, and I confessed (the sins of my nation), and I said, 'Please Hashem etc.. (verse 18) My G-d, incline Your ears and hear etc.. (verse 20) And I continued to speak in prayer etc.." see there his entire prayer at length.

And so Chanania, Mishu'el, and Azaria, when they were thrown into the fiery forge, it is written in the Zohar (Vayikra 57a); What saved them? On account of their prayer before the Holy One Blessed He etc. see there. And regarding this we pray (*Slichos*): He Who answered Chanania, Mishu'el, and Azaria inside the fiery forge, He should answer us.

And so with Ezra, it is written (Ezra 8:21-23), "And I proclaimed a fast there by the river etc. to request of Him a straight way etc. and we fasted, and we beseeched for our G-d etc. and He heeded us. And so when the Jews married gentile women, Ezra screamed bitterly over this, "I am embarrassed and ashamed my G-d to lift my face to You etc." see Ezra, chapter 9, his entire prayer at length.

And so *Mordechai* and Esther in the capitol city Shushan, they screamed and prayed copiously to Hashem Yisburach, as is explicated in *Megilas Esther*, and in Medrash Esther, and in the Second Translation (to Esther).

And so afterwards the *Anshei Kinnesses HaGedola* (Men of the Great Assembly) came and set down for us all the prayers, that every person should pray to Hashem Yisburach, in the morning prayer (Shacharis), in Mussaf (extra prayer of the holidays), in Mincha (afternoon prayer), and *Arvis* (evening prayer). And so all our holy Sages o.b.m., the *Tana'im* (Sages of the Mishna), and the *Amoaru'im* (Sages of the Talmud), exceeded profusely to pray before Hashem Yisburach, as is explicated in Tractate Brachos (16b-17a), prayers of the *Tana'im* which they arranged for themselves to pray after the prayer of the Eighteen Benedictions (*Shmoneh Esray*) And so they set down for us many specific prayer for every type of matter, like the prayer for the wayfarer (*Tifeelas Hadderech*) (Brachos 29b). And so they instituted (Tractate Taanis 8b); When a person enters to measure his granary, he should say, 'May it be the will before You Hashem our G-d that You send blessing upon this heap'. And when a person enters a bathhouse he should say, 'May it be the will before You, that you bring me in peacefully, and bring me out, and save me from this fire and what is similar to it in the future world' (Tractate Brachos 60a). And so when a person enters to let blood, he should say, 'May it be the will before You that this enterprise be a healing for me etc.' (ibid). And so when a person enters a city, he should say, 'May it be the will before You, that You bring me into this city peacefully' (ibid). And they made a resolution and said: 'If only a person were to pray the whole entire day' (Brachos 21a – t.n. the very resolution in form of prayer!).

And so too afterwards many tzaddikim came and engaged profusely in prayer, and they composed prayers and many *pi'yutim* (liturgical poetry), until the holy Arizal *za.tza.l.* (mention of the tzaddik for blessing) and his holy students came, and they composed for us as well, many prayers, like the book "Shaarei Tzion" (Gates of Zion) etc.. And afterwards the holy Baal Shem Tov *za.tza.l.* (mention of the tzaddik for blessing) came and engaged profusely in hisbodidus and seclusion, and he revealed the utter eminence of prayer, as is known from the holy books which were constituted upon the foundation of the wisdom of the holy Baal Shem Tov *za.tza.l.*.

And look in the book "Soor MayRah ViAssay Tov" (Steer Away From Evil and Do Good, part Do Good page 32b) of the rav the tzaddik Rabbi Tzvi of Ziditchov, who wrote there; You do not have a more choice time for hisbodidus, only this hour, after midnight, to stand and beseech for one's wretched soul, which on account of its sins has been distanced from the source of life. And he should review in this hour everything that transpired, and he should speak from his heart like a slave before his master, with outspread hands and feet, with soft words said like a son before his father, and pray in whatever language spoken in the native tongue, which he speaks its language and hears, so that he can speak fluently from a grieving heart, which is in pain from all its sins and transgressions, and he should request pardon and forgiveness. Like the words of the Zohar (Vayikra 122a); From when the temple was destroyed, we have not been left with anything other than confession alone. And he should request from his G-d that He should help him in His service and to fear Him with a full heart, and he should go at this at length, and certainly this is more choice than all the fasting etc., see there. And it is brought down there as well, in the name of the book Beis Midos (House of Traits), a handwritten manuscript attributed to the Arizal *zatza"l*, that a person needs to do hisbodidus between him and his Maker, and speak tenderly to the Blessed G-d, like a slave speaks to his master and a son with his father, end quotation.

And so too all the students of the holy Baal Shem Tov *zatza"l* went in this way, until his (great) grandson came, he is our Master, Our Leader, and our Holy Rabbi, the light of lights, the hidden esoteric light, the rav Rabbi Nachman, the mention of the holy tzadik for blessing, from Breslov, author of the books "Likutay Moharan" and other books, and he renewed this holy old way which our fathers from time immemorial traversed, and he engaged copiously in prayer, and entreaty, and hisbodidus in the fields and forests, as it will be told further on of his holy practices, see there. And he said that his entire enterprise is prayer (Likutay Moharan II:93). And he enlightened our eyes in our utter darkness, to teach us proper (straight) ways how to practice this. And he said to his men (on the first night of Shavuos, Saturday Night 5569 – Life of Rabbi Nachman 59, also see there 264): Give your hearts to me and I will lead you on a new path, which is the old path which our forefathers traversed from time immemorial; and he revealed to us that there is no remedy to be saved from the utter overwhelming (bad) inclination, that always quests and desires to cause man to stumble (-violate the Torah), except through hisbodidus, which every person wherever he may be, whenever, and whatever level he may be, as each one knows the wounds of his heart and the pains of his soul, should set for himself a special place to pour out his heart there before Him Blessed He about everything that he is going through, in our vernacular, and to request of Him that He should draw him close to His service Blessed his, and He should help him so that he is not ensnared in the net of the Accuser, Heaven forbid. And even if Heaven forbid he has already stumbled in what he violated, if he doesn't despair of himself from screaming and praying to Hashem Yisburach, he will certainly merit to rise from his fall. And he said in this language: "Even (*afeelloo*) when one falls (*az men falt*) into a mire (*in ablutteh arrayn*) one screams and screams and screams (*shrayt men un men shrayt un men shrayt*)." And so he spoke more of this in many many verbiages.

And so also for all of man's physical necessities, he warned strongly that a person should pray for everything that he is deficient, whether it be a big thing or a little thing, as this is explicated in the book Likutay Moharan (14:11) on the verse (Psalms 145:9) "Hashem is good to all," and he explained there, Hashem is good for everything, whether it be healing or livelihood and the likes. When one believes this, certainly his main endeavor will be after the Holy One Blessed He (i.e. just to pray to Him Blessed He for each and everything), and he will not pursue many contrivances, for they are not helpful at all; and the infinitesimal that are helpful, he doesn't know from them, and can't find them. But to call out to the Holy One Blessed He, this is good and beneficial for everything in the world, and this can be found always, for He Blessed He is always present, see there.

And he said that a person has to receive all his bounty and needs just through prayer, and for everything, whether a big thing or a small thing, he should pray to Hashem Yisburach, for otherwise, even though Hashem Yisburach gives him everything he needs, he is like an animal, which Hashem Yisburach also gives it all its needs without prayer. And especially in the matter of the service of Hashem, certainly there is no recourse, just prayer. And he said that prayer is a general remedy (/advice) and root for all the advice (/remedies) that are brought down in his holy books. For while indeed his holy books are full of awesome and wondrous remedies (/advice) for each and every matter in the service of Hashem, Divine advice which stand forever, however the remedies themselves are very hard to fulfill. And above all of them, the main remedy (/advice) is just prayer and hisbodidus. And he said, from small to big, it is impossible to be a Jewish man except through hisbodidus.

He also strengthened us very much, that a person should not lose heart at all when he sees sometimes that his heart has become sealed due to the great pressure and suffering which he is undergoing physically and spiritually, or because he is arduously caught up in business, and he is unable to speak out what is with his heart, for it is very precious in the eyes of Hashem Yisburach each and every utterance that a person merits to speak before Him Blessed He from the midst of his utter stress and poverty, physically and spiritually. And he said: even when a person does not merit to speak before Him Blessed He but one word, and even if it is only, "Master of the World," alone, even this is very precious by Him Blessed He. And he taught us to know, that when a person sees that he is very far from Hashem Yisburach, and his heart is very sealed, and he can't open him mouth, the person must search in himself for

21

good points which are still to be found in him, and he should enliven himself with them, and thank Hashem Yisburach for them, and through this he will open his mouth, and he will be able to pray and express his words before Him Blessed He properly, as is explicated in Likutay Moharan, vol. one, Torah 282, on the verse (Psalms 104:33, 146:2), "I will sing to my G-d with all I have (/with the very little bit of me left)", see there.

And so it is with the physical as well, when a person undergoes hardships and various suffering, and they seal his heart to the extent that it is difficult and cumbersome for him even to pray and express his words before Hashem Yisburach, specifically then, the person needs to search and find the latitude that Hashem Yisburach broadens for him in the midst of his duress, and the favors He did for him until now, and to thank Hashem Yisburach for them, and through this certainly his heart will open and he will be able to pray and scream to Hashem Yisburach as befitting. And see Likutay Halachos, the laws of crossbreeding animals (4:4-6), that this is the aspect that a person should always (Brachos 54a) give thanks for the past, and through this he will be able to - scream out for the future. The aspect of (Psalms 116:17), "To You I will offer up a thanksgiving offering, and in the name of Hashem I will call." And he explains with this what is written by David, (Psalms 3), "A song of David when he ran from before Avsholom his son. Hashem how abundant are my hardships etc.," because through this that he began to sing the song and give thanks to Hashem Yisburach for what Avsholom his son was chasing after him, for the common son has mercy on his father (Brachos 7b, thus if he had to be chased, best that it should be by his son), through this he was able to scream properly afterwards, "Hashem how abundant are my hardships," and without this remedy it would have been hard for him then to scream to Hashem Yisburach properly, see there. And see further on inside this book (item #49).

And he said that the main weapon of the Jewish man, to defeat his (evil) inclination, is just prayer and hisbodidus. And through each and every utterance of prayer and hisbodidus his victory is plentiful, as all this can be understood from Likutay Moharan (vol. 1, Torah 2). And even though that since, "there is not a moment without disaster <*pegga*>" (Shlu, entry of Yom Kippur, in Tochachas Chaim Derech Mussar), certainly this would necessitate to fulfill, "there is no moment without prayer <*pegga*> and beseeching," even still, also the few words that a person merits to speak before Him, from the thickness of his utter misery and poverty, any time of the day, and he raises his eyes to the Heaven, and spreads his hands before Him Blessed He, this also is extremely precious by Him Blessed He, as this is explicated also in the holy Zohar (Vayikra 195a, and see Shemos 86b) on the verse (Psalms 102:1), "A prayer of the pauper when he is overwhelmed," how enormously precious the prayer of the pauper is by Hashem Yisburach, even a pauper who prays for his physical needs, for his lack of livelihood and the like, see there.

And look in Likutay Halachos, the laws of the prayer of Mincha, law seven (items 40 and 44), where it is explicated that all the more so, and all the more so, when a person feels his poverty and his lowliness from his bad conduct, and especially when there falls upon a person two types of poverty; that he is bereft of *da'as* (realization of knowledge) due to his innumerous grave failures, and also his being poor and very much lacking sustenance, and the poverty and lack of sustenance severely confuses him. When he appraises his ways, and gives heart to the hints and proclamations which Hashem Yisburach calls out to him every day, and he sees that he has no hope, for from right and from left he has no support; his behavior is very degenerate, and his livelihood scrimpy, and his wife and children scream for bread, and sustenance, and clothing, and other basic necessary essentials, and when he overcomes all this, and pours out his words before Hashem Yisburach, from the midst of his poverty and misery, in the aspect of (Psalms 102), "A prayer of the pauper when he is overwhelmed etc.," this is extremely precious by Hashem Yisburach, as it is written (Psalms 22:25), "for He does not despise and does not detest the screaming (/humbling) of the pauper, and did not hide His face from him, and when he cries out to Him, He hears." From here it can be gleaned that it would have been appropriate to despise him, and detest him, and to hide His face from him, just that His mercy is abundant, and He does not despise him, and He does not detest him etc.. See there his words which are sweeter than honey, and understand for your own soul, how much a person needs to strengthen himself in this matter of hisbodidus and conversation between himself and his Creator, through everything that he undergoes.

And one time he said that it is possible to discern on someone if he does hisbodidus, that is, because through this his face reveals abashment and great fear from Hashem Yisburach. And not for not does the liturgist describe the visage of the high priest when he came out from the holy of holies: "Like someone sitting in a hidden place to entreat the face of a king, (such was) the visage of the priest." And from all this understand for your own soul the eminence of one who does hisbodidus and one who sits in a hidden place to pour out his heart and soul like water directly before the face of Hashem.

He also revealed to us that the main time for this is at night, that then – at night, a person should do hisbodidus between himself and his Creator, and he should express before Hashem Yisborach his whole heart, and he should search out the good spirit, that is the good points that he still has in him, and select them from the midst of the bad spirit, and through this he will always remember his ultimate purpose is for the future world, as is explicated in Likutay Moharan, vol. 1, Torah 54 (end of 6) on the verse (Psalms 77:7), "I remember my melody at night, with my heart I converse, and search my spirit (/my spirit searches)," see there.

And so he warned strongly to engage a lot in the recital of Psalms and other entreaties, and supplications, and to find oneself in all the chapters of Psalms that he recites, for the Book of Psalms was founded only on the matter of the war against the (evil) inclination, and it primarily addresses the concerns of each one of Israel, that he should be saved from the war of the evil inclination and its legions, for they are the main enemies and adversaries (lit. haters) of a person, that desire to bring him down to the depth of Scheol (-hell) Heaven forbid.

And so he warned strongly to make from the torahs (-holy teachings), prayers, that is, whatever (lit. wherever) a person is learning, he should begin to examine himself, how far he is from all this due to his bad conduct, and through this he should pour out his heart before Him Blessed He, and through this he should express the wounds of his heart and the pains of his soul at that time, from everything that he is undergoing. And he said that from this, great delights are made. And he said that there never were such delights before Hashem Yisburach like these delights which are made through these prayers, which are made from the torahs, and certainly he will merit through this to complete repentance and the eternal life. And so he said once to his student the rav, the tzaddik, the holy Rabbi Nussun mention of the tzaddik for blessing, the author of the book Likutay Halachos mentioned above, at the beginning of his drawing close to him (Rabbi Nachman) o.b.m., at the occasion when he (Rabbi Nussun) once entered by him alone, and he (Rabbi Nussun) spilled out his whole heart before him, and our master, leader, and rabbi o.b.m. commanded him then (to take upon himself) a few practices, and he spoke over with him many things which restore the soul, to give him life and strengthen him in the service of Hashem, and in the midst of these words, our master, teacher, and rabbi, mention of the tzaddik for blessing, took him with his holy hand around his (R' Nussun's) shoulders, and said to him these words, "*Un veyetur* (and further) *iz* (it is) *zehr* (very) *git* (good) *az men* (- when one) *ret zich* (speaks) *oyss* (out) *dus harts* (the heart) *far* (before) Hashem Yisburach *azoy vee* (just like) *far* (before) *ein* (a) *emmessen* (true) *guettin* (good) *fraynd* (friend)." And these words entered the heart of his holy student, our teacher the rav Rabbi Nussun, mention of the tzaddik for blessing, *mamash* (-really) like a burning fire, and he immediately understood, that just through this *aitza* (-remedy, advice), certainly he will merit to everything he needs in the service of Hashem. For all the various thoughts that the evil inclination will oscillate in his mind, and all types of obstacles that will prevent him, all of them he will recount before Hashem Yisburach, and he will request from Him mercy and endearment for each matter, that He should help him be as is truly proper for a Jewish man.

And our teacher the rav, the tzaddik, Rabbi Nussun *zatza"l*, also told over, that when our master, our leader, and rabbi *zatza"l*, spoke with him about the Cave of Elijah, which he had visited at the time he was in the Land of Israel, our master, our leader, our rabbi *zatza"l*, told him, that then, when he stood there, he pictured in his eyes the scene of Elijah standing there to pray and do hisbodidus there. And he said to him in these words, "*Ich* (I) *hub meer oyss gimult* (pictured for myself) *ut du* (that here) *iz gishtannin Eleyahu* (Elijah stood), *un hutt zich oyss garret dus harts* (and spoke out his heart) *far* (before) Hashem Yisburach." And our teacher the rav, Rabbi Nussun, mention of the tzaddik for blessing, told over, that then he was inspired, and renewed, and overly strengthened to always engage in expressing his words before Hashem Yisburach on every matter that was deficient in the service of Hashem Yisburach, because he understood then from these holy words of his, that also Elijah did not merit to his (high) level – that he didn't taste the taste of death and burial (Kings I:11, Moed Kutun 26a, Koheles Rabba 3), just through prayer and hisbodidus, for he had already said, that all the tzaddikim did not come to their (high) levels, only through hisbodidus, and prayer, and supplication before Him Blessed He.

Now behold our teacher the rav, Rabbi Nussun *zatza"l*, whom it was *mamash* fulfilled by him (Exodus 33:11), "he did not move from within the tent," the tent of Torah of Rabbainu Hakadosh, light of lights etc., author of Likutay Moharan zatza"l, he received his holy *daas* (-realization of knowledge) in wondrous completion, more than all his (other) students, the tzaddikim o.b.m.. For our master, teacher, and holy rabbi (Nachman) shined into him the light of his holy *daas*, like the large luminary to the small luminary. And our master, leader, and rabbi *zatza"l*, said of him, that he knows of me more than everyone. And he learned, and taught, and acted, and fulfilled all the words of our master, leader, and holy rabbi *zatza"l*, to the utmost completion, and he revealed to us the straight approaches to all the good traits, and especially in the matter of prayer and hisbodidus, according to what he received from our master, leader, and holy rabbi *zatza"l*. And he excogitated awesome and wondrous novelties to strengthen every person in the service of Hashem, behold they are the written in the holy books of Likutay Halachos, which he composed (them) on all the four (sections of the) Shulchan Aruch (Code of Jewish Law, lit. set table), as he was charged by our master, leader, and rabbi *zatza"l*. And he also composed the book Likutay Tifeelos which is comprised of prayers, entreaties and supplications, endearments and appeasements, confessions, and great arousal for the soul of every Jewish man, that the person will arouse himself to remember his end, which he founded upon the foundation of the holy discourses of the book Likutay Moharan, on assignment of our master, leader, and rabbi *zatza"l*.

And he said once regarding these prayers, the wording of the verse (Psalms 102:19), "Write this for the final generation, for the nation that will be created then will praise Y-ah." Namely, that these prayers were written for the final generation, and in the future there will be created a nation that will praise Hashem with these prayers. And he spoke radically of their stature. And he wrote in the introduction to the book Likutay Tifeelos these words, "Prayers such as these have never been in the world etc.." And he warned strongly to engage in them constantly, see there. And once, he said, "Now, that these prayers have went out into the world, in the future, judgment and accounting (*din vicheshbon*) will have to be given for every day that they were not said." [In Siach Sarfey Kodesh (6:40) it is brought down that they asked Rabbi Nussun if it was true that he said this. Rabbi Nussun replied, "I said it and I didn't say it; judgment and accounting everyone will give on what is necessary to be given, however, then, they will see for themselves that had they said these prayers they would have a lot less to be judged and accounted for."] And even still, he wrote in the introduction there, that also from this a person should not withhold (his hand), namely to engage every day in hisbodidus, to pour out his words before Hashem Yisburach in minute detail, on each and every matter that he sees he is deficient at that time, and to make for himself prayers from the Torah, in the language spoken, and only through this will he be able to come through in every matter, for it is impossible to explain in writing in detail all the needs of a person, especially according to the changes that always occur to a person at all times, see there.

And look in Words of Rabbi Nachman (229), he wrote there; in the beginning this was the main prayer, what each one would speak before Hashem Yisburach what was in his heart, in the spoken language. But afterwards the *Anshei Kinnesses Hagedoala* (Men of the Great Assembly) etc. and they set the arrangement of the prayer, as this is explicated in Maimonides' Laws of Prayer (1:3-7), see there. However, in any case, according to the law, this is the main prayer. Therefore, also now, that we pray the order of the prayer that the *Anshei Kinnesses Hagedola* constituted, it is very good for a person to regularly pray before Hashem Yisburach prayers, entreaties, and supplications from his heart, in the language he understands, that Hashem Yisburach should merit him to His service, for this is the main prayer, as mentioned above etc., see there. And behold it is herewith understood, that so too, also now that we have merited that the tzaddikim after them, arranged for us such awesome prayers, even still a person should not suffice for himself with this alone, rather he needs to abound profusely in expressing his words before Him Blessed He, from his heart, in the language he is familiar with, every matter in detail that he sees that he is missing, whether spiritual or physical.

We have surely seen in these end of times, when the horribly terrible darkness spreads out, that many of our nation have become very very distant from the service of Hashem, and they have been washed away by the torrent of incorrigible water of this lowly world, and they have drowned in the depths of mire, and there is no stance, as it is written (Psalms 69:3), "I have drowned in the depth of mire and there is no stance," and all this is just because they do not take to heart the holy *aitza* (advice/remedy/recourse) which is written afterwards (verse 14), "as for me, my prayer is to You Hashem etc.." And many don't know any way how to practice this. Even though it is true that whoever puts his heart and eyes to the books of our master, teacher, and holy rabbi and his holy student our teacher Rabbi Nussun *zatza"l*, certainly he will find in them a true, erect, and correct way how to conduct this holy matter, however their holy words which address this matter are spread about between the holy discourses, and not every person can find easily what he is seeking. And also, behold these books are not readily found and available in everyone's hand.

Therefore we have put our hearts to gather in this book many homilies from the books of our master, leader, and holy rabbi *zatza"l*, and from the holy books of Likutay Halachos from his holy student, which speak about the eminence of reciting Psalms, and the eminence of one who does hisbodidus and pours his heart like water directly before the face of Hashem, and straight ways which are critical for each person to know how to act, and to strengthen himself in this. And we named this book "Outpouring of the Soul," for it speaks entirely of how a person needs to pour out his heart and soul before Hashem, and this alone is the general *aitza* (-remedy, advice) for each and every matter, whether it be spiritual or physical.

And certainly when a person will put his eyes and heart to these words written in this book, his heart will be aroused to accustom himself to go in this holy old way, which our forefathers traversed from time immemorial, and it is going to be renewed in the future when the righteous Messiah comes, for only he will draw the world to this way, so that all the populace will practice it, as is explicated in Likutay Halachos, laws of Rosh Chodesh (First of the Month, 5:26), and as is explicated in Likutay Moharan (Torah 2), that the main weapon of Messiah is prayer, and all the wars that he will conduct, and all the conquest he will conquer, everything is from there. And also the entire future redemption is contingent on this, as it says (Jeremiah 31:9), "And I will bring them to my holy mountain, and I will bring them happiness in my house of prayer," quickly, in our days, amen.

Na Nach Nachma Nachman MeUman

Practices of Rabbi Nachman
Na Nach Nachma Nachman MeUman

Practices of our master, leader, and holy rabbi, the rav, Rabbi Nachman *zatza"l*, in the matter of hisbodidus, according to what is written in the holy recounting of his praises.

In the book "Praises of Rabbi Nachman," in the beginning, in recounting his practices and strenuous efforts in the service of Hashem (article 10), it is written: His main devotion, through which he merited to what he merited, was just the profusion of the prayers, and entreaties, and supplications, and endearments, and appeasements which he very frequently prayed and beseeched before Him Blessed He. And he would endear and appease Him Blessed He with all types of entreating and beseeching, that He in His Mercy should merit him to draw close to Him, to His service, Blessed He. And the main thing that was to his avail, was the prayers in the Yiddish language which is spoken amongst us, which he would very frequently designate for himself a place that he found, where there weren't any people, and he would articulate his words before Hashem Yisburach, in the vernacular, that is in the Yiddish language, and he would endear and appease Him Blessed He, and supplicate and entreat before Him Blessed He with many many types of arguments and justifications that it was becoming of Him Blessed He to draw him close to His service, Blessed He. And he was very very wont to doing this. And he would spend days and years on this.

Also he would hide himself, on top of his father's house, under the roof, where there was the likeness of a room with a partition of reeds, where straw and fodder are stored, and there he would hide himself, and would recite Psalms, and he would scream silently to Hashem Yisburach, that He should give him to merit to draw close to Him Blessed He.

And the general principle is, that all the types of supplications that are in the world, that are found in any book available amongst us, everything but everything, he didn't leave any entreaty or supplication that he didn't say many, many times. Whether it be Psalms, or the book Shaarei Tzion (Gates of Zion), and the supplications which are printed in the large prayer books, and other types of supplications and entreaties, and even the entreaties that are printed in Yiddish, all of them, he did not hold back from saying. And he was in the habit of saying all the entreaties that are after the *maamados* (- an arrangement of sections of the Torah which are unique to each particular day of the week, and commemorate the partaking of the standing over – *maamud* – the daily offering, which was incumbent in the time of the Temple), which are printed after each and every day, and he was sometimes in the routine of saying all the entreaties of all the days in one instance (t.n. these entreaties are very particular to their specific days, so I believe that Rabbainu must have prefaced each different day, with some sort of statement like: and on Tuesday we entreat etc.). Also he was accustomed sometimes to recite Psalms, only those verses which speak of entreaty, and supplication, and screaming to Hashem Yisburach, and he would say just these verses, and not say the rest, and he would say all these verses from the whole book of Psalms in one session.

And besides all this, the main thing was what he would pray from himself, that is, what he was accustomed to speak from his heart before Hashem Yisburach in Yiddish, which he would pray and argue before Hashem Yisburach with many many types of arguments, and entreaties, and supplications, which he said from his (own) mind and from his heart as mentioned above, that Hashem Yisburach should merit him to His service. And this was the main thing which availed him to merit what he merited. Thus we heard explicitly from his holy mouth.

[Praises of Rabbi Nachman, Article 11] And many times he would be speaking before Hashem Yisburach words of entreaty and supplication from his heart, and in the midst of his words he came upon nice argumentation and prayers that were ideal and in order, and they were good in his eyes, and he would write them so that they would be with him for a remembrance, so that he could pray them regularly afterwards as well. And so he was very accustomed in this matter, to speak between himself and his Creator a very very great deal. And all his prayers were that he should merit to draw close to Hashem Yisburach, and he had great vindications to Hashem Yisburach for this.

[Article 12] And even still it always seemed to him that no attention was being given to him whatsoever, and he wasn't being heard at all, just on the contrary, it seemed to him that he was being distanced from His service, Blessed he, with all types of estrangement from His service Blessed He. Yet even still he would strengthen himself very much, and did not resign his stance. And many times it happened, that he would fall discouraged from this that he saw that he prays, and pleads persistently, and presses urgently, so much, to draw close to the service of Hashem Yisburach, and no attention is paid to him whatsoever. And because of this he would fall sometimes dejected, and wouldn't speak so much anymore between himself and his Creator, for some days. Afterwards he caught himself, and was ashamed with himself for having second-guessed His measures, Blessed He, for in truth, certainly Hashem Yisburach is gracious and compassionate etc., and certainly He desires to draw him close etc., and he returned and strengthened his conviction, and began again to importune persistently and speak before Hashem Yisburach as mentioned above, and so it was many times.

It is further written there [Words of Rabbi Nachman, article 117]: In the town of Ossiatin, near the city of Medivedivikeh, his father in law o.b.m. lived, and his main growth was there [t.n. Rabbi Nachman married at the age of 13, which wasn't unusual for the times, and also he asserted that at that age he already attained the spiritual perception of the Baal Shem Tov, even still these are considered early years of life and growth, especially for Rabbi Nachman who continued to grow exponentially]. And there is a big river that runs there, upon which grow vast amounts of reeds and rushes. And the holy practice of our master, leader, and rabbi *zatza"l*, was to sometimes take a small boat, and row out by himself into the aforementioned river, even though he was not proficient at operating this boat, even still he would row out with it until after the reeds and rushes, till the place where he was no longer visible, and there he did what he did in prayer and hisbodidus, fortunate is he, for in truth he merited to what he merited, as is tangibly apparent from his holy books.

And in the book Life of Rabbi Nachman (230, His exertion in the Service of Hashem 1) it is written: that he would frequently take a horse from his father-in-law's house, and he would ride on it to some forest, and there he would come down from the horse and tie it to some tree, and he went into the forest to do his (part), to do hisbodidus there as was his practice. And many times the horse freed itself and fled from his place (back) to the house of his father-in-law. And when they saw there that the horse came back alone, they worried and were very fearful, for they said, certainly he fell from the horse, Heaven forbid. And many times heavy rains fell upon him when he was in the forest, and afterwards he would come home an hour into the night or later. And see below (inside this book, article 28) where I copied down there from his holy words, that in the place where vegetation grows, namely in the field or in the forest, it is very good to do hisbodidus there.

More from there (Words of Rabbi Nachman, article 154): he said, the main thing in his attainment of his (lofty) level, is (-was) just through the medium of *prustic* (common simplicity), that he used to speak a lot, and converse a lot between himself and his Maker, and recited a great deal of Psalms with simplicity, and through this specifically he attained what he attained. And he said, "If I had known that Hashem Yisburach would make of me what I am now (i.e. such a novelty), I would have done my devotions with such alacrity, to the extent that what I had done and served Hashem Yisburach in an entire year, I would have done in one day." And he yearned very much after the virtue of the devotion in the aspect of true *prustic*. And he said, "*Ay ay prustic*." He also said that he spoke with many great tzaddikim, and they said as well, that they didn't attain their (high) levels, only through the matter of *prustic*, that they engaged in their devotions with utter simplicity; in hisbodidus, and in communion between himself (-themselves) and his (-their) Maker etc., and through this they attained what they attained, fortunate are they.

More from there (Words of Rabbi Nachman, article 162). Rabbainu o.b.m., even though he had a private room in the town where he stayed – alone, even still he would usually go out into the field, into some forest, or so forth, and he would do a great deal of hisbodidus there. And one time I went with him, here and there, by the fields and mountains, and he inclined his hand upon the face of the fields and mountains, and he said to me, "On all of these fields and mountains that you see around the city, and all the places close to the city from all around, in all of them I went and circled about many many times," i.e. he would walk and do hisbodidus there in all the places mentioned above. And he told me, that there, on the top of the mountain, there is a place very high up, and there at the top of its height there is the likeness of a valley, and he would ascend to the top of the height of the mountain, and enter into the valley which was inside of it, and there he loved very much to do hisbodidus a few times. And sometimes he would go to other places as mentioned above. And all of this was in the congregation of Medivedivikke, when he was already a famous tzaddik at the time he lived there. Besides for what he profused abundantly to do hisbodidus when he lived in the town as mentioned before. And so too at the beginning, when he lived in Mezhbizh, and also afterwards when he lived in Zlatopole' and here, the holy Congregation of

Breslov, every single day he would do a lot of hisbodidus, and several times he would do hisbodidus the whole entire day.

And in the book "The Life of Rabbi Nachman" (107, The Place He Lived and His Journeys 4), it is written: One time, after he had become famous, Rabbi Shimon travelled with Rabbainu o.b.m. by way of the town of Ossaitin, where Rabbainu o.b.m. had exerted himself in his great devotions, in the house of his father-in-law, where he lived (there), and he traveled with him by way of the fields and so forth, and Rabbainu o.b.m. was yearning very much, and he said, "How good it was before me over here, for in every step and step I felt the taste of Gan (-Garden of) Eden." For there, in those roads, he would often go and do hisbodidus. And he was nostalgic and yearning very much, and he said, "Behold here it was very good before me, and for what do I need the present fame?" Also another time he told over before me, that when he was in his youth, when he went to do hisbodidus somewhere, in the forest or in the field, when he returned from there, the whole world was new in his eyes, and it seemed to him as if it was a completely different world, and the world did not appear in his eyes at all as it had previously.

More from there (Words of Rabbi Nachman, article 163): A person from Zlatopole' told me, that when Rabbainu o.b.m. lived in Zlatopole', one time in the summer, Rabbainu o.b.m. prayed early in the morning, and afterwards he sent his daughter, the child Sara may she live, and she called him to come to Rabbainu o.b.m.. And Rabbinu o.b.m. said to him, "come with me for a walk," And he went with him outside the city, and he went amid the vegetation etc.. Afterwards they went further, and they came close to a mountain called a "Mageelle," which was there, near the city. And he asked him, "What is this?" And the man told him the matter of that Mageelle [t.n. with the help of Hashem Yisburach I will publish this fascinating omission in Words of Rabbi Nachman]. And he said to him, that he should go with him there, and went in there. And when he entered there, they were not visible at all to the outside, because the aforementioned mountain was hollow inside, and somewhat deep inside. And Rabbainu o.b.m. went in there with this aforementioned man, and Rabbainu o.b.m. sat there on the ground, and he took from his sleeve the book Shaarei Tzion (Gates of Zion), and began to recite, and he cried very very much. And he continued saying further, from page to page, and he cried very profusely without cessation. And the man stood next to him and held his *tzubech* (pipe's bowl), and he stood confounded, and he saw his very great crying. And he spent a lot of time at this. And when he stopped crying, he commanded the aforementioned man to go and look outside, where the day stands. And he went out and saw that the day had already turned away, and the sun was declining to set. He tarried so much with his crying, almost a complete summer day (- in the Ukraine this can be over 16 hours) without cessation etc..

More from there **(Words of Rabbi Nachman, article 164)**: Also when he left to the Holy Congregation of Uman, which was very close to his passing away, approximately a half a year, and he had already merited to an eminent height that no person in the world ever merited, as is already explicated, also there he did a great deal of hisbodidus. And one time the homeowner whom Rabbainu o.b.m. lived by him as a neighbor (-it seems that they shared a semi-detached house), there in Uman, and there Rabbainu had a private room that the homeowner had access to, and the homeowner entered suddenly into the room, and he found Rabbainu o.b.m. lying with his hands and feet outspread on the floor. Even though he was very very weak then, without measure; his very life was a miracle, and he was close to dying at any time, even still he did not abandon his good practice of simplicity until the final hour, when he passed on high, high above, fortunate is he. And I heard that he said at the end of his days, "If I had known previously in the days of my youth, as I know now what is possible to merit through hisbodidus, I would not have destroyed and depleted my precious body so much with fasting and mortifications." The general construct is, that he didn't rest and didn't remain silent even in the days of his grandeur, even though he merited to perceptions of the Divine, to an extremely lofty, incredible, and awesome stature, even still he did not suffice himself to this, and he toiled and exerted at all times, at all hours etc., and he profused in prayers, and entreaties, and urgent pressing, and many supplications, and in very, very great and awesome yearning and longing, until he came to a loftier perception and level. And afterwards, immediately from when he merited to this perception and he was somewhat happy, immediately after he merited this, he forgot about the entire past, and he returned to begin from scratch, like he was beginning to go in the holiness of a Jew. And sometimes we heard explicitly from his holy mouth, that he said in an expression of passionate yearning and longing, "How does one merit to be a Jew?" And he said this with great *temimus* (unfeigned earnest simplicity), as if he still had not started at all. And he

41

profused to urgently press Hashem Yisburach with endearments, and longing, and arguments, until he merited to the level higher than him. And so it was each time, until he reached in the end such a lofty level, that inside a body it is impossible to attain more by any means, and therefore he was then forced to pass away. And he said in these words, "*Ich* (I) *vult* (want) *shoyn* (now/already) *giggerrin dus hemdil oyss gittun* (remove this tunic – referring to his body which dresses the soul) *vurren* (since) *Ich* (I) *kun oyf ayn madreigge nit shten* (cannot remain on one level)."

And even though he merited to what he merited, even still his prayer and hisbodidus between himself and his Creator was with extreme humility, and with a broken heart, with simplicity, and with *temimus*, as it is written in the book "The Life of Rabbi Nachman" (239, His exertion and toil in the service of Hashem 10), that one time he was asked by one of the young youths how to do hisbodidus, and he taught him how to say before Hashem Yisburach, 'Master of the World, have mercy on me etc., for is it conceivable that my life go by in such folly, and that this is what I was created for?! [And in Yiddish: *Ha-yittuchain az ess zul meer azzuy avvec gen dee velt, bin ich den foon dest veggen bashaffin givvurrin* etc.]. Afterwards, at some time, this guy stood behind the walls of Rabbainu o.b.m., and he heard that Rabbainu o.b.m. himself poured out his heart before Hashem Yisburach in similar words.

And so too after our master, leader, and rabbi *zatza"l* said the homily (Likutay Moharan 206), "I have strayed like a lost sheep (Psalms 119:176) etc." where he explains that the way of Hashem Yisburach is to call a person immediately when he sees him straying from the sensible way. There are those that He calls with a hint, and there are those that He calls with an actual calling, and there are those that He kicks and hits, because the Torah proclaims before Him (Zohar vol. 3, 36a, 58a), "Until when will the foolish be attracted after foolish persuasions (Proverbs 1:22)." And the Torah is Hashem Yisburach Himself, that He calls them, and requests them to return to Him. Therefore while he still has not overly strayed from the straight way, then it is possible for him to return with ease, because he still recognizes the voice of Hashem Yisburach and the Torah, and he is familiar with it, for he had recently been with Hashem Yisburach, and he had been hearing His voice – the voice of the Torah – and he still has not forgotten the voice, therefore it is possible for him to return with ease. And this is like the parable of the shepherd, when one sheep strays from the way, then immediately he calls it; and as long as the sheep still hasn't strayed much from the way, then it recognizes the voice and immediately follows it. But when it has strayed a lot from the way, then it has already forgotten the voice of the shepherd, and doesn't recognize it, and the shepherd also despairs from continuing to ask for it, because it was so long since it had went and strayed from him. So too when a person already tarried long, Heaven forbid, in his evil, and he turned and strayed a great deal from the straight way to those crooked and deviating ways, then it is difficult for him to return etc.. And this is (Psalms 119:176), "I strayed like a lost sheep," that is, I strayed from the straight way like a lost sheep that diverged from the way as mentioned above. Therefore I ask from before You (ibid: end of the verse), "request your servant, for Your *mitzvos* I have not forgotten." That is, You should hasten to call me immediately, as long as I remember, and have not forgotten yet the voice of Your *mitzvos* etc., see there. And it is written in the book "The Life of Rabbi Nachman" (ibid - 239, His exertion and toil in the service of Hashem 10), that when our master, leader, and rabbi *zatza"l* revealed this homily, he said to his holy student, the rav, Rabbi Nussun *zatza"l*, that this homily is now (in these times) his hisbodidus.

And if you know and heard a little of his utmost wondrous exertion and toil in the service of Hashem from his very youth (as is explicated somewhat in the books "Words of Rabbi Nachman," and "The Life of Rabbi Nachman"), and his utmost wondrous holy, and awesome, and extremely incredible, perceptions, as is known and understood somewhat to anyone who peruses his holy books, which the world merited to enjoy them, besides his other holy compositions which the world has not merited to enjoy (them), like the books which he ordered to be burned, and his "Hidden Book," in the aspect of (Genesis 1:4 with Rashi), "And G-d saw that the light was good – to put away in concealment, as this is explained elsewhere (The Life of Rabbi Nachman, 169 and onwards; His Trip To Lemberg 3-), aside from 'esoteric wisdom' (Job 11:6) which he merited to perceive, which we did not merit to know from them, even from hearsay (or conveyance/an idea - alone/), just knowledge of their existence alone. And after all this he entered the service of Hashem with such true *temimus*, to the extent that he said in hisbodidus before Hashem Yisburach, "I have strayed like a lost sheep etc.," in the construct explained in this homily mentioned above. And certainly if you reflect on this, you will be very amazed at the utter *temimus* of the righteousness of Rabbainu o.b.m.. But in truth, behold this verse itself was said by King David r.i.p. at the end of the eight faces (i.e. Psalms 119, which has eight verses for each letter of the aleph beth), which has in it very awesome and exalted secrets. And who doesn't know and believe in the enormous stature of the level of King David r.i.p., and even still he said of himself, "I have strayed like a lost sheep etc.," for His greatness Blessed He is unfathomable.

And so the greatness of the crying of our master, leader, and rabbi *zatza"l* before Hashem Yisburach, is impossible to explain and tell over whatsoever, but in short I will copy several things from his holy words.

In the book "Praises of Rabbi Nachman" (article 8) it is written that: he told over that all his learning came to him with great exertion. In the beginning he was learning *mishna'yos*, and he didn't understand what he was learning, and he would cry very profusely before Hashem Yisburach, that He should enlighten his eyes in His Torah, until he merited to be able to learn *mishna'yos*. And so afterwards, when he was studying the Talmud, in the beginning also he didn't understand, and he would cry also a great deal, until he merited to understand. And so afterwards when he grew older and began to work on learning the holy Zohar and the writings of the Arizal, he would cry also a great deal before Hashem Yisburach, until he merited to understand in every place that he learned, through his prayer and his crying as mentioned, see there. And from this it is apparent, that also in the days of his youth he was very accustomed to cry copiously before Hashem Yisburach over every devotion in the service of Hashem.

And so it is written in the book "The Life of Rabbi Nachman" (231, His exertion and toil in the service of Hashem 2), that when he was still a little boy, around six years old, he yearned very much to receive Sabbath in great holiness as would be proper. And he went to the bathhouse *erev* (-the day preceding) Sabbath immediately right after midday, and he ritually immersed himself with alacrity, and came right away to his house and put on his Sabbath clothing, and entered the *Bais Medrash* (House of Torah Study and usually prayers as well), and went here and there, wanting to draw upon himself the holiness of Sabbath, and the additional *Neshama* (soul). And he desired to see something, but did not see (anything) at all. In the interim, men began to come into the *Bais Medrash*, and some important man came and stood near his table where he prayed, which is called in Yiddish a *shtender* (lectern), and he began to recite Song of Songs, and he (Na Nach Nachma Nachman MeUman) o.b.m. went, and inserted his head below, inside the *shtender*, and because he was still a little child, they didn't take issue with him, and he was perched there, and he began to cry before Hashem Yisburach. And he cried very much with a deluge of tears, several hours until the evening, until his eyes became swollen (which is called *gishvullin*), and afterwards he opened his eyes and it appeared to him as if he saw some sort of aura, because the candles had already been lit, and his eyes were so closed up from crying, and then his mind was somewhat set at ease, see there. And so afterwards, when he got older, he didn't abandon this holy way of his, as I copied down above, that also when he lived in Zlatopole', after he came from the Land of Israel, he went to do hisbodidus outside the city with another man, and he cried then very much before Him Blessed He, until he tarried in his crying almost a complete summer day without cessation.

And I heard from my father and teacher o.b.m. (R' Asher Zelig of Teplic), that one time our master, leader, and rabbi *zatza"l* sat in his room and cried so very profusely before Hashem Yisburach, and the tears rolled down his eyes to the floor, until the floor became so damp from the tears that the heel of his shoe stuck to the floor because of the moisture of the tears. And so I heard further from him, that one time during the holy days of Succos, when our master, leader, and rabbi *zatza"l* circled the *beema* (large lectern in middle of the synagogue) with the *esrog* and his species (-*lulav* etc.), his men saw afterwards, on the floor, in the place that he went around the *beema*, the floor was damp from his tears, that he poured out then when he circled the *beema*.

And it is written in the book Words of Rabbi Nachman (article 172), that one time he gave his old *tallis* as a present to one of his foremost followers, and he said to him, "Be very careful to treat this *tallis* with respect, for as the number of strands that are in the *tallis*, so many tears I cried before Hashem Yisburach until I knew what a *tallis* is." And he said, that whenever he reveals Torah, he cries first. And regarding this he revealed a wondrous secret in his holy book Likutay Moharan, volume 1, Torah 262. And so he wrote there, since from the wellspring of the Torah which is originated (from them) flow out rivers, and the other-side and the evil spirits (lit. externals) come to drink from these rivers, therefore it is necessary to cry before originating in the Torah, (for) then from the crying, rivers are made, in the aspect of (Job 28:11), "From the crying He set up rivers," see there in Rashi. And then the other-side and the evil spirits drink from these rivers which were made from the crying, and through this they don't have any suckling from the Torah novelties. And therefore the composition of *halachos* (laws) and (Torah) novelties is called "*masseches*" in the aspect of (Psalms 102:10), "and my beverage I –*mussachti* (mixed/protected)-- with tears" because it is necessary to "*mussach*" <protect> the beverage of the novelties with crying (hence, it is called *masseches*, similar to *mussach*). And this is the aspect of (Psalms 137:1), "On the rivers of Babylon," the aspect of the rivers that are made from the (Torah) novelties which compromise the Babylonian Talmud. "There we sat <*yushavnu*> (continuation of the verse)," an aspect of the holy yeshivas (same as 'yushavnu' we sat) where these novelties are learned. "also (we) cried (continuation of the verse)," because it is necessary to first cry as mentioned above, see there.

And so he would always go with a very broken heart, and he wasn't accustomed to have a cheerful countenance. And we heard, that because his family, the family of the Baal Shem Tov o.b.m., came from the Kingdom of the House of David, as is known in the world, therefore also his (King David's) progeny are usually going with a very broken heart. Because King David r.i.p. founded the Book of Psalms which is mainly captivating (-in that they conquer and arouse the heart to repent) words which emanate from a broken heart, for all his words are just screams and entreaties with a very broken heart, therefore, also his progeny now, have a broken heart, for the most part. But for us, he warned very much to always be happy. And he said, "for men of your grade, from (going with) a broken heart can come to sadness, Heaven forbid," therefore it is necessary to designate some hour in the day in which one should have a broken heart and express his words before Him Blessed He, but the entire rest of the day he should be happy. And through the happiness it is will be easy for him to designate an hour of the day to break his heart before Him Blessed He. Fortunate is whoever merits to go in these ways and practices, then he certainly will merit to a good end.

Na Nach Nachma Nachman MeUman!

Na

NaCh

NaChMa

NaChMaN

Me ' Uman

Foreword

Above, I have already brought down in the introduction, that all our forefathers, and our prophets, and our holy Sages o.b.m., all of them went in this way, to profuse in prayers and entreaties, and to express their words before Hashem Yisburach about everything they underwent, and each and every person needs to go in this old way as well, and only through this he will merit eternal life. And being that I know that there exist some people who invert the truth and say, that for a person who stands on a low level it is not appropriate to engage in hisbodidus to express his words before Hashem Yisburach to ask Him to draw him close to His service Blessed He; this is only pertinent to the great tzaddikim. Therefore I decided to present here, at the beginning of the book, the homily which is printed at the beginning of the book Likutay Halachos, Orach Chaim (Way of Life – the first section of the Code of Jew Law), which begins with the laws of Sabbath (vol. 3), which proves from the words of our holy Sages o.b.m. the opposite of their sentiments, just on the contrary, the more a person knows in himself how utterly far he is from Hashem Yisburach, the more he needs to strengthen himself in this.

It is written in Tractate Avoda Zura, page 5b: Our Rabbis learned (Deuteronomy 5:26), "Who would give (-if only) that their hearts as such, will be with them to fear," Moses said to Israel, "Ingrates children of ingrates, when the Holy One Blessed He said to Israel, "Who would give that their hearts as such, will be with them," they should have said, "Give it to us Yourself." However Moses didn't hint this to them

[Rashi: this rebuke, until after 40 years, in the repetition of the Torah (*Mishneh Torah* - Book of Deuteronomy), in the plains of *Moav* he said to them, "And He didn't give you a heart to know" – that you should know to ask what He was asking from you, even *Moshe Rabbainu* didn't remember to take this matter to heart until 40 years (later)] only after forty years, as it says (Deuteronomy 29:4), "And I led you in the desert forty years," and it is written (verse 3), "and Hashem did not give you a heart to know etc.," Rabba said, from this it is established: a person does not grasp the mind of his teacher [Rashi: to have the realization of knowledge (*daas*) of the end of his mind and understanding] until forty years (later) [Rashi: for here Moses didn't hint it to Israel until forty years later].

And Tosfos (a primary commentary printed alongside the Talmud, opposite the commentary of Rashi) wrote: Until forty years a person doesn't grasp etc.. Rashi interpreted that even Moshe didn't remember. And if you say: Why (then) did Moshe get angry at Israel, behold he also didn't remember? It must be said (-answered), that since he didn't need this prayer, he didn't give it consideration until after forty years when he grasped the mind of his Master, but Israel, who needed this prayer, they should have contemplated from that time, for they had already sinned with the calf and the spies, end quotation.

And the Maharsha in Agguhdos (the section of his commentary pertaining to the *agadah*) wrote, in the heading, "You should have said give etc.": Even though our Sages o.b.m. said (Brachos 33b), 'everything is in the hands of Heaven, except for fear of Heaven," (-so why were they held responsible for not asking Hashem to give them fear of Heaven which is something not in the hands of Heaven but must be acquired and earned?), even still, it is elementary that it is in the hands of the Holy One Blessed He to incline the heart of people to good, for many verses purport to this, end of quotation.

And from all this it is clear to the eye of truth how much our Sages o.b.m. warned regarding hisbodidus, that is, to express one's words before Hashem Yisburach, and request from before Him that He give us fear of Heaven so that we do not sin, even though everything is in the hands of Heaven except for fear of Heaven, even still everything is in His hands. And one needs to request Him Blessed He specifically for this, as this is explained well in this (excerpt from the) Talmud, that Moses was very upset with them and called them ingrates for not having said to Hashem Yisburach, "Give (it to) us Yourself," that He Blessed He should give them fear of Heaven, as is clarified there in the Maharasha mentioned above. However, it is necessary to insert oneself very, very much into the discipline of hisbodidus, that is, to beseech Him Blessed He constantly: "Give it to us Yourself, the fear of Heaven," and not to fall discouraged in any way, to the extent that the Sages o.b.m. said there, that even Moses didn't hint it to them, only after forty years, because a person doesn't grasp the mind of his teacher until (the elapse of) forty years. See, and understand well, how much it is necessary to work at this, to understand the mind's end of our Rabbis o.b.m., who admonished us regarding this, for the Accuser very much disheartens the resolve of each and every one, as if our Rabbis o.b.m. were not referring to him, according to the murkiness of his conduct and stubbornness etc.. But in truth, this is not the case; Hashem Yisburach desires that we come to understand by ourselves His mind's end, that His will and His desire is that we should beseech him always, "Give us, Yourself, a good kosher heart to fear Your Name." And give careful consideration to what the Tosfos mentioned above wrote in their answer, that even Moses himself didn't put his heart to this so much, because he was a great tzaddik, and he didn't need this prayer, but Israel, who saw that they already stumbled with big transgressions, with the calf and the spies, they should have taken upon themselves to figure out the intention (*daas*) of Hashem Yisburach, that His desire is that they beseech Him that He should save them from sin, and that He should give them fear of Heaven, for this is the construct of, "Give it to us Yourself," mentioned above.

So there it is, explained in Tosfos mentioned above, the opposite of the sentiments of the some who invert the truth and say that no one is worthy of engaging in hisbodidus, to express his words before Hashem Yisburach, except for the greatest tzaddikim, but not the youth, especially earthly people etc.. For behold it is explained in Tosfos mentioned above, the exact opposite, that on the contrary, Moshe Rabbainu r.i.p. did not need this so much, because he was a great tzaddik, but specifically upon Israel he was extremely demanding, since they knew their lowly status, specifically because of this they needed to very much strengthen themselves in hisbodidus, and to understand well the mind's end of Hashem Yisburach, that even though He Himself said, "Who will give etc.," which implies that the matter is not in His hand, as our Rabbis o.b.m. said, everything is in the hands of Heaven except for fear of Heaven, even still His desire is that we request of Him, "Give it to us Yourself," which is the construct of hisbodidus, to express one's words between him and his Creator, and to entreat and beseech before Him for his soul, that He, in His mercy, should give him fear of Heaven so that he sins no more etc.. For the real truth is that everything is in His hand Blessed He, as many verses and homilies from our Sages o.b.m. purport (to this), and like the Maharsha mentioned above, wrote, just that He desires, Blessed He, that specifically one should beseech Him for this. And this itself is the intention of, "Who will give that their hearts," namely that they should put their hearts to this very well, to supplicate and plead before Him Blessed He constantly for this, and to say, "Give it to us Yourself etc.," and then certainly Hashem Yisburach will merit them to fear of Heaven and to everything good. And give careful consideration to the Talmud mentioned above, and understand how very much Hashem Yisburach desires that every one of Israel should request from Him fear of Heaven, which is the construct of hisbodidus which our master, leader, and rabbi *zatza"l* exhorted us countless times. Fortunate is he who adheres to this.

And look in the book "Ulim LiTrufa" ("Leaves for Healing," from our teacher the rav, Rabbi Nussun *zatza"l*, letter 28), where he writes also, that whoever is on a low level, needs to strengthen himself all the more in hisbodidus, to express his words before Him Blessed He, and on the contrary, the words of a very lowly person, on account of his improper conduct, are exceedingly more precious before Him Blessed He. And he writes there in these words: Be strong my son, and be strong to go in this way, to speak the holy longing every day with mouth (i.e. to actually say and enunciate the words), and force yourself very much to accustom yourself to this, and believe that however it may be, even your words are very precious in the eyes of Hashem Yisburach, for He, in His mercy, desires also for your prayer; because all the worlds with all their great service that they serve Him Blessed He, with unrelenting dread and fear, do not have any significance by Him Blessed He compared to one saying and one prayer of a person of this lowly world, as is explained in the Torah (Likutay Moharan vol. 2, Torah 7), "For he who is merciful, he can lead them (Isaiah 49)," And if the person is very low through his unpleasant conduct, on the contrary, when he expresses his words before Him Blessed He, and performs some devotion, it is all the more precious in His eyes, Blessed He. For this is His main honor Blessed He, when those who are very distant are drawn to His service Blessed He, as is explained in his holy books etc., see there (Likutay Moharan 10:2-3, and 14:2-3).

And while I am already engaged in copying this book, I will also copy some homilies of our Rabbis o.b.m. in the Talmud, and Medrashim, and the Holy Zohar, which speak of the great eminence of prayer, to beseech mercy, and pleading before Hashem Yisburach for every matter, which only through this one can have deliverance in every matter.

1. **Talmud, Brachos 32b.**

Rabbi Eluzur said, prayer is greater than good deeds, for you don't have anyone great in good deeds more than Moshe Rabbainu, even still he was not answered, only through prayer as it says (Deuteronomy 3), "Do not continue speaking to Me," (-for had Moshe continued to pray, Hashem Yisburach would have relented, even still due to the prayers of

Moshe to merit to enter the Holy Land, he at least merited to -) and adjacent to this, "Ascend the top of the summit." (-From where Hashem Yisburach showed Moshe all of the Holy Land, in merit of his prayers).

And Rabbi Eluzur said, prayer is greater than the offerings, for it says (Isaiah 1:11), "For what do I need your abundant sacrifices," and it is written (ibid verse 15), "and when you spread your hands." (-even though the prophet already disqualified the offerings, there was still need to disqualify their prayers, because prayers are even stronger).

[Rabbi Chanin said that] Rabbi Chanina said, "Whoever lengthens his prayer, his prayer will not return empty etc..
If a person saw that he prayed and was not answered, he should return and pray, for it says (end of Psalms 27), "Hope to Hashem, make your heart strong and courageous, and hope to Hashem."

Our Rabbis learned, four (things) needs strengthening, and they are these: Torah, and good deeds, prayer, and *derech eretz* (-vocation) etc.. Prayer, from where (is it learned that it needs strengthening)? For it says (end of Psalms 27), "Hope to Hashem, strengthen and embolden your heart, and hope to Hashem."

2. Talmud, Brachos 29

Rabbi Eliezer said, he who makes his prayer routine etc.. What is "routine"? Rabbi Joshua said in the name of Rabbi Oashaayu, whoever's prayer is considered to him as a burden. And our Rabbis said, whoever does not say it in a language of entreaty.

3. Talmud, Yomu 86b

Rabbi Yitzchuk said, they said in the west (-in the Land of Israel) in the name of Rabbu son of Murrey, come and see how the measure of the Holy One Blessed He is not like the measure of flesh and blood; the measure of flesh and blood, one who antagonizes his friend, there are prospects that he will be appeased by him, and it is plausible that he won't be appeased; and if you say he will be appeased by him, there are prospects that he will be appeased with words etc., but the Holy One Blessed He; a person does a sin in privacy, He is appeased by him with words, as it says (Hosea 14:3), "Take words with you, and return to Hashem." And not only that, but in addition He acknowledges this to him as (if he did Hashem) a favor, as it says (same verse), "and take good." And not only that, but in addition it is written of him above as if he offered up cows, as it says (same verse), "and our lips will be the payment (-replacement for the offering) of cows." Lest you say, obligatory (offerings of) cows (-which are not as significant as voluntary offerings), (therefore) it teaches, saying (verse 5), "I will heal their rebelliousness, I will love them graciously [-the word graciously, can also be translated as "a voluntary offering"].

4. Talmud, Rosh Hashana 16a

Rabbi Yitzchok said, Screaming (-prayer) is becoming (-beneficial) for a person, whether before the verdict or (even) after the verdict.

5. Talmud, Sanhedrin 44b

"Did you render your prayer (while you were still) not in duress (Job 36:19)," Rabbi Eluzur said, A person should always preempt prayer to distress etc.. Resh Lukkish said, whoever exerts himself in prayer below (-in this world), he will not have antagonists from above. Rabbi Yoachanun says, a person should always beseech mercy, that everyone should contribute to his strength, and he shouldn't have antagonists from above. And Rashi explains, that ('everyone' refers to) the ministering angels should help him beseech mercy.

6. Talmud, Brachos 31a

It is taught in the Braissu (-oral tradition similar to the mishna), Rabbi Yehuda said, such was the practice of Rabbi Akiva, when he would pray with a group etc., and when he would pray alone (-between him and himself), a person would leave him in one corner, and would find him in a different corner, and why such a drastic (movement), due to bowings and prostrations.

Rav Huna [-should be Hamnuna] said, how many significant laws [in the matter of prayer] can be learned from these verses of Chana (Samuel 1:1:13), "And Chana etc. her lips moved," from here (it is learned out) to one who prays, it is necessary that he enunciates with his lips etc., see there (Brachos 31) the prayers which Chana prayed.

And in the Medrash Shochair Tov in (the book of) Samuel, our Sages o.b.m. said on the verse (ibid 12), "And it was when she had prayed copiously to Hashem," from here (it is learned) that all who profuse in prayer, he is (-are) answered.

7. Talmud, Moed Kuttun 25

And Ruvu said, these three things I asked for from before Heaven; two they gave me, and one they did not give me: The wisdom of Rav Huna and the wealth of Rav Chisdu they gave me, and the humility of Rabbu son of Rav Huna they did not give me.

8. Medrash Rabbu, Torah Portion of Bishalach

"**Heeder** of prayer (Psalms 65:3)," flesh and blood, if a pauper comes to say something before him, he doesn't listen to him; if a rich man comes to say something before him, immediately he listens and accepts him; but the Holy One Blessed He is not like that, rather, everyone is equal before him, the women, and the slaves, and the poor. Know this for yourself, for by Moses, the teacher of all the prophets, it is written of him, what is written of the pauper. By Moses it is written (Psalms 90:1), "A prayer of Moses," and by the pauper it is written (Psalms 102:1), "A prayer of the pauper." To have you know that everyone is equal in prayer before the Place (-Hashem is called the Place, for all of space exists in Him, and He doesn't exist in Space).

9. Ibid

"**Heeder** of prayer," you find; flesh and blood, he cannot hear the conversation of two (people) at once, but the Holy One Blessed He is not like that, rather, everyone prays before Him, and He hears and accepts their prayers.

10. Ibid

"**Heeder** of prayer," Moses said before the Holy One Blessed He, "Master of the World, when Your children will be in pain, and there will not be anyone to beseech mercy for them, immediately answer them." The Holy One Blessed He said to him, "Moses, on your life, any hour that they call Me, I will answer them," as it is written (Deuteronomy 4:7), "Who is ... (a great nation which has G-d close to him) ... like Hashem our G-d in all our calling to Him.

11. Medrash Rabba, Torah Portion of Titzaveh

"**Take** words with you, and return to Hashem (Hosea 14:3)," He said to them, "Words – I request, cry and pray before me, and I am accepting (-will accept). Your forefathers, was it not through prayer that I redeemed them? As it says (Exodus 2:23), 'And the Children of Israel sighed from the labor, and they screamed'. In the days of Joshua, was it not through prayer that I performed miracles for them? So I do not request, not sacrifice and not offerings, just words," as it says, "Take words with you, and return to Hashem."

12. Tanchuma Torah Portion Vayishlach

The Holy One Blessed He does not desire to condemn any creature, rather He requests that they pray before him, and he will accept them. And even if a person isn't worthy for his prayer to be answered, and to do with him kindness, since he prays and profuses in pleading, I (will) do kindness with him.

13. Tunnu Divay Eliyahu (zuta-minor, chapter 6)

The Holy One Blessed He said, "Behold I will let you know a little of my ways; when I see people that don't have any recognition of Torah and good deeds; not of their own handiwork and not of their fathers' actions, but they stand and profuse in entreaties before Me, I attend to them," as it says (Psalms 102:18), "He has attended to the prayer of the desolate and has not despised their prayer."

14. Jerusalem Talmud, Brachos

Rav Yuden said, flesh and blood who has a patron, if he (the person) is confronted by a difficulty, he doesn't barge into him (the patron) suddenly, rather he goes and stands by the door to the courtyard of his patron, and calls to a member of the household and says, "so-and-so is outside." But the Holy One Blessed He is not like that. If you are confronted with hardship etc., scream to Him – and He will answer you, this is what it says (Joel 3:5), "whoever will call in the name of Hashem will escape."

15. Tunnu Divay Eliyahu (Rabba – Major, Chapter 13)

In that hour there will be an opening for the voice of the transgressors of Israel to ask for mercy to be accepted in repentance, and to say before Him, "Master of the World, it is revealed and known before You that the evil inclination incites us, accept us, in Your abundant mercy, in complete repentance before You." For all who profuse in conversations and prayers, they accompany him until he enters his everlasting home.

16. Agudas Tehilim

"Hashem I have called You (Psalms 141:1)," David said, "There is someone who is confident due to his pleasant deeds, and there is (someone) who is confident due to the deeds of his fathers; and I am confident in You, for I do not have (in me) good deeds, only that I called You – answer me. When David was in the cave, he knew and saw, that a person does not stand, not on his money and not on his strength, and what does he stand upon? Just his prayer, as it says (Psalms 142:2), "My calling to Hashem I scream."

17. Medrash Rabba Torah Portion of Vu-eschanan

The gates of prayer are never locked. There is a prayer which is answered after it has been prayed forty days. From whom do you learn this? From Moses, for it is written (Deuteronomy 9), "And I fell before Hashem the forty days." And there is a prayer which is answered after it has been prayed twenty days. From whom do you learn this? From Daniel, as it is written (Daniel 10:3), "refined bread I did not eat ... until the completion of three weeks (of days/years)," and afterwards he said (Daniel 9:19 – even though this is written in an earlier chapter, it is an event that took place later), "Hashem hear! Hashem forgive! etc.." And there is a prayer which is answered after it is prayed three days. From whom do you learn this? From Jonah, as it is written (Jonah 2), "And Jonah was in the belly of the fish three days, and Jonah prayed to Hashem his G-d from the belly of the fish." And there is a prayer that is answered after it is prayed one day. From whom do you learn this? From Elijah etc.. And there is a prayer which is answered after one instant (/time, calling). From whom do you learn this? From David, as it is written (Psalms 69), "And I, my prayer is to You Hashem at a time of favor." And there is a prayer, that while it still has not been prayed verbally, he is answered, as it says (Isaiah 65), "And it will be before they call, and I will answer." Rabbi Chiya Rabbu said, it is written (Psalms 27), "Hope to Hashem, strengthen and embolden your heart, and hope to Hashem," One should pray over and over again, and there is an hour that they will give it to you.

18. Zohar, Torah Portion Vayishlach, page 168b

Rabbi Yoassey opened and said (Psalms 102), "A prayer of the pauper when he is overwhelmed, and he pours out his words before Hashem." The prayer of a pauper precedes all the prayers of the world before the Holy One Blessed He, because it is written (Psalms 22), "For he does not despise and does not detest the callings of the pauper etc.." Come and see, the prayer of all people is prayer, and the prayer of the poor is a prayer that stands up before the Holy One Blessed He and breaks gates and doorways and goes up to be accepted before Him, this is what is written (Exodus 22), "And it will be when he screams to Me, and I will listen, for I am merciful." And it is written (Exodus 22:22), "I will surely listen to his scream."

19. Zohar, Torah Portion Bulluk, page 195a

Rabbi Abbu opened (Psalms 102), "A prayer of the pauper when he is overwhelmed etc.," These three are called prayer: "A prayer of Moses etc. (Psalms 90)," this is a prayer that has no counterpart by any other person; "A prayer of David (Psalms 17 and 86)," this is a prayer that has no counterpart by another king; "A prayer of a pauper etc.." Which is held in the most regard? Say that it is the prayer of the pauper, this prayer precedes the prayer of Moses, and precedes the prayer of David, and precedes all the other prayers of the world. What is the reason? Because the pauper is broken hearted. And it is written (Psalms 34), "Hashem is close to the broken hearted etc.," when (/since) he prays his prayers, he opens all the windows of the heavens, and all the other prayers which ascend on high, are pushed aside by that broken hearted pauper, as it is written, "A prayer of the pauper when he is overwhelmed <yaatoaf> etc.," he procrastinates (-yaatoaf can mean to slow down or be late, as in Gen. 30:42) all the prayers of the world, and they do not ascend until his prayer ascends etc.. And the Holy One Blessed He said, "let all the prayers of the world tarry, and this prayer ascend to Me, there is no need for a court to judge between us, let his complaints come before me, and I and he alone etc. as it is written, "and before Hashem he pours forth his words," "before Hashem," for certain! All the legions of the heavens inquire from one another, "The Holy One Blessed He, with what is He busy, what is He working at?" They say, "He is alone with what He desires, with His vessels." Everyone do not know what is done with that prayer of the pauper and with all his complaints, because the pauper has no desire (-satisfaction) but when he pours tears of complaint before the Holy King, and the Holy One Blessed He has no desire (-satisfaction), only when He accepts them and they are poured before Him, and this is the prayer which delays all the prayers of the world, see there, for it goes to much more length about this.

And see in Likutay Halachos, at the end of the laws of tefillin, law 5, that he brings down there the words of the Zohar mentioned above, and he concludes there, that all of this is said even of a regular pauper who prays for his material needs and his destitution and poverty, all the more so, and all the more so, when a person begins to have mercy on himself, and feels his poverty and destitution of good deeds, and argues with Hashem Yisburach for not drawing him close to Him, and he pours out his words and his heart before Him, until he is aroused to cry etc., how utterly precious this prayer is in the eyes of Hashem Yisburach. And it is more precious than all the prayers of the world etc.. And in the very end, certainly he will merit to achieve his request to draw close to Hashem Yisburach, to be equal to all the kosher ones and the tzaddikim, see there all of this at length.

20. Zohar, Torah Portion Vayishlach, page 169

"**Save** me now (/please) from the hand of my brother, from the hand of Esau, for I am afraid of him, lest he come and smite me, mother upon children (Genesis 32:11)," From here (it can be learned) that someone who prays a prayer, needs to explain his words properly. "Save me now," and if You say that You saved me from Lavan, "from the hand of my brother." And if You say, other relatives are generically called brothers, "from the hand of Esau." What is the reason? In order to explain the matter properly. And if You say, why do I need this? "For I fear him, lest he come and smite me," in order to make the matter known above, and to explain it properly, and not to leave any ambiguity in the matter.

Behold I have shown you in the Introduction and in the Forward, to know a little of the words of our holy Torah, and from our holy prophets, and from our holy rabbis o.b.m., who all went in this holy way of prayer and hisbodidus, to beseech mercy and grace (/entreaty) from Hashem Yisburach for everything. And now if you desire as well to have mercy on your eternal life, and to come inside the ark (which are the) words of prayer, in order to be saved from the waters of the flood, turbulent waters which roar and rush in these end of days, that the waters have *mamash* come to the soul, I will lead you, I will bring you to inside the book, and put your eyes and your heart to the holy articles which are brought down in it, from the books "Likutay Moharan," "Words of Rabbi Nachman," and "The Life of Rabbi Nachman," from our master, leader, and holy rabbi, the light of lights etc., our leader the rav, Rabbi Nachman *zatza"l*, and from the holy books of "Likutay Halachos" from his holy student, the rav, the tzaddik, Rabbi Nussun o.b.m., who renewed this holy old way, and you will find straight ways how to practice and strengthen yourself at this, and your eyes will be opened in this holy way, as it is written in his "Legendary Tales", in the story of the Prayer Leader (Story 13), that the group that chose for themselves that the main purpose is just to engage in prayer and entreaties, they also had several collections of prayers even before they drew close to the Prayer Leader, and through this that they engaged just in prayer, they were tzaddikim. Just, afterwards, when they merited to draw close to the Prayer Leader, and he revealed to them the arrangements of his prayers, and his compositions, and his constructs, then their eyes were enlightened, and he made them into consummate tzaddikim etc., see there. And Hashem Yisburach will (/should) help us, that we merit to spend all our days just on Torah, and prayer as is His true desire Blessed He, amen.

Na Nach Nachma Nachman MeUman!

Outpouring of the Soul

1. Reciting Psalms Is Intrinsic To Repentance

Whoever wants to merit to repentance, should recite Psalms frequently, because the recital of Psalms is *mesugal* (propitious) for repentance. For there are fifty gates of repentance; forty nine gates, everyone is capable of entering and attaining, however the fiftieth gate is the aspect of the repentance of Hashem Yisburach Himself – so to say, for also by Him Blessed He we find the aspect of repentance, as it is written (Malachi 3:7), "Return to Me and I will return to you (plural)." And these forty nine gates of repentance are an aspect of the forty nine letters which compose the twelve names of the tribes of G-d (-the sons of Jacob), for each and every gate has a letter of the forty nine letters of the tribes.

Now behold, everyone desires to fear Your name, and even still not everyone merits to repent, for there is one who has absolutely no arousal for repentance, and even someone who has arousal for repentance, does not merit to reach the letter and the gate of repentance which is applicable to him. And even if he arrives there, it is possible that the gate of repentance will be closed, and because of all this, the person will not merit to repent. And through the recital of Psalms, even someone who does not have any arousal to repent, he will be aroused to repent, and will also merit through the Psalms to reach the gate and the letter pertaining to him, and to open the gate. It comes out that through Psalms one merits to repent.

And this is the aspect of (Samuel 2:23:1), "the words of the man who was raised high," and our Rabbis o.b.m. expounded (Moed Kuttun 16b), that (the words "raised high"-*hookam oal*, infer that) he raised (-established) the yoke (*oal*) of repentance, "and the pleasant songs of Israel (end of the verse)," because through the aspect of the pleasant songs of Israel, namely the Book of Psalms which he enacted, through this he established the yoke of repentance. Because through Psalms one merits to repentance, as mentioned above. And this is what our Rabbis o.b.m. said (Avoda Zura 4b), David was not behooving of that incident (-with Bas Shevah), only in order to teach repentance to the individual etc.. It comes out, that the main instruction of repentance that is through King David is the Book of Psalms, which he said with tremendous arousal and Divine Inspiration, to the extent that each and everyone, according to his standing, can find himself inside the Book of Psalms, and merit to repentance through the recital of Psalms, as mentioned above.

And the main refinement of the twelve tribes of G-d, which are forty nine letters, which are the aspect of the forty nine gates of repentance, was in Egypt, which is the aspect of the narrowness of the throat, which is the aspect of superior repentance (as is brought in the writings of the Arizal (Shaar Hakavanos, Sfiras Hu-omer, Drush 11), see there and understand well). And therefore after they were refined there in Egypt and they merited to go out from there, they counted forty nine days of the *sfira* (-'counting'- the Torah commands to count from the second day of Passover), which correspond to the forty

70

nine letters mentioned above, which are the forty nine gates of repentance. And on the fiftieth day, then (Exodus 19:20), "And Hashem descended on Mount Sinai," this is the aspect of "and I will return to you", the aspect of the repentance of Hashem Yisburach himself so to speak, the aspect of the fiftieth gate, as mentioned above.

And this is (Exodus 1:1), "And these are {*Vi-aileH*} the names {*shimoaT*} of the children {*binaI*} of Israel {*YisroeL*} that are coming {*habu-iM*}," the last letters of these words are the letters "TeHiLIM" – Psalms. "To Egypt {*mitzraimU*}, with {*eS*} Jacob {*YaakoV*}, each person {*eeSh*} and his household {*oobaysOa*}," the last letters of these words spell out "TeShOoVUh" – repentance. Because through Psalms one merits to repentance, which is the aspect of the names of the Children of Israel that are coming to Egypt etc., because the forty nine gates of repentance are the aspect of the forty nine letters that comprise the names of the Children of Israel that are coming to Egypt to be refined there, as mentioned above.

And this is what we see, that in the days of repentance, that is in (the month of) Elul and the Ten Days of Repentance (-from the New Years till Yom Kippur), all of Israel is occupied then in the recital of Psalms, for the recital of Psalms is *mesugal* (-propitious) for repentance, as mentioned above. Therefore it is a very great thing to always be engaged in the recital of Psalms, because Psalms is an enormously great arousal to Hashem Yisburach. Fortunate is one who adheres to it **(Likutay Moharan vol. 2, Torah 73).**

The copier [R' Alter of Teplik] said: See Likutay Aitzos (A Collection of Advice; Entry on Teshuva – Repentance, article 32), where this matter is written in short, with these words: And there is (one) that doesn't know (how) to reach the gate intended for him, that specifically in that way he needs to return to Hashem Yisburach etc., and through the recital of Psalms he will merit etc. and to come to the gate of repentance indigenous to his *neshama* (soul) etc., see there. And it becomes apparent from his holy words there, that the forty nine gates mentioned above, are an aspect of forty nine ways to repent, for each person, according to the root of his soul, has a unique way and a unique service, that he needs to traverse specifically in that way, and through this he will merit to return to Hashem Yisburach, as this is understood from the Torah "Unoachi" ("I", Likutay Moharan, Torah 4) on the homily of our Sages o.b.m. (Sota 21a), "and he doesn't know which way he is going," see there. And not everyone merits to find his unique way, according to the root of his soul, to return with it to Hashem Yisburach. And on this King David r.i.p. screamed (Psalms 119:9), "With what will a youth merit (/make meritorious) his <specific> way to guard as You prescribed." And our master, leader, and holy rabbi *za.tza.l.* revealed to us that through the recitation of Psalms, Hashem Yisburach will bestow him with wisdom, and understanding, and realization of knowledge to perceive for himself his own unique way, specific to him according to the root of his *neshama* (soul), what to do in this world, until he merits through this to complete repentance, and see below article 75.

Na Nach Nachma Nachman MeUman!

2. Hisbodidus

Hisbodidus is a great virtue, higher than everything. Namely, to set for himself, in any case, an hour or more to do hisbodidus alone by himself in any room or in the field, and to express his words between himself and his Creator, with arguments and reasoning, with words of charm, and endearment, and appeasement, to beseech and entreat before Him Blessed He, that He should draw him close to Him, to His service, in truth. And this prayer and conversing should be in the spoken language, that is, in our country, in Yiddish ("*lushon Ashkenaz*", today this can very readily refer to English vernacular), for in the Holy Tongue it is difficult for him to express all he has to say, and also the heart is not drawn after the words because he isn't accustomed so much to speaking in that language, for it isn't our practice to speak in the Holy Tongue. Whereas in Yiddish, which is spoken and used in conversation, it is easily and much more readily spoken, for the heart is drawn and closer to Yiddish because he is fluent in it. And in Yiddish he can express all his words, and everything that is on his heart he should converse and tell over before Him Blessed He, be it regret and repentance on the past, and be it a pleading request to merit to truly draw close to Him Blessed He from today onwards, and so forth, every person according to his level.

And he should be very vigilant to accustom himself to be diligent with this every day, for one designated hour as mentioned above, and the entire rest of the day to be joyous (as it is written in the previous article (i.e. Likutay Moharan vol. 2, Torah 24) which begins: It is a great mitzvah to always be joyous). And this practice is very extremely great in stature, and it is a way and an extremely beneficial *aitza* (advice/remedy) to draw close to Him Blessed He, for this is a general *aitza*, which includes everything, for whatever he is missing in the service of Hashem, or if he is altogether completely distant from His service Blessed He, for everything he should express his words, and request from Him Blessed He, as mentioned above. And even if sometimes his words are suppressed and he absolutely cannot open his mouth to speak before Him Blessed He, even still, this itself is extremely good, namely the preparation that he is ready and standing before Him Blessed He, and desires and yearns to speak, even though he is unable, this itself is also extremely good. And he can also make from this itself, a conversation and prayer, and over this itself he can scream and plead before Him Blessed He, that he has become so distance to the extent that he can't even speak. And he should beseech from Him Blessed He mercy and compassion, that He should have mercy on him and open his mouth so that he can express his words before Him Blessed He.

And know that many, many great and famous tzaddikim told over, that they didn't come to their level, only through this practice. And one who is intelligent will understand for himself the great eminence of this practice, which reaches very far above, and it is something equal for everyone, from little to big, because everyone is able to practice this practice, and through this they will come to a great height (/quality), fortunate is the one who adheres to this.

It is also good to make from the Torah (-holy teachings), prayer, that is, when one learns or hears any homily of Torah from the true tzaddik, then he should make a prayer from this, that is, to request and plead before Him Blessed He regarding everything that was discussed there in that homily, when will he also merit to achieve all of this, and how far he is from this, and he should ask from Him Blessed He that He should merit him to come to everything that was discussed there in that homily.

And one who is intelligent and desires truth, Hashem will lead him in a true way, and he will understand for himself, one thing from another, how to practice this in such a way that his words will be words of grace and correct arguments to gain His will Blessed He, that He draw him close to His service in truth. And the matter of this conversing reaches a place extremely high up, and especially when he makes from Torah, prayer, from this is made enormous delights above **(Likutay Moharan vol. 2, Torah 25)**.

See in the book "Ulim Litrufa" ("Leaves for Healing", letters written by Rabbi Nussun, Letter 397) what is written there: And the main thing is to make from the Torahs, prayers. To beseech every day, and to express his words before Him Blessed He according to whichever Torah he is learning in his (Rabbi Nachman's) holy books, for in all of them he can find himself every day. Aah, Hashem! When will we merit to this? For all our days are flying and passing as a passing shadow, and like a dissipating cloud, and like a rushing wind, and like a fleeting dream (from the liturgy of the High Holidays, "Oonisaneh Toakef") etc.. And we don't have the wherewithal to grab them and hold on to them, so that they stay set up for us, that we live in them forever, just through prayer and entreaty. And the main thing is, through this holy way, which is old and very new, which is to make from the Torahs, prayers, as mentioned above. And it appears to everyone, in their own eyes, that they are far from this, but in truth this is not so, "for this matter is very close to you, with your mouth and your heart to do it (Deuteronomy 30:14)." And if even still, one is unable to begin speaking at all, behold we have spoken a great deal about this as well, with true *aitzoas* (advice/remedies) which are proven and tested, which have already helped us profusely etc.. Fortunate are we that we have merited to hear all this, and to engage a little in this. Who would give that we merit to truly fulfill His will and go in all His ways, to be joyous everyday, and to beseech and scream to Hashem, and to make from the Torahs, prayers etc., see there (see at the end of this book, the awesome discourse from the book Likutay Halachos, Orach Chaim, laws of Rosh Chodesh, law 5, which is based on these two homilies presented above in article 1 and article 2).

His holy words which are written at the end of the book Likutay Moharan

3. Crying in Prayer

And regarding the matter of hisbodidus, and conversing between oneself and his Maker, and the recital of Psalms, and entreaties, and supplications, it is very good when one merits to say them with a truly whole heart, until he merits to cry before Hashem Yisburach like a son who cries before his father. However, he said, that when a person says Psalms, and entreaties, and supplications, and he thinks in his heart and anticipates crying, this thought isn't good, and it also confuses his mind, for because of this he isn't able to say the requests with a completely whole heart. For it is necessary when saying entreaties and supplications, to distant from oneself all types of exterior thoughts of the world, just to concentrate one's mind on the words that he is speaking before Hashem Yisburach, like a person speaks to his friend, and then naturally his heart will be aroused readily until he comes to a truly profound crying.

But when he thinks about this and anticipates crying, then this (-the attempt to cry) and this (-the concentration on the prayer) will be unsuccessful. For the very reciting gets mixed up through this, as mentioned above. For this, that he is thinking and awaiting to cry, is also a form of foreign thoughts that confuse the *kavana* (concentration), because through this he cannot hear well what he is saying. For, the main thing is to speak the words in truth before Hashem Yisburach, without any extraneous thoughts whatsoever, as mentioned above, and if he merits to cry in truth, wonderful, and if not, not. And he should not confuse his speech for this, as mentioned above (**Likutay Moharan vol. 2, Torah 95**).

4. Adherence to Hisbodidus

In addition, he said about hisbodidus – for his way, of blessed memory, was to encourage this very much, to be very accustomed to doing hisbodidus, to express one's words before Hashem Yisburach every single day – and he said, that even if one is unable to speak at all, even the utterance of a single word is also extremely good. And he said, that even if one cannot speak, only one word, he should have strong resolve to say that word many many times, without limit or bounds. And even if he spends many many days with this word alone, this is also good. And he should be strong and emboldened, and profuse to speak that word countless times, until Hashem Yisburach has mercy on him and opens his mouth, and he is able to express his words.

And he said, that speech has enormous power, for behold it is possible to whisper (an incantation) on a gun so that it can't fire, understand (this). And at that time, when he spoke about this, he spoke a lot about hisbodidus, and he spoke at great length in a wondrous talk, with all types of expressions, and he strengthened and exhorted us very very much in this, to strengthen ourselves to profuse in hisbodidus and conversing between one and his Maker. And he said that he desires that we have the whole entire day for hisbodidus, to spend the entire day on this, except not everyone is able to fulfill this. Therefore it is incumbent to instruct them that in any case they should have some hours for hisbodidus, because this is also good. However someone who's heart is strong in this, and desires to truly accept upon himself the yoke of His service blessed He, he (Rabbi Nachman) desires that he (this person) should have the entire day for hisbodidus. And he mentioned then the homily of our Sages o.b.m. (Brachos 21), if only a person would pray the whole entire day (**Likutay Moharan vol. 2, Torah 96**).

5. Original prayer is a new undetected secure route to Hashem Yisburach

In addition I heard in his name, that he said regarding the eminence of conversing between oneself and his Maker; for (of) the prayers, and entreaties, and supplications that were already standardized, they are already known to all the destructive forces and prosecutors, and they wait in ambush on the ways of these prayers, because they are already familiar with them. Just like for example, a well trodden road which is known and familiar to everyone, the murderers and thieves always wait in ambush there, because they already know of this road. But when going on a new path and road, which are still unknown, there they do not know to ambush (there) at all. Similarly with the matter at hand, because the conversing that a person speaks from himself, between him and his Maker, is a new way and a new prayer that the person is saying new from his heart, therefore the prosecutors aren't very prevalent to ambush. And even still, he also very much admonished regarding the reciting of other entreaties and supplications, as is explicated in our words many times **(Likutay Moharan vol. 2, Torah 97).**

6. Speech has great power of arousal

In addition he said regarding the matter of encouragement to do hisbodidus, and entreaties, and supplications, that the spoken word has great power to arouse a person, even though it appears to the person that he doesn't have any heart, even still when he speaks a great deal of words of arousal, and entreaties, and supplications, and so forth, this itself that he is speaking, is a revelation of his heart's and his soul's arousal for Hashem Yisburach, in the aspect of (Song of Songs 5:6), "My soul went out when he spoke," that the speaking itself is a manifestation of the soul and the heart. And sometimes through speaking a lot, even though it will be without any heart at all, even still, afterwards through this he will come to great arousal with heart and soul. And the general principle is, that the speaking itself has a great power **(Likutay Moharan vol. 2, Torah 98)**.

7. Speak out your very soul, and Gd is right there listening

He said, that the main hisbodidus and conversing between one and his Maker in completion, is when one expresses his words so much before Hashem Yisburach until he is very close to expiring his soul Heaven forbid, until he is about to die Heaven forbid, until his *nishuma* (-soul) isn't bound to his body, only by a thread, from his utter loss, and yearning, and longing for Hashem Yisburach in truth. And so it is clarified in the words of our Rabbis o.b.m. (Taanis 8a) who said, a person's prayer isn't heeded unless he places his soul in his palm, that is as mentioned above. And he said, behold, when Hashem Yisburach helps in hisbodidus, one can express his words before Hashem Yisburach like a person speaks with his friend. And one needs to accustom himself to speak with Hashem Yisburach like he speaks with his Rabbi and with his friend, for (Isaiah 6:3), "the

entire world is filled with His glory," and Hashem
Yisburach exists everywhere.

(Likutay Moharan vol. 2, Torah 99).

8. The level one attains is achieved through hisbodidus

They told over to me that he said, that from little to big, it
is impossible to be a truly kosher person except through
doing hisbodidus. And he mentioned many many famous
true tzaddikim, and said, that all of them did not come to
their (high) level except through hisbodidus. And he also
took (for example) a simple person who was from the
progeny of the Baal Shem Tov *za.tza.l.*, and he said, also
this (person) expresses his words at all times before Hashem
Yisburach with great crying. And he said, that the progeny
of the Baal Shem Tov are exceedingly regular at this, for
they are the progeny of King David r.i.p., and the whole
occupation of David was this affair, that he would very
much break his heart before Hashem Yisburach always, for
this is the main (-way it came about) Book of Psalms that he
founded, as is explained elsewhere (See Likutay Moharan vol. 2,
Torah 101, Words of Rabbi Nachman article 68).

(Likutay Moharan vol. 2, Torah 100)

9. Find yourself in the prayer –
Prayer is the single catch-all fail-safe vital critical remedy

He said, that through saying Tikun Chatzos (-Midnight
Rectification) it is possible to express one's words, everything

that is on one's heart, similar to doing hisbodidus. For presumably one doesn't say it on the past, rather the main reciting of *chatzos* ('midnight' – referring to the rectification mentioned above) concerns what is happening with the person now. And when he says *chatzos* in this perspective, it is possible to find everything that is on his heart, in the recital of *chatzos*. And so with the reciting of Psalms and so forth, one needs to see to it that he finds himself in all the chapters (/songs) of Psalms, and all the entreaties, and supplications, and *sleechoas* (veniality – liturgy of petitions for forgiveness), and so forth. And easily, and simply – without contrivance, one can find himself in all the entreaties and supplications, and especially in the Psalms which were said for the general populace of Israel, for each and every one in particular. And every person, all the battles of the inclination which are upon him, and everything that is being done with him, everything is laid out and explicit in Psalms, for it was principally said regarding the battle against the evil inclination (*yetzehr hurra*) and his legions, for they are a person's main enemy and hostility, that want to bar him from the way of life and cast him down to abysm of scheol (-hell) Heaven forbid, if he doesn't guard himself from them. And exclusively regarding the matter of this battle, the entire Book of Psalms was founded. For the main principle, and root, and foundation of all the *aitzoas* (advice/remedies) to draw close to Hashem Yisburach is just the recital of Psalms and other entreaties, and supplications, and hisbodidus, to express one's words between himself and his Creator, to request from before Him, that He should draw him close to His service Blessed He, and just through this one merits to win the battle; if he will be very strong and emboldened always to plead persistently, and to pray,

Outpouring of the Soul

and to entreat before Hashem Yisburach constantly, come what may, then certainly he will win the battle. Fortunate is he. Thus was what we understood from the words of Rabbainu o.b.m..

For even though there are many good *aitzoas* (advice/remedies) to be found in the books of Rabbainu o.b.m., which are full of *aitzoas* to draw close to Hashem Yisburach, even still, in most cases it is difficult for a person to carry out the remedy itself. Therefore the main thing is prayer, and entreaty, and supplication. Come what may, no matter what, one should speak verbally in whatever condition, and he should beseech from Hashem Yisburach constantly that He should take him out from the darkness to the light, and He should return him in truly complete repentance, and not give remittance until He answers him. And even though he calls and screams to Hashem Yisburach for the longest time, and he still is very, very distant, even still, if he will be strong and bold with prayers and supplications, certainly without doubt Hashem Yisburach will answer him, and He will draw him close to His service in truth, certainly without doubt. Just be strong and courageous, as our Rabbis o.b.m. said (Brachos 32a), that prayer needs encouragement, as it says (Psalms 27:14), "Hope to Hashem, be strong and embolden your heart, and hope to Hashem," and Rashi explains, if your prayer was not accepted, go back and hope (-pray). And so (one should do) forever, until Hashem looks and sees from the Heavens, as it is written (Psalms 130:7), "(Put) hope Israel to Hashem from now until forever."

And all this is already laid out clearly in our words numerous times, however it is necessary to go over and repeat this, and to remember this every single day. For there are many, many types of demoralization and confusion on this, without limit, what the mouth cannot verbalize nor the heart fathom. Therefore it is necessary to go over this a thousand times in order that one should strengthen and embolden himself to stand his ground, to pray and to entreat before Hashem Yisburach constantly, that He should draw him close to His service, come what may. "Let us lift [even] our hearts with our outstretched hands to G-d in Heaven (Lamentations 3:41, according to one interpretation of Rashi),""For Hashem will not abandon His nation, and His inheritance He will not forsake (Psalms 94:14),""The benignities of Hashem, for they have not depleted, for His mercy has not come to an end (Lamentations 3:22)."

(Likutay Moharan vol. 2., Torah 101).

10. When praying one should be aware of G-d and nothing else

When praying, as long as a person still hears someone (then), that is, that while he is praying, he hears and senses that another person is also standing there, this is not good. Because every person when praying needs to picture in his mind that there is no one there except I and Hashem Yisburach alone. And in Likutay Moharan (vol. 1, Torah 55:6) it is clarified even further, that a person must abnegate himself while praying, so much so, that he doesn't even retain any awareness of himself whatsoever, just of Hashem Yisburach alone, see there.

(Likutay Moharan vol. 2., Torah 103).

11. Importance of common simple devotion

He loved very much the simple devotions of ordinary people, the simple kosher people. And he loved very much someone who could say a lot of entreaties and supplications from inside the large prayer books, as is the practice of the kosher common people. And he would admonish and exhort us many times to sing songs (*zmiros*) on Sabbath. And he held culpable and was very upset with someone who was wise in his own eyes and didn't make the extra effort to sing the songs (*zmiros*) on Sabbath and Saturday night (*motzai Shabbos*), or any of the other simple devotions. For the essential of Judaism is with simplicity and complete *temimus* (wholeheartedness, unfeigned, sincerity) without any contrivances, as delineated by us many times already (Likutay Moharan vol. 2; 12, 19, 44, 78. Words of Rabbi Nachman, articles 5, 15, 19, 32, 51, 101, 124, 235 and more). And he himself also, his whole life, before he was met with the severe illness through which he passed away, would sing a great deal of songs (*zmiros*) every single Sabbath and on Saturday night (*motzai Shabbos*). **(Likutay Moharan vol. 2, Torah 104).**

12. Through prayer one can achieve everything - and it is therefore the main accounting

Someone asked him, in the matter of the conduct of drawing close to Hashem Yisburach, and he instructed him to learn etc.. And he asked him, "but I am not able to learn." He answered him, "through prayer one can come to everything, to everything good: to Torah, and to service (of

Hashem), and to all the holiness, and to all the devotions, and to all the good of all the worlds.

[**The** copier (R' Alter of Teplik) says: see in the book "Yerach HuAisuneym" (Month of the Powerful/Forefathers – the month of Tishrey), handwritten manuscript of the holy Rav of Tcherin *za.tza.l.*, on the torah "the depth cover them (Exodus 15:5)" in Likutay Moharan, vol. 1 (torah 9), where he writes regarding the day of judgment of the New Years (Rosh Hashana), that the main judgment on a person is for what he was not vigilant in the matter of prayer, for through prayer it is possible to come to everything desirable: to Torah, and to good deeds, and to repentance, and to be saved from sin, just as our Rabbis o.b.m. issued many prayers for (all) this. And this is understood from the words of our Rabbis o.b.m. (Eruvin 65a), that Rabbi Eluzur Ben Azaria said: "I can absolve the whole world from judgment" etc., and they concluded there, what is (the meaning of) "I can absolve" that he said, (he was referring to) from the judgment on prayer. For the judgment on prayer is the aggregate judgment and accounting of a person, for if he had only been vigilant and accustomed to pray properly, he would have merited to rectify everything, as this is similarly explained also in the commentaries there (see Ein Yaakov there). And like this is explained by us elsewhere (see Siach Sarfey Kodesh 4:116), that this is learned from the matter of the betrothed damsel, whose main liability for capital punishment, may the Holy Merciful One spare us, is "on account of her not screaming (Deuteronomy 22:24)," etc., see there.]

One time he said: If they would let a dead person in this world pray, certainly he would pray very (/nicely,) nicely with all his strength. (**Likutay Moharan vol. 2, Torah 111**).

13. Prayer is bonding and attachment to G-d

He said, that the essence of the prayer is the binding (*divaikus*) to Hashem Yisburach. And it would be better to pray in the Yiddish (-English) that is spoken, because when one prays in the spoken language, then the heart is very close and attached to the words of the prayer, and he can attach himself all that more to Hashem Yisburach. However the Men of the Great Assembly (*Anshey Kinnesses HaGedolah*) enacted the order of the prayer (because not everyone is able to arrange the order of the prayer for himself, as is brought down (Maimonides, laws of prayers 1:4)), therefore we are obligated to pray in the Holy Tongue as they arranged for us. But the main thing is just to concentrate on the simple meaning of the words, for this is the essence of prayer, to pray before Hashem Yisburach for every single thing, and through this one binds (himself) to Him Blessed He. (And someone who prays with the *kavanos* (intentions) of the Kabbala for the words of the prayer, and he is not worthy of this, it is a great defect etc. (Words of Rabbi Nachman articles 75 and 249; Life of Rabbi Nachman 526, avodas Hashem – the service of Hashem 83), see there). Now, someone who always speaks in the Holy Tongue, like a Jerusalemite, doesn't have to think in his mind the meaning of the words, just to incline his ear to what he is saying, and this is the main intention (*kavana*) of his prayer. And by the true tzaddikim of great stature, by them all the *kavanos* (intentions) of the Arizal etc. are the (simple) meaning of the words, for in their meaning of the words are encompassed all the *kavanos*.

(Likutay Moharan vol. 2, Torah 120).

14. Encouragement for passionate prayer – to appreciate the importance of even a small segment

He would strengthen his men who complained before him with great protest against that which they were so distant from prayer, and it was so difficult for them to pray. And he would encourage them and console them with many expressions, that they should not be disheartened because of this.

He said: Behold, by a convert (that converted), what an achievement it is by him, to know how to just recite the words until "*Baruch SheUmar*" ("Blessed is He Who said" – the second part of the morning prayers), therefore it is befitting to console oneself, and cheer oneself, that in any case he merits to say the words of the prayer.

And I heard, that he was speaking with a simple person about the matter of prayer, that it was very difficult for him to pray, and he gave him an *aitza* (advice/remedy), and said to him, that he should think in his heart, that he doesn't need to pray, just until "*Baruch SheUmar*" ("Blessed is He Who said" – the second part of the morning prayers), because perhaps in this *gilgul* (form of reincarnation) he needs only to rectify this section of the prayer, because perhaps in an earlier *gilgul* he had already prayed with *kavana* (intention) the other sections of the prayer, just this section – until "*Baruch SheUmar*" he needs now, in this *gilgul*, to pray with *kavana*, and therefore he should insert all his strength into this small amount, to pray with *kavana* until "*Baruch SheUmar*". Afterwards, when he reaches "*Baruch SheUmar*", he should think, perhaps he needs to rectify this section, such as from "*Baruch SheUmar*" till "*VaYiVurech Duvid*" ("And David blessed" – second half, of the second section of the morning prayers), and he should again pray with *kavana* that section, and so forth further on. And the general rule is, that one should not confuse himself at the beginning with (consideration of) the whole prayer, for it will be difficult and heavy upon him, he should just strive each time to say a little with *kavana*, for it is possible to pray a little with *kavana*, and afterwards a little more etc., as mentioned above. **(Likutay Moharan vol. 2, Torah 101).**

[**And** also it is already explained in The Words of Rabbi Nachman (article 75), that the reality is that usually it is not possible to pray the entire prayer, just a little, for each one prays some section of the prayer according to his aspect, for there is a master of the hands and there is a master of the feet etc. (Tikunay Zohar 18, page 32a). And this is the aspect mentioned above, that everyone is aroused and merits to pray with *kavana* a section of the prayer according to his aspect. Therefore a person should not be disheartened when he sees that he merited to pray a little with *kavana*, some part of the prayer, and suddenly it comes to cessation, and he cannot pray properly anymore by any means, for usually it was compelled to be like that, as mentioned above. And he should endeavor to pray the rest of the prayer with complete simplicity etc., and through this he will merit with His Mercy Blessed He to arouse from this, until he returns, and his heart will fire up, and he will begin to pray properly again with inspiration etc.. And if sometimes he doesn't merit to have passion throughout the entire prayer, what can be done? If he merits, he can say afterwards some chapter of Psalms, or another supplication or entreaty with *kavana*. For certainly every single person, according to what he knows in his soul of his lowliness, it is becoming of him to realize that he is very, very distant from prayer, which is very, very lofty. And from where does he merit to such a lofty devotion which is higher than learning Torah; and therefore he must do his part; if he cannot pray properly with *kavana*, he should begin to pray the words of the prayer with utter simplicity, and he should incline his ear to what he is saying, and usually through this he will come to the appropriate arousal etc., see there.

And also see in Likutay Moharan (vol. 1, Torah 99) what is written there, that a person has to be strong with prayer even when he doesn't merit to pray with attachment (*divaikus*), and his prayer is not fluent in his mouth Heaven forbid, even still he should be strong even then to pray with all his might and concentration (*kavana*), for when he merits to pray with attachment (divaikus), and his prayer will be fluent in his mouth properly, then all his prayers will ascend with that prayer which he prayed properly. And this is, "**And I pleaded to Hashem** (Deuteronomy 4:23)" – always, both with *divaikus* (attachment) and without *divaikus*. "**At that time saying** (same verse)" – that is, because when I merit to pray with attachment (divaikus), and the words will be said fluently in my mouth in the aspect of "my prayer is fluent (Brachos 4:3 – this is a sign that it will be answered)," then all the prayers that he prayed until now not properly, will also ascend with that worthy prayer.

And see in The Words of Rabbi Nachman (article 74) what is written there regarding prayer, that sometimes a person does not have any passion in his prayer, and it is necessary to fire himself up with emotion and a fiery heart for prayer. Like, for example, it is found that a person sometimes makes himself upset, until he comes to anger and is angry, like people say in Yiddish, "*ehr shnitzt zich a roagez*" (he made himself angry), the same exact thing with holiness, regarding prayer, it is sometimes necessary to make oneself worked up, and make for himself emotion and a fiery heart with the words of the prayer, "*azoy vey ainer* (just like someone) *shnitzt zich a roagez* (works himself up)," and through this he will actually come afterwards to true vigorous fervor in prayer.

15. Capitalize on the exact spot you received inspiration and act upon it before moving on

I heard in his name that he said, that sometimes a person is visited with a thought of repentance and longing for Hashem Yisburach, in some place, it is necessary there, specifically in that place, to strengthen (with) this thought of repentance and longing, for instance, to say there some words of entreaty and supplication, or words of longing, with mouth and with heart, according to the matter, and not to wait and not to move from his place, even though this place is not disposed for such, such as a place that isn't designated for Torah (study) and prayer, just on the way and so forth, because when he moves from his place it is possible that it will cease. And so we saw this matter by him o.b.m. himself, many times.

(Likutay Moharan vol. 2, Torah 124).

16. Seeing oneself in the Psalms, even the praises

Regarding the recital of Psalms, he spoke with someone and said to him, that the essence of saying Psalms – is to say all the chapters of the Psalms referring to oneself. And Rabbainu o.b.m. explained this to him a little, that all the wars (that) King David r.i.p. beseeched that Hashem Yisburach should save him from them, one needs to depict everything on himself, referring to the battle he has with the evil inclination (*yetzehr hurra*) and his legions (as this is explained above, article 9). And the person asked him o.b.m., how to depict on himself the verses that King David r.i.p. praised himself, such as (Psalms 86:2), "Guard my soul for I am pious (*"chusid"*)," and so forth. He replied to him, this as well one needs to read on himself, because it is necessary to judge oneself favorably, and to find in oneself, some merit and good point in which this, he is in the aspect of pious, and so forth. And Rabbainu o.b.m. said to him, behold by Yehoshufat it is written (Chronicles 2:17:6), "And he lifted his heart (-ego) in the ways of Hashem," that in the ways of Hashem and His service Blessed He, he lifted his heart a little. In addition Rabbainu o.b.m. said to him, behold in the morning we begin by saying, "What are we? What are our lives? Etc.," and we extremely efface ourselves, and afterwards we say, "But we are Your nation, the Children of Your Covenant etc.," for afterwards we strengthen ourselves and relate our greatness, that we are His nation the Children of His Covenant, the progeny of Abraham, Isaac, and Jacob etc., because this is the necessary conduct in the service of Hashem, as mentioned above. And see Likutay Moharan (Torah 282), what is written on the verse (Psalms 104:33, 146:2), "I will sing to my G-d with all I have (/with the little bit (of good) remaining in me)," and it is brought down further on, article 67.

(Likutay Moharan vol. 2, Torah 125).

17. Speak to G-d like an enamored toddler cajoles his father

It is very good for someone who is able, to pour out his words before Hashem Yisburach piteously and pleadingly, like a son who yearns before his father, for behold Hashem Yisburach already called us sons, as it is written (Deuteronomy 14:1), "You are sons to Hashem your G-d." Therefore it is very good to express one's words and troubles before Him Blessed He like a son who complains before his father with cute and endearing motions which are called *"piyostin"*- (playing, cooing), and even if it seems to someone that in accordance to his conduct he is not like a son before Him Blessed He, even still, behold Hashem Yisburach called us sons, as mentioned above, because (Kedushin 36a), either way (-whether or not Israel act befittingly) they are called (by You) sons etc., (so) it is on me to do my part, to make myself as a son, as mentioned above. And how good it is when one can arouse his heart with entreaties until he cries and sheds tears like a son before his father. **(Words of Rabbi Nachman 7).**

And see the book "Ullim LiTrufa" (Leaves for Healing, letter 254), where it is written there: And I saw in Medrash Rabbu (Vayikra Rabbu 2-3), that it brings down (there) the verse (Jeremiah 31:19/20), "Is Ephraim a dear son to me? Is he a child of (my) delight? For whenever I speak of him (/for it is sufficient the words (of Torah) which I put in him, to effect), I surely remember him more." And it says there: Which (age) is a delightful child? Around the age of two or three years old. And another said, around four or five years old. And the commentaries (see Eitz Yosef) there explain, that one said around the age of two or three year old, for even though such a young toddler cannot speak, only hintingly, or partial words, even still his father delights in him, with his speech, and fulfills his desire. And one said, around the age of four or five years old, for then his speech is complete, and he makes requests from his father with full verbalization: "Give me such a thing or such a thing." And his father fulfills his request. And even though it is not explained so much over there, I explained the matter more, because I, in my poverty, took out from here a great deal of inspiration regarding what he o.b.m. admonished us, for one to express his words before Him Blessed He every day etc., because thank G-d, I understood from this Medrash powerful encouragement and arousal for this. Because it is understood and conveyed from this, that even when a person cannot speak at all before Him Blessed He, or to express his words well, even still it is precious in His eyes Blessed He, even if he speaks only hintingly and with partial words like a two or three year old baby, and sometimes Hashem Yisburach helps, and he speaks entire phrases like a toddler of four or five years old. And in this way Israel is precious in His eyes Blessed He, when they speak and converse their needs before Him Blessed He, and they are called a "child of delight". And see there what is written (there) on the end of the verse, "for when I speak of him;" My Word (the Torah) that I put in him is sufficient etc.. It can be understood from there the utter preciousness of the spoken word, and it is impossible to explain so much in writing, and it is compulsory to be brief, however, you can understand for yourselves from this, hints to strengthen oneself, in the matter of speaking and conversing between oneself and his Creator, however possible. True, it is certainly better to speak explicitly with complete articulation, however, even when one cannot speak properly, it is precious in His Eyes Blessed He even the speech which is called "*piyestin*" (playing, cooing), like a delightful child of two or three years old. And understand this well to fulfill all this with simplicity, for it is your eternal life, for it is impossible to pass through this world peacefully, only through this which is written here, for our strength is only with our mouth etc. (Medrash Shocher Tov 22:20), see there.

18. Joy is a pathway to do hisbodidus

When a person is happy the entire day, then he can readily designate an hour of the day to break his heart and converse everything that is on his heart, before Hashem Yisburach, as explained by us many times; but when he has sadness Heaven forbid, it is very difficult for him to do hisbodidus and to express his words before Him Blessed He.

(Words of Rabbi Nachman, article 20).

19. Have a broken heart but never be sad

A broken heart and sadness are not at all the same thing. For a broken heart is of the heart, whereas sadness comes from the spleen (Tikunay Zohar 3 of the final additional 11, and see Likutay Moharan 23:5), and it is the other (-evil) side, and the Holy One Blessed He hates it; however, a broken heart is cherished before Hashem Yisburach, and is very dear in His eyes Blessed He. And it would be good for a person to have a broken heart the entire day, however, people of your standing are not able to hold this up, because it is possible from having a broken heart to come to sadness Heaven forbid, which is completely forbidden for a person. Therefore it is necessary to designate some hour in the day in which one should have a broken heart, that is, to do hisbodidus and break his heart before Him Blessed He, but the rest of the whole day entirely he should be just happy. **(Words of Rabbi Nachman, article 41).**

20. Difference between a broken heart and sadness

Sadness is like someone is angry and upset, like someone who resentfully finds fault and complains against Him Blessed He, Heaven forbid, for not doing for him as he wishes; however, a broken heart is like a son who expresses his yearning before his father, like a baby who complains and cries before his father for being distant from him etc.. **(Words of Rabbi Nachman, article 42, and furthermore see below article 34).**

21. A Broken heart brings joy

After having a broken heart comes joy; and this is an indication if one had a broken heart, when afterwards he comes to joy. **(Words of Rabbi Nachman, article 45).**

22. Take the time to settle yourself and take stock everyday

One must have great merit, for him to merit, to settle himself one hour a day, and for him to have regret for that which necessitates regret, because not everyone merits to this, for the day passes and whisks by him and he doesn't have the opportunity to settle himself even one time in all the days of his life. Therefore it is necessary to rise and take charge, to see to commit time for himself to settle himself well, concerning all his action which he does in this world, if it is appropriate for him to spend his days in such a fashion, with this conduct.

(Words of Rabbi Nachman, article 47).

[**And** see in the book "Nachas HaShulchan" (Savoring the Table- Code of Jewish Law), handwritten manuscript of the holy Rav of Tcherin o.b.m., in the laws of passover, where he explains that the main insurrection of the other (-evil) side is to blind a persons eyes so that he does not give any contemplation whatsoever to his ways, in the aspect of (Proverbs 18:3), "A fool does not desire understanding etc.." However, immediately when there is an awakening of the power and the radiance of the *neshama* (-soul), which is the aspect of the light of the candle, the aspect of (Proverbs 20:27), "The candle of Hashem is the *neshama* of a person (searching all the chambers of the innards)," and he begins to examine his actions and to contemplate his ways, then (Avoda Zura 55a), one who comes to purify himself (from above) they help him, and a little light repels a lot of darkness (Tzaidah LaDerech 12). And this is what we make the blessing on the obliteration of *chumetz* (-leaven and foods which were fermented, which must be eradicated before Passover) at the time of the *bedika* (-the search for *chumetz* the night before Passover, all the *chumetz* found is destroyed the next morning, yet the blessing on the destruction is made before the search), because the very *bedika* (-search, examination) for the *chumetz* (which is a construct of the evil inclination), that is, when one begins to

search and examine his actions, this itself is already the
beginning of the obliteration].

23. Hisbodidus in bed and sighing

He said: King David r.i.p. founded the Book of Psalms
from this, that he was very strong in the matter of
hisbodidus. And he said, that the main hisbodidus of King
David r.i.p. was when he lay on his bed and covered
himself with a sheet, then he would speak and converse
everything on his heart before Hashem Yisburach, as it is
written (Psalms 6:7), "I converse (/spoil, ruin/swim) every night
(in) my bed with my tears I drench my bed." Fortunate is
whoever accustoms himself to fulfill this practice which
surmounts everything. **(Words of Rabbi Nachman, article 68).**

In addition, it is written in his holy words (article 275, see also
Life of Rabbi Nachman 587), that it is good for a person, when
he lies down in his bed to sleep, to accustom himself to
pour out his words before Hashem Yisburach and to request
from Him that He draw him close to His service Blessed
He. And if he doesn't merit then to speak outright before
Him Blessed He due to the preponderance of his stone
heart, in any event he should accustom himself to sigh and
groan, many groans continuously one after the other, over
his great distance from Hashem Yisburach and that he
should merit to draw close to Him Blessed He (Life of Rabbi
Nachman 510, and see below article 47). And it is already laid out
in his holy book Likutay Moharan many torahs (teachings; 8,
22:4, 56:9) what one can merit through a holy sigh, see there.

24. G-d helps and provides words for one to prevail and be victorious despite all

Our Rabbis o.b.m. said (Pesachim 119), sing to Whom one is victorious over Him, and He rejoices, for it is necessary to best Him Blessed He, so to speak. For even though it seems to a person that Hashem Yisburach does not want to draw him close because he was very delinquent (/did a lot of damage) and even now he does not behave properly as He desires Blessed He, even still a person must bolster himself exceedingly, and prostrate himself before Him blessed He, and spread out his hands to Him, that He should have mercy on him and draw him close to His service, "for despite this, I desire to be a Jewish man." It comes out, that he wants to defeat Hashem Yisburach so to speak, and Hashem Yisburach has joy from this, that they defeat Him so to speak. **(Words of Rabbi Nachman, article 69).** [And see Likutay Moharan (vol. 1, torah 124), that it is written there, that because of the joy that Hashem Yisburach has from this, therefore He Himself sends him words in his mouth so that he can defeat Him, for short of this it would certainly be impossible for flesh and blood to defeat the Holy One Blessed He, just, Hashem Yisburach Himself helps him with this, as mentioned above].

25. A Jew who turns to G-d, G-d puts all edicts aside giving him undivided attention

When a Jew desires to speak with Hashem Yisburach, to express his words before Him blessed He, and to ask from Him that He should draw him close to His service blessed He, then Hashem Yisburach so to speak throws aside all

His affairs, and all the edicts that He wishes to decree Heaven forbid, and all His engagements that He blessed He is involved in, so to speak, and He casts everything aside and turns Himself to attend just to this person who desires to speak with Him, and express his words before Him to request from Him that He help him to draw close to Him blessed He. The upshot is, that through this the natural result is that the Jews are saved from all harsh decrees, may the Merciful One save us.

(Words of Rabbi Nachman, article 70).

26. Through good tidings it is possible to recite Psalms.
(Words of Rabbi Nachman, article 97).

27. Psalms and trust in G-d are a life support which heal.
The surrounding vegetation yearn and are included in one's prayer.

Reciting Psalms is a great quality (/height), as if they were (being) said by King David r.i.p. himself, because he said them with Divine inspiration (*ruach hakodesh* -holy spirit), and the Divine inspiration is resting (innate) inside the words. And when one says the chapters of Psalms, he arouses with the breath (*ruach*) of his mouth the *ruach hakodesh*, to the extent that it is considered as if King David r.i.p. himself had said them. And it is extremely propitious (*mesugal*) to heal the sick, for him to have trust solely in Hashem

Yisburach, that through the reciting of Psalms, Hashem will save him. And the trust is an aspect of a cane (/support), just like a person is supported on the cane, so he is supported on the trust, that he trusts that Hashem will save him, as David said (Psalms 18:19), "And Hashem is a support for me." And therefore through this the sick person is healed, as it is written (Exodus 21:19), "If he rises (from his sickbed) and walks outside on his cane, then exonerate (the attacker)." And this is the aspect of (Isaiah 11:1), "And a staff (/shoot) will come out from the lineage (/stump) of Jesse (-*Yeesheye*)," which is said of Messiah, who is from the progeny of David. And this is the aspect of (Pesachim 68.): In the future the tzaddikim will resurrect the dead, by means of the cane, in the aspect of (Zechariah 8:4), "And a man with his cane in his hand," in the aspect of (- based on the verse - Kings 2:4:29), "And you should place (the) my cane on the face of the youth."

He also said then: Winter is the aspect of pregnancy, at which time all the grasses and the vegetation perish, for their vitality is dormant in the winter, and they are then in the aspect of death. And when summer comes, which is the aspect of birth, then all the grasses awaken and come to life, and at this time it is good and very fine when one goes out to converse in the field, "conversing" being prayer, and entreaties, and yearning, and longing for Hashem Yisburach, and then all the vegetation of the field which are beginning then to live and burgeon, all of them are yearning and including themselves inside his words and his prayers. **(Words of Rabbi Nachman, article 98).**

[And see in Likutay Moharan (vol. 2, torah 1), that this is the aspect of (Genesis 24:63), "And Isaac went out to converse <*lu-suach*> in the field," that is, his prayer was together with all the vegetation <*siach*> of the field, for all the vegetation of the field restored (returned) their vitality in (to) his prayer, see there].

28. Do hisbodidus in the fields

He said: If a person would merit to hear the songs and the praises of the grasses, how each and every grass says song to Hashem Yisburach without any ulterior motive or any foreign thoughts whatsoever, how beautiful and pleasant it is when one hears their song. So therefore amongst them it is very good to serve Hashem with fear [and he said in these words: "*es iz zehr git frum tzoo zayn tzivishin zay*"], and to do hisbodidus on the face of the field between the growth of the earth, and to truly pour out one's words there before Hashem Yisburach. And further see in the Words (of Rabbi Nachman, article 227), that he also said, that it is better for the hisbodidus to be outside the city in a place of grasses, as mentioned above, for the grasses are an impetus to arouse the heart. **(Words of Rabbi Nachman, article 163).**

29. Scream to G-d as if your life is in peril

He said: It is necessary for every person to scream to Hashem Yisburach, and to lift his heart to Him blessed He, as if he were hanging on a thread in middle of the ocean, and powerful storm winds (are) blowing to the heart of the sky, to the extent that he doesn't know what to do, and there is barely even an opportunity to scream. But in truth, certainly he has no *aitza* (advice, solution, course of action) or recourse except to lift his eyes and heart to Hashem Yisburach. For a person is in grave and dire danger in this world, as every person knows for himself (-in his soul).

(Words of Rabbi Nachman, article 29).

30. Scream to G-d from the depth of Hell

One time I (Rabbi Nussun) stood before him, and he o.b.m. was resting on his bed, and the following words were discharged from his holy mouth, and he said these words: "*Dor* (the) *ikur* (main thing) *iz* (is), '*meebeten* (from the belly of) *scheol* (-hell) *sheevaatee* (I screamed) (Jonah 2:3)'." And see in the book Ullim LiTrufa (Leaves for Healing, letter 60), which brings down there this statement, and writes there the following: And every person is so despondent to the extent that it appears to him as if this was not said regarding him, as if he descended lower than the belly of scheol (-hell) Heaven forbid, and as if he is no longer able to scream, and as if he has already screamed a very great deal and it was to no avail, and many more such excuses and denial. And the truth is not so, for I know the truth, that he o.b.m. intended in all his words also etc. and pertaining every single person etc., see there.

(Words of Rabbi Nachman, article 302).

31. Hisbodidus is for everyone, every single unique soul

Every single person has unique practices, that he needs to practices according to his needs, to rectify what he defected, and according to the root of his *neshama* (soul). However, hisbodidus and to pour out one's words before Hashem Yisburach every day (and) in the spoken language, this is a general practice of which every single Jew is obligated every day, all the days of his life. And so, learning the Shulchan Aruch (Code of Jewish Law) every day, this is also a general practice, as mentioned above. **(Words of Rabbi Nachman, article 185).** [And see below, the end of item 61, where it explains there that these two are contingent one upon the other].

32. Hisbodidus prepares a person for Messiah

He said: Certainly there are kosher people to be found even though they do not do hisbodidus, however I call them perturbed and disconcerted (shocked), and suddenly when Messiah comes and calls them – they will be confused and disconcerted. But he who conducts the holy practice of hisbodidus, will resemble a man well rested whose mind is collected and very settled, so he will have calm presence of mind, without agitation or confusion.

(Words of Rabbi Nachman, article 228).

33. It is appropriate to be enraptured with yearning for G-d even when amongst people

It is appropriate for a Jewish man, that his heart should be so drawn to Hashem Yisburach, to the extent that even when he is amongst people, he will be aroused time and again to Hashem Yisburach with great longing and intensive awakening, and lift his hands and his heart to Hashem, and scream to Hashem Yisburach with all (lit. with the expiration of) his soul, and with wondrous arousal: "Do not leave me Hashem, my G-d (Psalms 38:22)." And he lifted his hands then and said this verse with a pleasant voice of entreaty and longing before Hashem Yisburach.

(Words of Rabbi Nachman, article 229).

34. With a broken heart one can turn intimately to G-d even when amongst people

He said: The difference between a broken heart and depression is; a broken heart is such that even when one stands amongst people, he turns his face away and says: "Master of the World etc.," and at that exact time simultaneously, Rabbainu o.b.m. himself said, "Master of the World," with wondrous arousal, with upraised hands in intensive yearning, as was his way. **(Words of Rabbi Nachman, article 230, also see above articles 19-21).**

35. Speaking to G-d is a mighty endeavor and it is ludicrous to back down due to some minor dejection or deterrent

He said: A parable, a warrior girded his loins to conquer a bastion, and afterwards when he came to the gate there was a tapestry woven there from spider webs which blocked the gate. Is there anything more ridiculous than this, that he should retreat from his battle due to the blockage of spider webs? And afterwards he said: The main thing is the speech, for through speech one can conquer everything, and be victorious over all the battles. And he said: Even though it is possible to do hisbodidus by thought, [but] the main thing is the speech.

The meaning of the parable is readily explanatory, addressing the difficulty a person has to speak before Hashem Yisburach what is in his heart, and all of this is due to his shame and heaviness, for he does not have holy brazenness. And certainly this is a great folly, for behold he desires to conquer with his speech an arduous battle, which is the battle of (-against) the (evil) inclination, and now, when he is close to begin to speak before Hashem Yisburach and conquer, and break walls, and open gates by means of the speaking, and because of a minor deterrence, from his dejection and so forth, he will hold himself back Heaven forbid, from speaking. Behold this restraint is tantamount to the blockage of a spiderweb in contrast to a rampart, for what he desires to break with his speech!

And he said, that it is good for a person to do hisbodidus two hours a day; one hour – for him to go and yearn and prepare himself to speak, and to arrange and forge his heart for this, and afterwards he should speak for one hour. **(Words of Rabbi Nachman, article 232).**

36. Pray for everything, even the smallest concern

He said, for every matter it is necessary to pray, that is, if one's garment is torn and he needs clothing, he should pray to Hashem Yisburach that He should give him clothing to wear. And so forth with everything similar. Something big or small, for everything, one should accustom himself to pray always to Hashem Yisburach for everything he is lacking. Even though the main thing is to pray for the fundamental, namely, for the service of Hashem Yisburach, to draw close to Him blessed He, even still, also for this one needs to pray. And he said: He who does not practice this, even though Hashem Yisburach gives him clothing, and a livelihood, and all his needs in life, nevertheless his whole life is like an animal, which Hashem Yisburach also gives it food etc.. Because since he does not draw all his sustenance through prayer from Hashem Yisburach, consequently all his vitality is *mamash* (-really) like the life of an animal, because a person needs to draw all his sustenance and his needs from Hashem Yisburach specifically through prayer and entreaty. And one time he (Rabbi Nachman) said to his student, our teacher the rav, Rabbi Nussun *zatza"l*, regarding a small and very trivial matter that he somewhat required, "Did you prayer for this to Hashem Yisburach?" And he stood flabbergasted, for this matter was wondrous in his eyes, to pray to Hashem Yisburach for something infinitesimal such as this, and also because it was not overly necessary. He (Rabbi Nachman) spoke up and said to him (with an inquisitive inflection), "This is beneath your dignity, that you should pray to Hashem Yisburach for such a trite matter?" And the general principle is, that for everything in the world one needs to pray to Hashem Yisburach.

(Words of Rabbi Nachman, article 233).

37. Hisbodidus can take time to show its effect like dripping on a stone until it carves a niche

He said regarding encouragement in hisbodidus and conversing between oneself and his Creator: Even if many days and years pass by, and it seems to him that he still has not accomplished anything with his conversing and his words, even still he should not fall from this whatsoever, for the truth is that certainly the words are making an impression. An allegory for this: Like water coming down on a stone, even though it would seem that the water doesn't have power against the hard stone, and the water has no apparent impression in the stone, even still, when the water comes down on the stone many, many times consecutively, they bore a whole in the stone, as can be seen outright. Similarly, even if one's heart is a heart of stone, and shows no sign of his words and his prayers, even still with the accumulation of days and years his heart of stone will be pierced through his conversing and his words, like (Job 14:19), "stones withered by water," as mentioned above. **(Words of Rabbi Nachman, article 234).**

38. The Psalm recited before Sabbath is an opportunity to really articulate oneself

He said: In *"Hoadoo"* ("Praise" - Psalms 107) which is said before Sabbath, before *mincha* (-the afternoon prayer), it is possible to break one's heart very much, and to express all one's words there, because it speaks there regarding the hardships of the soul and regarding screaming (to Hashem) over every matter. **(Words of Rabbi Nachman, article 270).**

39. Designate a special private place to do hisbodidus

It is very good for a person to have a room designated for him alone, to engage there in the service of Hashem, and particularly in hisbodidus and conversation between himself and his Creator. And he said, that even the sitting itself, that one sits in a room allocated for him alone, this also is very good. However, even someone who doesn't merit to have his own room, even still, he too can come up with many schemes to carry out this practice of hisbodidus and to speak between himself and his Creator. And he said, that under the *tallis* it is also like a private room, for when one lowers the *tallis* over his eyes, it is possible to speak between himself and his Creator whatever he desires. Also it is possible to express one's words before Him blessed He when he lies down in his bed and covers himself with a sheet, as pointed out above (article 23), that this was the practice King David r.i.p. chose for himself. It is also possible to sit with a book, and others will think that he is learning, and he can speak then between himself and his Creator. Additionally, many ruses can be found (by) he who truly desires to conduct himself in this practice of hisbodidus which is higher than everything, for it is an essential root of holiness and purity, as has been explained already many times. However, it is better for one to endeavor to have his own room, as mentioned above. **(Words of Rabbi Nachman, article 272-4).**

40. It is possible to scream silently

It is possible to scream to Hashem Yisburach in a silent whisper, screaming tremendously, and no one will hear anything, because one does not release any sound outside, he just visualizes distinctively the scream in thought. See the whole matter inside. **(Words of Rabbi Nachman, article 16).**

41. Put down prayers and Torah study for a future time of need

He said: Behold the storekeeper is in the practice of selling on credit, to be paid some time after, so why does a person not say some chapters of Psalms, or learn (Torah), or do other *mitzvos*, and they will remain ready by him for a time of need; for there will be a time when he will need it, when he will collect his wages and his accomplishments, so why should he not do as the storekeeper who gives merchandise on credit. **(Words of Rabbi Nachman, article 271).**

42. Encouragement to pray strongly even when one seemingly has reason to be disheartened

He said: Even if a person is the way he is, even still he should strengthen and embolden his heart to pray to Hashem Yisburach. And he said, that one should think in his heart, "Behold, if in my eyes I am so distant from Hashem Yisburach due to my plethora of sins, in that case, on the contrary, the main completion of the prayer – is specifically through me, for behold our rabbis o.b.m. said (Kreesus 6:), every prayer that doesn't include in it, (something) from the prayers of the iniquitous of Israel, is not (considered) prayer, and we learn this from the Incense (*Kitoaress*), which contained *chelbinnu* (galbanum). So if this is the case, if I am like the iniquitous of Israel Heaven forbid, if so, on the contrary, the entire completion of the prayer is specifically through me, as mentioned above, so certainly I need to strengthen (myself) all the more so, to pray to Hashem Yisburach, and be confident in Hashem's kindness, that He will listen and receive my prayer as well, for on the contrary, specifically through me there is the main completion of the prayer, for it is impossible to burn the *Kitoaress* without *chelbinnu*, hence *chelbinnu* is also the completion of the *Kitoaress*. And so too regarding prayer, as mentioned above, without my measly prayer which joins the prayer of Israel, the prayer would not have completion." **(Words of Rabbi Nachman, article 295).**

And see additional strong encouragement regarding prayer in Words of Rabbi Nachman (article 283) what he said regarding the youth, who are usually perturbed in their prayers due to their not having merited to sanctify themselves properly in the holiness of conjugation, and therefore when they stand afterwards to pray, it is very difficult for them to pray. And he o.b.m. warned of this many times, not to fall in resolve from this whatsoever, and what was, was, and during the prayer it is necessary to forget everything completely, and rally to always pray with joy as is befitting, whatever state he is in, and to trust in Hashem Yisburach that in the very end he will merit through the prayer to win the battle, and to sanctify himself as is befitting. And he said, that regarding this Abba

Binyumin took pains (Brachos 5b) that his prayer should be close to his bed; "*bed*" is a term for conjugation, and this is the meaning of "on my prayer, that it should be close to my *bed*," namely, that I should be able to pray afterwards, immediately following, and this matter should not disconcert my prayer whatsoever.

43. Hisbodidus is a taste of paradise and you will see the world in a completely new way

The person who merits to accustom himself to truly do hisbodidus and express his words before Hashem Yisburach properly, especially if he merits to do hisbodidus in the fields and forests, (then he) will feel with every single step he takes there, the taste of paradise (*Gan Eden*). Also subsequently when he returns from there, (then) the whole world will be brand new in his eyes, and it will appear to him as if it is a different world, completely new, and the world will not appear at all in his eyes as it had before.

(Life of Rabbi Nachman, article 107).

44. Hisbodidus is a super way of receiving Divine help despite the restriction of "free choice."

When he (Rabbi Nachman) made known the matter of hisbodidus and conversing between oneself and his Creator, our teacher, the rav, the tzadik Rabbi Nussun *zatza"l* spoke with him, and asked him: Behold a person has free choice (-t.n. so how can simply relating matters to Hashem effectuate the changes which should be incumbent on the person himself to achieve)? And he did not answer him explicitly, just offhandedly, as if to say, even still. That is to say, that is impossible to explain this matter to you completely, (and) even still it is necessary to practice this. And our teacher, Rabbi Nussun *zatza"l*, was not able to question any further, because he knew that this question could be asked also pertaining the prayers that were already set for us by our Rabbis o.b.m. addressing repentance and drawing close to Hashem Yisburach, like the blessing "*Hasheevainu*" (-of the 18 benedictions, return us in repentance) and so forth. (**Life of Our Master Rabbi Nachman, article 436**; And see below, article 93, what I brought down from the book Likutay Halachos, Choshen Mishpat, laws of deposit, law 3).

45. Always start anew

He said: It is good for a person to say during hisbodidus, when he is secluding himself with his Creator, he should say: "Today I begin to bind (*divaikus*) to You." And every time he should initiate a beginning, because all continuations follow after the beginnings. And even the rationalist scientists say that the beginning is paramount to half of the phenomenon of the entire process. Consequently, either way he should make a new start every time, and he should say as mentioned above, for either way (*mima nafshuch*); if it was good before – now it will be better, and if Heaven forbid beforehand it was not good – certainly it is necessary and incumbent to launch a new beginning. (**The Life of Rabbi Nachman, article 437**).

46. Rabbi Nachman's grandson took his watch and asks G-d to heal grandfather.

On the last Rosh Hashana (Jewish New Years) in Uman, his wise grandson, the son of his righteous daughter Mistress Sara o.b.m., Master Israel, was by him. And his grandson was still a young boy, three or four years old, and at that time Rabbainu's o.b.m. sickness was very critical, for it was close to his passing away, for he passed away right afterwards on Chol HaMoed (intermediate days of) Succos. And Rabbainu o.b.m. said to his aforementioned grandson, "Yisroel, pray for me to Hashem Yisburach that I should return to my health." He replied (to him), "Give me your watch and I will pray for you." Rabbainu o.b.m. responded, "Did you (plural – addressing everyone present) see that he is already a 'Good Jew' (an appellation reference for a Chasidic Master), for he is ordering that I give him an item in order that he pray." And he gave (it) to him. And the boy took the watch, and he progressed and said these words, "G-d, G-d, *luz* <let> *der* <the> *zaide* <grandfather> *zayn gizund* <be healthy>." And the people standing there began to laugh. Rabbainu o.b.m. responded, "This is the way necessary to beseech from Hashem Yisburach, and how is there any other way to pray to Hashem Yisburach?!" That is to say, that this is the main (method of) prayer to Hashem Yisburach, with utter simplicity, like an infant before his father, like a person speaks to his friend.

(Life of Rabbi Nachman, article 439).

47. Even to just say Master of the World is very good.
It can be discerned on a person if he does hisbodidus.

He said, even when one is unable to speak during hisbodidus, just the word "Master of the World" alone, this is also very good. (And see above, article 2, elucidated that even the preparation alone, that one prepares himself to speak but cannot speak at all, is also very good.) And he said, that it is possible to recognize on a person if he does hisbodidus. **(Life of Rabbi Nachman, article 440)** [And regarding this see the Introduction and below article 58].

48. Multiple daily sessions of hisbodidus. Sighing. Lifting the heart. Speaking to the limbs. Speaking exhaustively.

To one person, Rabbainu o.b.m. ordered that he should do hisbodidus, one period in the day, and one period in the night. Once Rabbainu o.b.m. asked one of his followers if he was accustomed to groaning and sighing, which is called '*krechtzin*', when he does hisbodidus. And he replied (to him), "yes." And Rabbainu o.b.m. said to him, "When I make a groan or a sigh, if I am holding my hand on the table at the time of the sigh, then is it impossible afterwards for me to lift my hand from the table, and I need to wait some time (hour) until my strength is restored (see Brachos 58b, and Likutay Moharan 22 and 109, and in the additional handwritten torahs published at the end, Rabbainu uses the word NeNaCh - sighing). Once Rabbainu o.b.m. grasped the rav, the tzaddik, Rabbi Shmuel Isaac o.b.m. against his heart, and said to him, "Because of a little blood such as this (i.e. the vascular of the heart) you will abolish this world and the next world." And in Yiddish, "*Ibber a bisselleh blit zulst uhn verin dey velt uhn yenne velt; krechtz dus ois*," accustom yourself to sigh a lot before Hashem Yisburach, until you are relieved of this blood, and put down the evil in it, and you merit to the aspect of (Psalms 109:22), "And my heart is hollow inside of me."

Once, Rabbainu o.b.m. spoke with Rav Yaakov Yosef regarding the service of Hashem, as was his practice always, and he told him a parable of a king who sent his son far away to learn wisdoms. Afterwards the son came to the king's house erudite in all the wisdoms. Once, the king commanded the son to take a certain extremely large stone (like a millstone) and carry it up to the higher floors of the house, and probably the son was unable to carry and lift the stone, because it was a very large and heavy stone. And the son was anguished for not being able to fulfill the desire of his father the king, until the king revealed to him afterwards his purport, and said to him, "Is it conceivable to you that I would command you something so arduous like this to take the stone as it is and carry it and lift it; are you able to do such a thing with your great wisdom?! Rather my entire intention was that you should take a sledgehammer and bash and break apart the stone into small pieces, and in this way you would be able to bring it up to the higher floor." Similarly, Hashem Yisburach commanded us (Lamentations 3:41) that we lift our hearts up to hands (stretched out) to G-d in heaven, and our hearts are very large and heavy stone (heart), and it is impossible to lift by any means, just, by taking a hammer, which is speech, and through this it is possible to bust and break apart the heart of stone, and then we are able to lift it to Hashem Yisburach, and understand (this).

Another time Rabbainu o.b.m. spoke about the necessity to engage abundantly in the recital of Psalms, and entreaties, and beseeching, and hisbodidus etc.. And the rav, the tzaddik, Rabbi Yuddel *zatza"l* asked him, "How does one garner heart (meaning to say, how does one merit that the words will be with arousal of the heart)?" Rabbainu o.b.m. answered him, "Tell me, by which tzaddik did you receive arousal of the heart? The main thing is the speaking with the mouth, words of entreaty and beseeching, and the arousal of the heart will come of itself.

(Life of Rabbi Nachman, article 441).

To one of his greatest followers, in the youth of this follower he instructed him, that during his hisbodidus he should speak a great deal individually with all the limbs of his body, and he should explain to them that all the desires of the body – (are) emptiness, for behold the end of every man is death, and the body is brought to burial, and all the limbs will decay and rot etc., and additional words similar to these. And he practiced this for some time, and afterwards he spoke with Rabbainu o.b.m. and he apologized before him that his body doesn't listen or feel whatsoever all his argumentation and words with it. Rabbainu o.b.m. said to him, "be strong in this matter and do not let up from this, and you will see afterwards what will be from these words." And he heeded his advice and fulfilled his words, until he merited afterwards, that every single limb which he spoke to individually was so drawn to his words, to the extent that *mamash* (-actually) all the life would leave the limb he was speaking with, and remained with out any vitality or sensation. And this he saw empirically in his external limbs such as his fingers and toes and so forth, until he began to speak with his inner organs which are vital, such as the heart and so forth, he needed to be very succinct in order that his life wouldn't expire *mamash*, as mentioned.

And I heard that once, this person spoke with those close to him about how this world isn't anything, and what is the *tachlis* (-purpose, end) of all the matters of the body etc. as mentioned above, and in the middle of speaking he fainted and began to die (and in Yiddish: he remained weak), and with ardent effort he revived and returned to life. And he said then that he merited through the holiness of Rabbainu o.b.m. to this (spiritual) level that whenever he reminds himself well of the fear of (Heavenly) retribution and the end and the *tachlis* of all the matters of this world, then all his limbs, even the smallest of his toes, feel *mamash* like they are already lying (in the grave) and rotting etc., to the extent that he needs to greatly bolster himself to retain his life inside of him, (so) that his soul does not depart *mamash*, as mentioned above. And I heard in the name of Rabbainu o.b.m. that he said to several other people as well, "Because your body is very coarse and strong with desires, therefore *darft eer* <you must> *un dulen* <badger/burden/exhaust> with holy words regarding the *tachlis*." And accordingly it is understood that it is also necessary to speak with oneself at great length in the matter of encouragement, so that he shouldn't abate completely, Heaven forbid (And see above, article 16). **(Life of Rabbi Nachman, article 442)**.

Additionaly it is brought down there (Life of Rabbi Nachman, article 545), that once, our teacher the rav, Rabbi Nussun *zatza"l* said to our Master and Leader, Rabbainu Hakadosh (-the holy) *zatza"l*, complaining (Psalms 69:4), "I have become exhausted with my calling out (to You), my throat has become parched (hoarse), my eyes longing disappointed, hoping to my G-d." And our Master and Leader, Rabbainu *zatza"l* lifted his hands slightly and said in a soft tone, "If so, what can be done?" That is to say, for certainly it is forbidden to have suspicion of Him Blessed He, and certainly Hashem is righteous. Afterwards he (Rabbi Nachman) said to him, "Behold, if King David r.i.p. said, 'I have exhausted myself with my calling out (to You), my throat has become parched (hoarse)', it literally was so, that he had called out so much until he was *mamash* (-actually) fatigued and exhausted with his calling, and his throat was *mamash* parched (hoarse), literally, but you, thank G-d, are still strong etc..

Likutay Aitzoas

Homilies which talk about prayer and hisbodidus as they are written in the book Likutay Aitzoas (A Collection of Advice/remedies) which flow out from the wondrous teachings that are in the book Likutay Moharan (Collection of Our Master and Leader, the Rav, Rabbi Nachman) volume one. And I recorded by each article its source, from which torah (-teaching) it originates, so that if the reader desires to know the material in their root and their substantiation, he can read inside the book Likutay Moharan itself.

49. One's main weapon is prayer.

- The teachings of Rabbi Nachman themselves empower a person to fulfill them.
- Every single word of prayer counts.
- Prayers accrue until there is made a complete structure and then there is salvation.
- Do not attribute the salvation solely to your own merit and prayers.

The main weapon of a Jewish person is prayer, and all the battles that a person needs to conquer, be it the war of the evil inclination or other battles with the obstructionists and the adversaries, everything is through prayer, and from there, is all his vitality. Therefore whoever desires to merit to the true holiness of an Israelite, needs to abound in prayer, and beseeching, and conversation between himself and his Creator, for this is the main weapon to win the battle. **(Likutay Moharan, Torah 2; Likutay Eitzos, Prayer 2).**

[**And** see in the book Ullim LiTrufa (Leaves for Healing, letter 117) from our holy teacher, the rav, Rabbi Nussun *zatza"l*, where he writes that every single holy expression of Rabbainu o.b.m. that he mentions by every matter, has special power to arouse and strengthen the heart of the Israelite to engage in it. And whoever takes to heart that all his armament is prayer etc., is aroused anew to engage in this, because he will consider in his heart: "If I do not have the strength to fight so much like great officers, nevertheless behold I am like a simple soldier who also takes arms from the royal ministry, and must learn warfare etc. every day, and everything is with (-through) the power of the king and the officers that train him etc., and whatever the case may be, I know that the battle is lengthy and ferocious, and I don't have any weapon etc. just the few words of my mouth, and even this is with the salvation of Hashem and His tremendous wonders etc.," see there].

And if a person abounds in prayer and hisbodidus for many days and years, and even still he sees in himself that he is still very far from Hashem Yisburach, and it seems to him that Hashem Yisburach is hiding His face from him Heaven forbid, he should not be mistaken Heaven forbid that Hashem Yisburach doesn't listen, hear, and heed every single word of every prayer, and entreaty, and conversation, and not a single word is lost Heaven forbid, rather, every single word makes a small impression above, and arouses His mercy Blessed He every time, but the holy structure that he needs to enter still has not been completed; and with the accrual of days and years, if he isn't foolish, and does not fall from his resolve in any way in the world, then through the abundance of prayers His mercy will be welled up, until Hashem Yisburach will turn to him, and shine His countenance upon him, and fulfill his desires and wishes, by the power of the true tzaddikim, and He will draw him close with great mercy and compassion **(Likutay Eitzos, Prayer 3).**

And even if a person merits sometimes to some relative salvation and reception of closer connectedness, he should not think to attribute that he merited this through his prayer and good deeds, for all the good deeds are from Him blessed He, as our Rabbis o.b.m. said (Vayikra Rabba 27:2) on the verse (Job 41:3), "Who proceeded me that I should pay

(/complete) him?" Who set for me a *mezuza* before I gave him a house etc.. And if not for His great kindness, he would already have drowned Heaven forbid in what he was drowning, may the Merciful One save us **(Likutay Eitzos, Prayer 6).**

50. The main source of life is prayer.

- Prayer sustains the three world formations.
- Prayers empowers G-d to provide bounty.
- Through prayer a person can find his soulmate.
- When one stands to pray the evil forces surround him, the *aitza* is to speak whatever it is he can, with truth, and the truth will illuminate the way out, even for others.

The main vitality is received from prayer, as it is written (Psalms 42:9), "a prayer to the G-d [of] {-is-} my life." (*). Also through prayer one endows vitality to all three world formations, which are, the lowly world, the world of the stars, and the world of the angels, and therefore through prayer one arouses the power of the angels who conduct the stars which are appointed over the grasses and the vegetation of this lowly world, and hit them, and say to them that they should grow, as our Sages o.b.m. said (Beraishis Raba 10:6), "You do not have a (single) grass below, that doesn't have a star and an angel which hits it and says to it, 'grow!'." Also, Israel endows their Father Who is in Heaven, with their prayers, and in accordance to his endowment to his Father Who is in Heaven, with his prayer, so the person will merit to find his sustenance. This is what the verse says (Psalms 99:7), "they guard his testament," that is, they guard the prayer, through which we *testify* on His Unity, and through this (continuation of the verse), "and law {*chok*} given to them," and law (*chok* – numerical value of NaNaCh) is a term for sustenance (Tractate Baitza 16). Also through prayer a person merits to find his soulmate.

However, when a person stands to pray, (then) foreign thoughts and *klipos* (husks – impure forces) come and surround him, and he is left in darkness, and he cannot pray. And the ultimate remediation for this is to see that words leave your mouth with truth, and through this, the word that leaves your mouth with truth, it will set for you an opening in the darkness that entraps you, and you will merit to pray well. And the main thing is, that in his prayer, and entreating, and conversation between himself and his Creator, even though it is impossible for him to say anything due to the utter darkness and confusion which surrounds him very, very much, from all sides, even still, at any rate, he should see to it to speak words with truth in whatever low level, like for example, he should say, "Hashem save etc.," truthfully, even though he cannot speak with proper vitality, even still he should force himself in any case to speak the words with truth, with simplicity, as he is (-in the paradigm that he is found in), and through this the truth will illuminate for him (so) that he can pray and express his words well, with His great kindness blessed He, and through this he fixes and upholds all the worlds. Also, through this he merits to breach openings to return others as well in repentance, to extricate them from the traps that ensnare them. **(Likutay Moharan, Torah 9; Likutay Eitzos, Prayer 15-19).**

(*) Tangentially, I will record here what the rav, Rabbi Naftoli *zatza"l* told over regarding this word. At the beginning of his drawing close to our Master and Leader, Rabbainu *zatza"l*, he saw in a dream that someone from the supernal world came to him and asked him which tzaddik he was drawn to. He answered, to the *Admu"r* (-Chassidic master) of Breslov *zatza"l*. And he (-from above) asked him to relate some word of Torah that he had heard from his (-Rabbi Nachman's) mouth. Being that this was right after he had heard from our *Admu"r zatza"l* the torah, "The depth will cover them" which is in Likutay Moharan (vol. 1, Torah 9), which begins: For the main vitality is received from prayer, as it is written, "a prayer to G-d of {-is} my life" etc., Rabbi Naftoli told him this word from the beginning of this torah. And when he heard this he became extremely inflamed with fiery intense passion and tremendous intense longing, and from the greatness of his fervor and yearning he lifted himself – the man from the supernal world – higher and higher, until he disappeared from him (- R' Naftoli). Afterwards Rabbi Naftoli *zatza"l* came to our *Admu"r zatzvk"l* and told him over the vision of this dream. Our *Admu"r zatzvk"l* answered him and said, "Do you think that also in the supernal world they hear the words of torah I say in the same way you hear it here?; It is not so. Over there, when they hear any word in my name, it is an altogether different matter!"

And see in the book "Ullim LiTrufa" (Leaves for Healing, letter 119), where it is written: Please (I) implore, my son, beware and heedful to fulfill the *aitza* (advice, remedy) mentioned above, in such a way that you will be able to grab from the midst of the darkness, to pray with *kavana* (concentration, intention), for this *aitza* is tried and tested, a thousand times. However, even still, the litigator (*ba'al duvur – Satan*) rallies very, very much each time with intense darkness at every prayer, and sets in one's mind numerous confusing thoughts without limit, and it is necessary by every prayer to remember this *aitza* many times, to turn one's back to the darkness and the confusion, and to strive to speak the words in truth, as one is (-in the paradigm the person is found in), and then Hashem Yisburach will illuminate for him openings etc., to the extent that he will uphold all the worlds with his prayers.   See my son, and comprehend the difference that takes place by a person in a single instant, for at first the darkness surrounded him exceedingly, and in a mere instant that he drew himself to speak a true word, he merited to uphold all the worlds, "for this is man in his entirety (end of Ecclesiastes)," that all the world are contingent on him every second, just, the magnitude of the onslaught that besiege him is without limit. However, Hashem Yisburach has already preempted a cure through the true tzaddikim etc.. And after G-d has made all of this known to us (Genesis 41:39), it is proper for us etc. at every time, to tunnel to fulfill their words truthfully, see there.

51. Pray for every single thing, G-d is "good for it." Prayer is the *hishtadlus*!

It is necessary to accustom oneself to pray at all times for everything he is lacking; whether it be livelihood, or children, or when he has someone sick Heaven forbid, at home who needs healing etc., for everything his main *aitza* (advice, remedy) is just to pray to Hashem Yisburach, and to have faith in Hashem Yisburach that He is good to {-for} all, as it is written (Psalms 145:9), "Hashem is good to {-for} all," that is for all things; whether for healing, or for livelihood, or for anything. When one believes this, certainly his main endeavor (*hishtadlus*) will be after the Holy One Blessed He, and he will not chase after many schemes, for most of them do not help whatsoever, and the minute minority of them which are helpful, are not known to him and he will not be able to discover them; however, to call out to the Holy One Blessed He, this is good and beneficial for everything in the world, and this can be found always, for He blessed He is always to be found. **(Likutay Moharan, Torah 14, Likutay Aitzos, Prayer 25).**

52. Hisbodidus is a gateway to the Secrets of the Torah

One who wants to taste a taste of the *ohr haganuz* [cached light], that is, the secrets of the Torah that will be revealed in the future, he should abound in hisbodidus between himself and his Creator, and judge and adjudicate himself (-all the time- Likutay Aitzos) regarding all his affairs and conduct, if this is proper and befitting for him to do, and to conduct like this against Hashem Yisburach, Who deals out to him goodness all the time and at every instance. And he should "manage his affairs {/dispense his words} judicially (Psalms 112:5)," and bring himself to account for everything. He himself should judge and adjudicate himself over all his affairs and deeds, and by this, he will remove from himself all fright, and he will be saved from the fallen fears, meaning that he'll not be afraid or frightened from any officer or lord, or dangerous beast, or bandits - nor from anything in the world, only from Hashem Yisburach alone he will fear and be frightened. And by this he will raise the fear to it's root, which is *da'as* (realization of knowledge) – that he will merit complete *da'as* (realization of knowledge), that he will know from whom to fear, namely to fear the Glorious

Name (-alone – Likutay Aitzos), [with a] fear of [His] loftiness. And through this, he will merit an attainment [of perception] of the revealed Torah, and through this he will merit to true humility, and through this he will merit to prayer with *meseeras nefesh* (giving over of the soul, self-sacrifice) to abnegate all his physicality and ego at the time of prayer, and he will pray without any intentions of self-benefit, and he will not think of himself as anything – just, he will annul his essence (/ego) and his physicality, as if he isn't in the world. And through this, he will come to the attainment [of perception] of the Hidden Torah, which is the *ohr haganuz* (cached light) which will be revealed in the future. And all this is attained through hisbodidus, as mentioned.

(Likutay Moharan, Torah 15; Likutay Aitzos, Hisbodidus 1).

53. G-d desires the prayers of the Jews

The Holy One Blessed He desires the prayers of Israel. And when Israel prays before Him, they fulfill His desire, and He receives exquisite enjoyment from them.

(Likutay Moharan, Torah 15; Likutay Aitzos, Prayer 28).

54. Meaningful prayer facilitates:
* one's ascent to continually unclothe loftier heights,
* attain holy brazeness,
* and to draw close to the true tzaddikim to receive the holy faith completely.

Every person has an aspect (-their own parameters) of the *revealed* and the *hidden* etc., and every person needs to rise

127

every time from level to level, to make from what is *hidden, revealed*. And this, one merits to through the study of Torah and copious prayers, for it is necessary to learn Torah and abound in prayer before Hashem Yisburach until He reveals to him what is hidden from him, and from what was *hidden* will be made *revealed*, and he will have a loftier (aspect of) *hidden*. And afterwards he needs to pray more until this *hidden* is revealed to him, and so every time, to go from one level to a higher level, to request each time from Hashem Yisburach to attain perception of the loftier *hidden* etc.. And through this one merits to joy and holy brazenness (*azoos di'kiddoosha*), through which one enters into holiness to draw close to true tzaddikim to receive from them the holy faith in great completion. And all of this, one merits through prayer with complete *kavana* (-concentration, intention), for prayer with *kavana* encompasses everything etc., see there. **(Likutay Moharan, Torah 22; Likutay Aitzos, Prayer 33).**

55. Prayer demands holy brazeness

The quintessence of prayer is through holy brazenness (*azoos di'kiddoosha*), for it is necessary to be brazen faced against Hashem Yisburach to ask from Him concerning everything one needs, even for the making of miracles and wonders, for it is impossible to stand in prayer before Hashem Yisburach except by means of holy brazenness, because every person, to the extent that he fathoms in his heart the greatness of the Creator blessed He, and sees his own lowliness and inferiority, how can he stand and pray before Him? Therefore at the time of prayer, a person needs to dispel the shame, and be brazen faced to ask from Hashem Yisburach everything that he needs, as mentioned above. And this is the aspect of (Psalms 22:6), "to You they screamed out and they escaped, in You they trusted and were not embarrassed." **(Likutay Moharan, Torah 30; Likutay Aitzos, Prayer 36).**

56. Yearning creates potential souls, verbalizing the yearning actualizes them

Through the conversation that one converses and speaks between himself and his Maker, and he verbalizes his yearnings and good desires, that which he yearns, and quests, and longs to get out of his baseness and merit to the true good, and he prays and pleads before Hashem Yisburach for this, through this he produces the good souls from their state of potentiality (*bikoaach*) to actuality (*bifoaal*). For through the longing alone, potential souls are made, because the yearning is the soul, in the aspect of (Psalms 84:3), "my soul yearns and pines (-even to the extent of expiration)," and through the speaking mentioned above, they are completed and produced from potential (*bikoach*) to actuality (*bifoal*), in the aspect of (Genesis 2:7), "and the man became a living soul," and the *Targum* (aramaic translation of Unkellus) is, "a speaking spirit," and as it is written (Song of Songs 5:6), "my soul departed with his speaking." And through this one merits to effectuate his request, and he merits to configure the letters of the Torah for the good, and sustain and give to everything, and to draw goodness and blessing in all the worlds, and good implementations are carried out in the world, and many souls are aroused to repentance through this speech, that one speaks between himself and his Maker. For this matter of yearning and good desires, and to fully verbalize them, is extremely precious, and every person needs to accustom himself to engage in this plentifully every day, and through this it is possible to return the whole world to the better (-Likutay Aitzos ends here). And this is (Ecclesiastes 8:14), "There is *hevel* (vanity/vapor/breath) which takes place in the world," that is *hevel* (breath) that leaves the mouth, from the holy speech mentioned above, "that there are evil people that are visited with (/attain) the likes of the conduct of the tzaddikim," meaning, as mentioned above, because through this many evil people are aroused to repent. And there is the opposite, the discharge in the *hevel* that leaves the mouth, utterances of bad yearnings Heaven forbid, and through this, "there are tzaddikim that are visited with (/come to) the likes of the conduct of the evil people." For speech, which is the soul, which is the speaking spirit (*ruach mimallila* – cited above from the *Targum*), transposes to other people, according to the *hevel* which is carried out in the world. **(Likutay Moharan, Torah 31; Likutay Aitzos, Hisbodidus 3).**

[**And** see in Likutay Halachos, laws of craftsmen, law 4:12, where it is explained that therefore it is necessary to guard oneself very much from bad yearning, and especially from verbalizing them, because they go and arouse people in the world to bad desires. And this is what King David r.i.p. said (Psalms 17:3), "You examined (/tested) my heart, You attended (to me at) night (see Malbi"m there – night is a time of thought and extra precaution is necessary q.v.), You have purged (/tested) me, and did not find (what You desired – Rashi; alternately explained: so that there is not to be found in me any improper thoughts)," that is that he said on behalf of *Klal Yisroel* (All of Israel): "I know that I did not withstand the test properly, because I still have not merited to be saved from yearnings of this world, however (continuation of the verse), 'my thoughts (/intrigues) will not pass my mouth,' for no matter what, I guard myself not to release these yearnings verbally Heaven forbid, so that there shall not be carried out through this bad implementations in the world Heaven forbid, rather, I accustom myself to always speak holy words of good yearning, to call out to You always, that You should return me to You in truth, and through this good implementations and blessing are drawn to all the worlds." And this is (verse 4), "for the implementations of man are (/will be) to the words of Your lips;" - "For I am guarded to speak only holy words, which are 'the words of Your lips', in order that through this all the implementations of man will be completed for the good." And this is (continuation of the verse), "I guarded (against) breached ways," - "For by virtue of this, that I regulate my language to speak always words of good yearning as mentioned, through this I merit to be saved and to be guarded from all breached ways, which are all the bad ways, may the Merciful One save us, just (verse 5), 'support my steps in Your path etc.', for the good spoken words support and assist me, to secure my steps in Your path." And this is what is explained even more; "Through what have I merited to this?": "I called out to You, for You answered me, G-d (verse 6)," for this is the whole matter of hisbodidus and conversation between one and his Maker, that it is necessary to accustom oneself to this copiously, to yearn constantly good yearnings and to verbalize them every day, as mentioned above].

And see further in the book Ullim LiTrufah (Leaves of Healing, letter 323), from our teacher, Rabbi Nussun o.b.m., where it is written: For it is possible to accomplish everything through desires and yearning, and to accustom oneself to speak out the yearnings and desires with his mouth. Get up now (/please), stand now (/please), arouse now (/please) your good hearts, very very well, to accustom yourselves to go in this way, to yearn and long profusely to Hashem Yisburach at all times, and to speak the yearnings verbally, for through this, worlds and wondrous novelty are woven through the permutation of the letters in the 231 gates which join and conjugate in wondrous new permutations through the spoken words of yearning to Hashem, and to His Torah, and to His holy ways, as understood and explained in Likutay (Moharan) I, Torah 31:6. 'For it is not an empty matter for you, for it is your life etc. (Deuteronomy 32:47).' And because today I learned in the books of Kabbala regarding the coming into existence and weaving of all the worlds through permutation of the letters in the 231 gates, front and back etc., (and) through this I was very profusely aroused now, while talking with one of our youths of the many, many good qualities (/heights) of one who merits to go in the ways of Rabbainu o.b.m., in the matter of desires and yearning to Hashem Yisburach, and to His Torah, in general and in detail, and to speak them out verbally; be it in a general fashion – that his desire is to be a Jew in truth, or be it in particulars – what he is specifically lacking at that time etc. etc.. Fortunate is one who holds to this. Not any mind can harbor what is done and woven from this in the supernal worlds, and the wonders of the delights which go up before Him through this. Strengthen and embolden yourselves to fulfill this practice at all times, so that it will be good for you eternally.

57. Connect the heart to its point to save it from the shame of fallen desires

In every Israelite there is an extremely precious good point, whose desire is always strong, to do the desire of its Maker, but the (worldly) desires break his heart, and through this his heart is distant from the point. Therefore it is necessary for every person to speak between himself and his Maker, in order to light up the aspect of the point which is in his heart, and through this his uncircumcised heart will be nullified, that is, the bad loves (-affections) which are the heart's disgrace, which break a person's heart, in the aspect of (Psalms 69:21), "disgrace broke my heart."

(Likutay Moharan 34; Likutay Aitzos, Hisbodidus 4).

58. Speaking to G-d will bring one to be embarrassed before Him with such holy connection that his face will shine

A person needs to accustom himself to speak between himself and his Maker, frankly with great and utter truth, until his heart is truly aroused, until he begins to speak with a passionate heart words of truth that are in his heart with great arousal, with repentance, until he sees his negligibility and the greatness of the Creator, until he is very embarrassed before Him blessed He. For until now he threw his sins behind his shoulders (-turned his back on them) and did not pay attention to them, and now that he acknowledges them, in this way he is inoculated with great embarrassment over the severity of his sins against a master and ruler, the essence and root of all the worlds, and this embarrassment is revealed on his face, and this shame is the aspect of the light of the tefillin, which are the sign of attachment (*divaikus*) Israel has with the Creator blessed He, and it is the aspect of (the) beam of light of the face, and through this shame all his sins are forgiven. **(Likutay Moharan, Torah 38; Likutay Aitzos, Embarrassment and Brazenness 2).** [The transcriber says: From here there is support to what is brought down above in article 47, what he said that it is possible to discern on someone if he does hisbodidus, because through this, there is revealed on his face great humiliation from Hashem Yisburach, as mentioned above].

59. Go out at night, alone, somewhere people never go, and completely nullify yourself to G-d. There is no danger to be feared.

The primary hisbodidus is at night, for then everyone is sleeping, and also that the place should be outside the city, that he should go on a solitary way, that is, in a place where people do not go there even in the day. And through this that one does hisbodidus at night on a solitary way as mentioned above, and clears his heart and mind from all engagements of this world, and abnegates everything, until he nullifies himself completely; meaning, that first he prays copiously until he abnegates this vice, and afterwards he continues to pray copiously until he abnegates a different vice, and afterwards he continues to pray copiously until he utterly nullifies himself, that he should not retain any haughtiness or any entity, until he is in his (own) eyes as literally nothing and void, and through this he merits to come to the aspect of true nullification – through this his soul is included in its root in His infinite (*Ain Soaf*) unity blessed He, which is called the *michoo'yuv hamitzee'oos* (imperative <of> existence), as is known. And through this all the worlds that are contingent on his soul are also included in His Infinite (*Ain Soaf*) Unity blessed He, which is called *michoo'yuv hamitzee'oos* (imperative <of> existence). And this is the interpretation of the Mishna (Ethics of Our Fathers 3:5): **One who is awake at night and (one) who goes alone on a path (/goes on a lone path)**, as explained above, **and clears {turns} his heart** – from all concerns of this world, in order to achieve the state of true nullification. And this is: **to nullification {emptiness}**, as mentioned above, **behold this** person **is the imperative {culpable}**, that is he is included in His Unity blessed He, which is called *michoo'yuv hamitzee'oos* (imperative <of> existence). And this is: **with his soul**, meaning that his soul, with all the worlds contingent on his soul, are included in the *michoo'yuv hamitzee'oos* (imperative <of> existence), as mentioned above. **(Likutay Moharan 52; Likutay Aitzos, Hisbodidus 7).**

And see in the book "Ullim LiTrufah" (Leaves for Healing, letter 113), after it brings there a brief synopsis of the torah "One who is awake at night," mentioned above, these words are written there: "Where are we in the world that (even though) we merited to hear such a thing, (and) we are still distant from his torah?! I scream in my heart now over the days that transpired, many years that I didn't merit to fulfill this due to the inundation of obstacles, but I cheer myself up with the very little that I merited at times to fulfill a bit of this. And also what we merited to express our words during the day, before Him blessed He, is also very extremely precious, for not every person merits to fulfill wholly everything mentioned above. And fortunate is one who merits to do hisbodidus even (if it is only) in the day. However, fortunate and fortunate is one who merits to fulfill straightforwardly 'One who is awake at night etc.', until he merits through this to be included in the *chi'yoov hamitzee'oos*, and to raise the entire universe which is contingent on him, to be included in Him blessed He, for he is *michoo'yuv hamitzeeyues*. May my lot be with them forever etc.," see there the whole letter.

And one time our teacher, the rav, Rabbi Nussun *zatza"l* spoke about this holy way of "One who is awake at night," as our master and leader, Rabbainu HaKadosh *zatza"l* revealed it, and he said these words: "There will yet be a time when this way will be viable for (/traversed by) the masses (just like now there is an established way to don a tallis and tefillin every morning)." And regarding the fears which this entails, our master, leader, and rabbi *zatza"l* said, that if he had an only son, he would send him out alone at night to the field, and he would have no worries. And he said this regarding every person, that one should not have any fear (for one on an assignment of a *mitzvah* will come to no harm (Pesachim 8b)). And our teacher, the rav, Rabbi Nussun *zatza"l* elaborated on this, and said regarding this, that it is like what is written in the holy Zohar (Parshas Shelach, Bamidbar 158b) regarding Caleb's (*Kullaiv's*) expedition to Chevron to prostrate on the tomb of the forefathers, and how he was not afraid of the giants that were there. And the holy Zohar writes there: "A person who is under duress doesn't pay any attention; so it was with

Caleb, since he was in duress, he paid no attention, and he went to pray on the tombs of the forefathers etc.," see there. And so too in this matter, whomsoever knows and evaluates himself well – that in a blink of an eye his days will fly by, and he will need to stand judgment and give an accounting for all his actions, and they will not let him by for anything etc., whoever reckons himself on all this, certainly will not look upon any fear of the fears and the likes, and all the more so since in truth there is no (concern for) fear entailed whatsoever, as mentioned above.

Our teacher, the rav, Rabbi Nussun *zatza"l* also told over a story of the holy Baal Shem Tov *zatzvk"l*: Once, he prayed with his *chevra* (ensemble), and they prayed with very great fervor, as was their way. Afterwards, when they finished their prayers they saw that the holy Baal Shem Tov *zatzvk"l* had a very grim countenance. And afterwards he (the Baal Shem Tov) spoke up and said to them, "When you prayed, the Litigator (*baal duvur* – Satan) inoculated in each of you thoughts of arrogance and haughtiness with regard to your praying with such fervor and clinging (*dvaikus*), and through this prosecution was invoked above against you, and I had to exert myself arduously until I sweetened (- mitigated) this. He told this over so that it should be known how very much it is necessary to abound in prayer to be saved from pride which is despised by Hashem (Proverbs 16:5), for it is possible that even when one is free of all the desires and the bad traits, even still it is possible for there to remain in the heart hidden pride Heaven forbid, as is delineated in the torah "One who is awake at night" (Likutay Moharan, torah 52) mentioned above. Therefore, it is necessary for this, to abound profusely in prayers and screaming to Hashem Yisburach at night and in a solitaire venue, until one merits to the aspect of true nullification, that he should not harbor any pride or any ego (lit. substance/entity), until he merits through this to be included, with all the worlds which are contingent on his soul, in His Infinite (*Ain Soaf*) Unity blessed He, which is the *michoo'yuv hamitzee'oos* (imperative <of> existence), as mentioned above.

60. Hisbodidus at night, crying to G-d and building ones good points from out of the bad, bring joy, and holds lust at bay, and cultivates a consciousness of the future world

At night, then is the main time for hisbodidus to express one's words before Hashem Yisburach, and to pour out his heart like water directly before the countenance of Hashem (Lamentations 2:19), and to seek out the good spirit, that is, the good points that he still retains, and to extract them from within the bad spirit, and through this he will merit to joy and to quell the imagination, from which all the desires ensue. And through this he will merit memory, to always remember the coming (-future) world, and to think at all times of his purpose and ultimate end, of the coming (-future) world, until he merits to truthfully return to Him blessed He. **(Likutay Moharan, Torah 54; Likutay Aitzoas, hisbodidus 8).**

61. Doubts in the heart are removed through learning *halacha*

Through learning the decisions of the *halachic* (-relating Jewish law) authorities (*poaskim*) one merits to pray properly, with all his heart. For in truth, if a person would know and believe with a complete heart that the whole world is full of His glory, and He blessed He stands above him during the prayer and listens, hears, and heeds every single word of the prayer, certainly he would be very particular to say his words with *kavana* (-intention, meaning, and concentration), and he would pray with great passion, but because his heart is divided, in the aspect of (Hosea 10:2) "their hearts are divided (from Me)," and he is not strong in this knowledge with a complete heart, because of this he is not so particular, and does not put his heart to pray with *kavana*. And all of this stems from the problems and heresy which are in the heart, which are the aspect of the quarrel ('division' – same root as "divided" above) of the evil inclination (*yetzehr hurra*) which is in the heart. Therefore the *tikun* (rectification) for this is learning the decisions of the *halachic* authorities, for through this the quarrel of the evil inclination which is in the heart, is neutralized in its root (Likutay Aitzos ends here stating: and through this one merits to pray properly, truthfully with all his heart), because the root of the quarrel of that evil inclination which is in the heart is in the evolution, step by step, degeneration from holy discord ('division'), which is the disputes ('division') between the *Tana'im* (Sages of the Mishna) and the *Amoaru'im* (Sages of the Talmud), which this one forbids and this one permits, and through learning the decisions of the *halachic* authorities one rectifies the discord which is in holiness, as mentioned, for the final *halachic* decision is the harmony and reconcilement of the dispute between the *Tana'im* and *Amoaru'im*, and therefore through this the dissent of the evil inclination which is in the heart, is also neutralized, and one merits a straight heart, that his heart will not be divided (upon him), just, believing that Hashem Yisburach hears all the words of the prayer, and then he merits to pray properly. And this is (Psalms 119:7), "I will praise You with a straight heart {*laivuv*}," 'laivuv' (heart in Hebrew is laiv, and can also be with an additional 'uv', our Sages denote meaning from this seeming redundancy) precisely, with both inclinations (as our Sages o.b.m. (Brachos 54a) inferred on the verse (Deuteronomy 6:5), "with all your heart {livuvichu}" - with both of your inclinations). When? (continuation of the verse), "when I learn the laws of Your righteous justice," see there. (**Likutay Moharan, torah 62).**

[**The** transcriber says: From here there is support to what is brought down previously, article 30, from his holy words, that these two matters, namely to pray and express one's words before Him blessed He, and also the learning of the Shulchan Aruch (Code of Jewish Law), are general practices for each and every man, every single day of his life, because according to what was mentioned above, they are contingent upon each other].

62. Speech is like a mother who is always available for her child even in dirty places – always use it

Speech is like the mother of children, meaning, just like a mother always accompanies her son even to filthy places, and she doesn't forget them, so too the spoken word accompanies a person always even in the filthy places and reminds him constantly of Hashem Yisburach, in the aspect of (Jeremiah 31:20, and see below end of article 96) "for whenever I talk of him I remember him so much more," that is, that even if a person is stuck, Heaven forbid, in very low standing, in the place that he is, Heaven forbid, even still,

140

by means of speech he can always remind himself of [-by/with] Hashem Yisburach, meaning, that even if he is where he is, if nevertheless he strengthens himself even there to speak holy words of Torah, and prayer, and conversation between himself and his Maker, or to speak with his rabbi or with his friend in fear of Heaven, he can always remind himself of (/by) Hashem Yisburach even there, in the filthy places, even if he fell to the place where he fell – may the Merciful One save us, for the spoken word doesn't let him be, to forget Hashem Yisburach. Understand this matter well, of the great power of speech, it is a wondrous and awesome *aitza* (remedy/advice) for someone who truly desires not to forfeit his world entirely, Heaven forbid. **(Likutay Moharan, torah 78; Likutay Aitzoas, speech 19).**

63. Sighing – to regain one's standing

When a person prays or does hisbodidus properly, and in the middle he falls from his level, this stems from defection of (the) faith, and so it is necessary then to break his heart inside, and to be ashamed of himself for falling from heaven to earth, and he should pity himself until he sighs, and through the sigh he will return to his level.

(Likutay Moharan, torah 108; Likutay Aitzos, sigh 2).

64. Personal words to G-d are Divinely inspired

The words that a person converses and speaks between himself and his Maker are the aspect of *ruach hakodesh*

(Divine inspiration), for through undertaking this, and forcing himself, and preparing himself to speak before Hashem Yisburach, Hashem Yisburach sends him words in his mouth which are the aspect of *ruach hakodesh* (Divine inspiration). And it is necessary to see to it, and to constantly endeavor at all times to request with new words of appeasement and entreaties, and one merits this through purity of the heart, which one merits through the holy motion of the intellect (Likutay Aitzos, hisbodidus 2). And this is (Psalms 51:12), "A pure heart create for me, G-d," then (continuation of the verse), "and a resolute (/correct/established) spirit create (/renew) inside of me," that he should merit every time to come up with new original words which are the aspect of *ruach hakodesh* as mentioned above.

(Likutay Moharan, torah 156).

65. Not to be overly insistent even in prayer

A person is forbidden to be obstinate about anything, that is, it is forbidden to be adamant in his prayers that Hashem Yisburach should do for him specifically as his request, whether it be livelihood, or children, or other necessities, it is necessary to just pray before Him blessed He with (-in such a fashion that invokes) mercy and entreatingly; if Hashem Yisburach gives – He gives, and if not – not (Likutay Aitzos, prayer 31). And this is (Ethics of Our Fathers 2:18), "Do not make your prayer routine <keva> (rather invoke mercy)," <keva – routine> is a term for theft, as it is written (Proverbs 22:23), "and He will steal <vikuva> the soul of those who steal from them," meaning, to take the item with coercion, with theft, "rather, compassionately and entreatingly," as mentioned above. **(Likutay Moharan, torah 196).**

66. Candidly unburdening oneself to G-d evokes Divine consolation

When a person does hisbodidus and expresses his words and his pain before Hashem Yisburach, and confesses and regrets the severity of the defects he impaired, then the *Shechina* (Divine Presence) directly across him expresses before him Its words and pain, for every single infraction and infringement that he violated in his *neshama* (soul), he inflicted by Her, so to speak, and She consoles him, that he should seek contrivances to rectify all the damages.

(Likutay Moharan, torah 259; Likutay Aitzoas, hisbodidus 11).

67. Gaining passion from one's own momentum

Just like a person can be inspired by his friend, such as when one sees someone saying supplications and *slichos* (veniality – liturgy of petitions for forgiveness) with an enlivened heart, similarly there is inspiration by the person himself, in and of himself, that he is aroused from the phenomenon of his own words (Likutay Aitzos, prayer 74); that is, that he says supplications and entreaties with vivacity, and screams 'woe on me', and in the midst of this he is aroused from this and begins to look himself over, "Where am I? Who is screaming like that? Behold, it is *mamash* (-actually) woe on me!" And he begins a second time to scream "woe on me," "on me – distinctly." And even though at the beginning it also seemed to him as though he was also speaking really properly, nevertheless, afterwards the difference between before and after will be apparent, understand (this).

(Likutay Moharan, torah 270).

68. Importance of speaking to G-d especially when it is difficult, which usually brings expansion

Even though a person cannot speak at all, and it seems to him that he is unable to open his mouth in his prayers and his hisbodidus due to his utter physicality and from the weight of the hardships of his body and soul he is undergoing, even still it is necessary specifically then, to strengthen and force himself to call out to Hashem from the midst of his pain and duress, in the aspect of (Psalms 118:5), "From distress I called out to Hashem," for the main awakening is for the person to first be aroused from the distress and duress, and through this he will usually merit subsequently to come to great expansion, until he is able to pray and express his words properly, until he is able to come to the aspect of *ruach hakodesh* (Divine inspiration) specifically through this, that he was aroused to Hashem Yisburach from the grips of such distress and moroseness (Likutay Aitzoas, prayer 75). Like we find by King David r.i.p. in all his prayers, that the beginning was from distress and duress, that it was very difficult for him, such as due to the troubles of Absalom or the troubles of Nuval and the likes, and afterwards, in the same prayer he achieved *ruach hakodesh* (Divine inspiration). And this is the aspect of the *shofar* (-ritual horn), that the wideness is above, and the narrowness is below by the mouth. And this is the aspect of (Psalms 66:14), "and my mouth spoke when it was difficult for me," as mentioned above. **(Likutay Moharan, torah 279).**

69. No matter how fallen, find some good point

When a person begins to look upon himself, and he sees that he is distant from being good, and that he is full of transgressions, then it is possible that through this he will fall, and will not be able to pray and do hisbodidus whatsoever. Therefore he must search, and seek, and find in himself some good, for how is it possible that never in his life he did some *mitzva* or something good. And even though when he begins to look at that good which he did, he sees that the good itself is full of wounds, for the good is mixed with ulterior intentions and a lot of rot, even still, how is it possible that there will not be in the little good some good point. And so he should search and seek further, until he finds in himself some other good points. And through this that he finds in himself some (sort of) merit and good, through this he will actually decamp from the measure of guilt to the measure of merit, and he will be able to return in repentance through this, in the aspect of (Psalms 37:10), "and a little bit [more] and there is no longer an evil person," that is, through finding in oneself a(nother) little bit in which he is not evil, through this (continuation of the verse), "and you will contemplate his place and he is not there," on his original level. And through this he can

145

vitalize himself and bring himself, (even) the way he is, to joy, and then he will be able to pray, and sing, and express gratitude to Hashem. And this is (Psalms 104:33, 146:2), "I will sing to my G-d with my little bit {/while I am still living/ with my very being}," namely, with the little bit (more) – the good points which I still have, through this I can sing and pray to Hashem Yisburach. **(Likutay Moharan, Torah 282; Likutay Aitzoas, encouragement 26).**

[**And** see in the book "Ullim LiTrufah" (Leaves for Healing) from our teacher the holy rav, Rabbi Nussun *zatza"l* who wrote there in Yiddish, in letter 235, how our master, leader, and rabbi *zatza"l* said this matter, in order that the words would enter the heart of every person, to adopt this with *temeemus* (unfeigned simplicity/wholesomeness) and simplicity, and he wrote there, "And this is what our master, leader, and holy rabbi *zatza"l* would say: *az* <when> *a mentch* <a person> *zeht* <sees> *ehr iz zehr shuffil* <he is very low>, *tor ehr nit arup fallin* <it is forbidden for him to fall (despondent)>, *nor* <rather> *ehr mooz* <he must> *zich micha'yeh zain* <vitalize himself> *in zul zich mi'yashev zain* <and settle himself>: *vey hub ich nit eppes amitzva gittun* <did I not do some mitzva>, *vey hub ich furt nit amuhl eppes gitz gittun* <did I not do, at any rate, one time, some good thing>; *ich fast in Yoam Kippur* <I fast on Yom Kippur>, *in Tishu Bi'Uv oych* <on the ninth of the month of Av as well>, *un kul hadalled taanaisim oych* <and all the four fast days as well> *chutsh* <even though> *dus hartz tit mir zehr vay* <this heart pains me very much (-it is very painful)>. *Un gai amuhl in mikva arain* <and at times I go into the *mikva*>, *un afeeloo in kul hakilkoolim* <and even (despite) all the defections> *Rachmuna litzlun* <may the Merciful one save us>, *mootshe* *ich mich zehr* <I try very hard> *un vil mich zehr matzil zain vichooloo* <and I want very much to save myself etc.>. *In vey seh iz* <And however it may be>, *al kul punim* <nevertheless> *eppes nikoodoas toavoas* <some good points> *hub ich in mir* <I have in myself>, *vus ich hub kamuh pumim gitten* <that I have done several times> *rutzoan Haboaray yisburach* <the will of the Creator blessed He>. *In dehr mit miz men zich micha'ye zain* <With this one must vitalize himself> *nisht mi'ya'ish zain bishoom oafen vichooloo* <not to despair no matter what etc.>. See there in Likutay Moharan all these things, and internalize these words in your heart anew. And If Heaven forbid, the litigator (*baal duvur* – Satan) surmounts, it is necessary afterwards to go back and take this up, and so (too) every single day and every time, and in the process Hashem Yisburach helps substantially.

"And specifically to be resolute and converse and say all of this before Hashem Yisburach, and to say, 'Master of the World, *vey azoy ich bin* <the way I am>, *vey azoy ich bin* <the way I am>, *azoy vey dee vaist* <like You know> *in ich vaist mine vaytug* <and I know my pain>, *dee hust zich furt mit mir chessed oalum gittun* <You have nevertheless done with me a world of kindness> *in hust mich bashaffen mee'zerra Yisroel viloa usannee vichooloo* <in creating me from the progeny of Israel and not making me etc.> *oon meh hut mich furt gishnitzin* <and I was nonetheless circumcised> *oon bleet far gussin tzey acht tug* <and given to bleed on the eighth day>, *in oon chaider* <and in religious Jewish elementary school> *hub ich gillerint aleph bais* <I learned the Hebrew alphabet> *in siddur* <and the prayer book> *in chumash* <and five books of the Torah> *in gimura vichooloo*

<and Talmud etc.>. *Veefil yisoorim* <abundant suffering> *in shmitz* <and hitting> *hub ich gilliten foon dee milamdim* <I endured from the teachers>, *oon alain* <and of my own right> *hub ich mich oich gimitchin* <I toiled> *kamu pi'umim* <several times>. *Vus tit men* <what can be done> *ritzoanee laasoas ritzoanchu* <my desire is to do Your will>, *ach si'or shebu'eesa mi'akkev oasee* <but the leaven in the dough (-the evil inclination) restrains me> (Brachos 17a), and if the holy *Tana* (-sage) of the Talmud was not embarrassed to say this, *badarfin mir zich bivaday nisht shemmin* <we certainly should not be ashamed> *shrayin* <to scream> *dus* <this> *far* <before> Hashem Yisburach, in all types of expressions of vociferation: bitter, bitter, bitter etc., *givald* (-woe/alas/catastrophic), *givald* etc.. And if Heaven forbid, Heaven be merciful, the *baal duvur* (litigator – Satan) overbears, it is necessary to scream still more and more, and so every time, until Hashem overlooks and sees from the Heavens, "for Hashem will not forsake forever (Lamentations 3:31)." And that which the salvation is delayed, entails extremely esoteric matters, for His thoughts blessed He are very deep (Psalms 32:6; see below article 100), and certainly the impediment is on our part, what we don't arouse to properly surmount over everything which needs to be overcome, and also (because) Hashem Yisburach wants and desires the prayers of Israel (Yevumoas 64, Shemos Raba 21:4), even the worst of the worst, and wants that he should pray copiously and scream to Him blessed He more etc.," see there.

70. Holy speech tempers the tempest of libido ultimately resulting in a radiant countenance

Through the wholeness of the Holy Tongue (i.e. that one guards the language to sanctify it with holy words of Torah, and prayer, and entreaties, and beseeching, and conversation between him and his Maker, even in the language that he speaks (-not Hebrew), for on the contrary, when he speaks between himself and his Maker he needs to speak specifically in the language of his vernacular, for through this he arouses his heart surpassingly, as mentioned above), through this one merits to rectification of the *bris* (-circumcision-covenant) and to quell the evil which encompasses all the bad desires, which is the desire for promiscuity, for he cools his heat (-libido) with speech of the Holy Tongue mentioned above, in the aspect of (Psalms 39:4), "My heart is feverish inside of me etc. I spoke with my tongue," but whoever does not cool his heat (-libido) with speech of the Holy Language mentioned above, then the storm wind cools (*mikarrehr*) him with a nocturnal emission (*mikreh*), may the Merciful One save us. And so too the converse, through the rectification of the *bris* (-circumcision-covenant) one merits to the wholeness of the Holy Language mentioned above, for they are contingent upon each other **(Likutay Aitzoas, bris (-covenant/circumcision) 10-14).**

And through this a person merits to sublimate his countenance, so that his face radiates so much, to the extent that it is possible for one to see himself (reflected) in the face of this person who merited to rectification of the *bris* and wholeness of Holy Language mentioned above, like a mirror, how his (own) face is sunken in darkness, and he will return in complete repentance to Hashem Yisburach even without rebuke and without *mussar* (moral, morale, and ethical criticism), just through looking at his face alone. **(Likutay Moharan, torah 19).**

71. Sweetness of prayer and interference from people and from foreign thoughts

Everyone, according to their rectification of the *bris* (-circumcision-covenant) and according to his connection to the true tzaddikim who guard the *bris*, so too he can taste the sweetness in the words of the prayer. And then "a lion alights to eat his offering (Tikunay Zohar, tikun 3 of the 11 posterior tikunim)," that is, his prayer; but on account of the defection of the *bris*, he is is in the aspect of bitter water etc., and then he cannot taste the sweetness of the words of the prayer, and then "a dog alights to eat his offering," that is, his prayer. And know, that the brazen faced of the generation, they (distinctly) are the dogs which stand (against) and oppose the prayers of the Israelite who still has not amended his *bris* completely **(Likutay Aitzos, prayer 48-9; Likutay Moharan, torah 50).**

[**Upon** this, the book Likutay Aitzoas (Collection of Advice), in the entry of prayer, article 49, writes: And from here you can understand how great is the sin of those who oppose the prayer of an Israelite and desire to confuse his prayer, for even though this person who is praying has not yet merited to rectification of the *bris*, and consequently was beset with this dispute, which is the aspect of "a dog alights etc." as mentioned above, but the opposers are not vindicated because of this from their punishment, for they uproot their souls from holiness and set themselves to be called by the designation of actual dogs, may the Merciful One save us, in the aspect of (Isaiah 56:11), "and the dogs brazen with desire," through this that they oppose his prayer, even though he did not reform his *bris* completely as mentioned above, for certainly a person has to exert himself to pray with all his might even though he is the way he is, and (he) cannot feel the sweetness of the words of the prayer, and also, the exertion itself is very precious, for regarding this it says (Psalms 44:23), "Because for Your sake we are killed all day etc.," as is explained elsewhere (Likutay Moharan vol. 2, torah 46, and see Words of Rabbi Nachman article 12) in his words o.b.m.].

And behold it is further understood from his words o.b.m. in Likutay Moharan, volume one, torah two, that whoever defects the *bris*, prayer is taken from him by means of an insurgency of foreign thoughts which come to confuse his prayer, and so it is written there in torah thirty, that all the befuddlement in the world, and all the trivialities, and all the confusion that a person has throughout the day, whatever time it may be, absolutely everything comes specifically during the prayer, and makes itself heard specifically then, to confuse the person during his prayer, in the aspect of (Psalms 106:2), "Who (can) tell[s] over the mighty acts of Hashem?" That is, whoever says over the

151

mighty acts of Hashem during the prayer, then (continuation of the verse), "make{s} heard all his *teheelah* {praise?; *tuhulah* – confusion!}," meaning, that he makes heard to himself all his mixed up sentiments and all his confusion. Because "*teheela*" (-praise) is a term for disarray and confusion, like it is written (Job 4:18), "and in his angels he puts obfuscation <*tuhulah*>," therefore extremely great surmounting is necessary during the prayer, over these confusions and foreign thoughts that come and rise in one's heart, particularly then.

And there is (written) in his words o.b.m., in Likutay Moharan volume two, torah 122, regarding foreign thoughts during prayer, that every foreign thought is a husk (*klipa*) with full stature, as is brought down (see Poras Yosef page 50), and when a person stands to pray in order, and doesn't pay attention to the foreign thoughts, then in the progression of his prayer he knocks them down; to this one he severs a hand, and to this one he severs a leg, and so forth with the other limbs. This is allegorical to the enterprise of war, when it is necessary to go and pass through many killers and ambushers, and (when) he is valiant and passes through them, then on his way he fells them; to this one he severs a hand, as he proceeds on course, and knocks him down, and to this one, a leg etc.. And so it is *mamash* (-really) with the enterprise of prayer, when one prevails to pray in order and not give any regard to the foreign thoughts, then he kills them or cuts them up limb by limb as mentioned above.

And so it is additionally exposited in his words o.b.m. (Likutay Moharan, vol. 1, torah 72), that one need not look upon them at all, and not look behind him at all, (he should) just go in order in his prayer, and through this they will depart automatically. And if he doesn't ignore them, then on the contrary, they will engulf him even more, like a person running away from something, and he side-glances off handedly on the thing he ran from, then this thing bears down upon him even more, so it is *mamash* (-exactly) in the matter of the thoughts.

And so it is exposited further in his words o.b.m. (Likutay Moharan vol. 2, torah 50) that thought is in the hands of the person to incline it as he wills. And even if his thought is already accustomed to go out of bounds plentifully, even still it is in the hand of the person to direct it each time to the straight (-proper-just) way, for it impossible by any means for there to be two thoughts simultaneously, see there. Therefore, certainly when one strengthens to think only of the words of the prayer, certainly the foreign thought will be cast away.

And see in Likutay Halachos (Laws of Tefillin, law 6:32) that this is the aspect of the (offering of the) *Oamehr* (Biblical measurement) *of Barley* (brought on the second day of Passover), which one needs, after leaving Egypt (-every year on the first day of Passover), to count the days to (-from) the *Oamehr*, that is because the barley, which is fodder for animals, which is the aspect of the power of imagination, from which all the confusion, and (improper) rumination, and all the foreign thoughts which are the aspect of hairs ('*si-u-roas*', same base as barley – '*si-oa-rim*') which are from the excess of the brain(s), as is known (see the Lurianic Kabalistic works: Mivoa Shi'urim 5:1:13, and Aitz Chaim 13:5 principle 2. And see Likutay Moharan

67:6). All of these are in the aspect of the *Oamehr* and measurement, just like a vessel that can hold a certain measurement, and it is impossible to put more than this into it, likewise the brain is a vessel which cannot be loaded except with one thought, and more than this is impossible to charge it concurrently. And this is barley ('*si-oa-rim*') which has the same etymology as hairs ('*si-u-roas*'), which are the thoughts, as mentioned above. And this is (a construct of) what we count the days to the *Oamehr* (-from the day of it's offering till the holiday of Shivuos 50 days later), that is because days are the life of a person, for all the days of a persons life are included in days and in time, and the essence of life is the intellect of the brain, as it is written (Ecclesiastes 7:12), "the intellect gives life," and all the thoughts are from there, and they are all in the aspect of the *Oamehr* and measurement.

And therefore after leaving Egypt it is necessary to bring an *Oamehr of Barley*, and wave it, and count the days of *sfeerah* (-counting) from that day, because the main purification from the putrid contamination of Egypt, which is the *nakedness of the land* (Genesis 42:9,12), defection of the *bris* (-circumcision, covenant), is through purification of the thought, as is known (see Likutay Moharan, torah 36:5, and the introduction to the Tikun Haklali (-General Rectification). And in Keheelas Yaakov – for *beena* (-understanding) is called thought (*machshuva*), and the Exodus from Egypt is from the realm of the *jubilee* which is *beena*), and through the mitzva of the *Oamehr of Barley* and the days of the *sfeerah* (-counting) it is possible to merit to clarify the imagination, from which come all the thoughts and confusion, and to draw upon oneself holiness, that he should guard himself, at least from now, to grasp his thought so that it doesn't go outside, and that he should know well, that it is impossible by any means for there to be two thoughts together, and the brain is just an *oamehr*, and measurement, and vessel which cannot have placed into it, just, one thought. And therefore it is possible to flee from the bad thoughts just by *shev vi'al taaseh* ("sit and don't do" – inaction), that is, not to think that (foreign) thought, rather set one's thought well, in the words of his prayer, and through this certainly the bad thought will be pushed away, as mentioned above.

And see in the book "Ullim LiTroofah" (Leaves for Healing, letters 312-3), where it is written: And the indication of the *Oamer of Barley* should not pass from your mind. And with this a person is strengthened also regarding hisbodidus and conversation between himself and his Maker. And it writes there: And the main thing is not to overly think of the past or the future, just to look at the *tachlis* (-ultimate purpose) at that hour, and do what you can, that which will bring you success for eternity, for every single word of Torah, and prayer, and conversation between oneself and his Maker, everything is the soul's success, wondrous success which is infinite, "no eye has seen etc. (Isaiah 64:3)." And especially since we see that the *baal duvur* (litigator – Satan) does his thing, may the Merciful One save us, we are obligated to do our part, to speak between oneself and his Maker, to express his words before Him blessed He, and through this one draws upon himself radiance and holiness of the good point he has inside, to bind it to his heart with a tight and strong knot etc., see there, and through this he will merit to remove from his heart all the degradations, which are the bad desires and bad loves which break a person's heart, in the aspect of (Psalms 69:21), "degradation broke my heart," as mentioned above in article 57, see there.

Articles Regarding Hisbodidus From The Books of

Likutay Halachos

72. Persistence in prayer

The essence of the consciousness of *tefillin*, which is the aspect of *divaikus* (binding) (as mentioned above, article 58), is the aspect of prayer and hisbodidus, for the main *divaikus* is prayer, as explained elsewhere (Likutay Moharan volume 2, torah 84), and on account of this they are called *tefillin*, a term denoting *tefilla* (-prayer), an aspect of (Genesis 30:8), "*naftoollee* (-same etymology as *tefillin* and *tefilla*) *Eloakim* (G-d) *niftaltee* (-same; I have surely grappled with G-d)," and Rash"i explains: "from the language of (Deuteronomy 32:5 "*eekaish oopisaltul*"), "crooked and spiral"; I have been persistent and have made many importunities and grapplings with G-d (-'The Place' – for all space is in G-d), to be equal with my sister. 'And also I prevailed' (continuation of the verse, with Rashi's commentary), that He agreed to my motion." And in this aspect it is necessary to profuse in prayer and hisbodidus very, very much all of one's life, for this is paramount. And it is necessary to be very extremely stubborn at this, that even though it appears to him that his words are absolutely

to no avail, and he is very far from (the fulfillment of) his
words, and it is days and years that he is busy with this and
has still not accomplished anything, even still it is
necessary to be stubborn with this; exactly like someone
who is stubborn, who does something without reason (/gain),
so too very great stubbornness is necessary in all service of
Hashem, in every act and remedy, but the primary extra
stubbornness is needed with prayers and entreaties, and the
main thing is with conversations of hisbodidus, for it is
necessary to strengthen (oneself) very much to abound in
hisbodidus and conversation between oneself and his
Maker, even though it will be in a crooked and spiral way,
many times without taste or smell (-appeal). For (Psalms
22:25), "He did not despise and did not abhor the pauper's
callings," even though it is befitting to despise him and to
abhor him, even still, Hashem Yisburach is full of mercy at
all times.

And see in the holy Zohar (Torah portion of Bulluk, page 195)
where it writes at great length of the greatness of the
preciousness of the pauper's prayer, see there, and all of this
is said even of a regular pauper who prayers for his needs;
over his materialistic inadequacy and poverty, all the more
so, and all the more so when a person begins to have mercy
on himself, and feels his poverty and inadequacy in good
deeds, and argues before Hashem Yisburach, and pleads to
Him to draw him close to His service, and pours out his
heart before Him cryingly and entreatingly, how very
precious this prayer is in the eyes of Hashem Yisburach
more than all the prayers of the world, even though for
some time already he has been praying and doing
hisbodidus and it seems to him that he hasn't accomplished

anything, even still every single word is not lost, and they are all enumerated and tallied, and cached in His treasuries. And also (take into consideration) that it is entirely impossible for a person to know, in this body, if he accomplished in the service of Hashem or not, and even if he did not accomplish in his entire life, just one hairbreadth, this also is more precious than all the life of this world, therefore it is necessary to strengthen in this very much, immeasurably. And when he is strong as delineated above in the aspect of "grapplings with G-d I have grappled," then at the very end he will certainly merit to achieve his request and to truly draw close to Hashem Yisburach, and to be consistent with his brothers, the kosher and the tzaddikim.

(Likutay Halachos, Laws of Tefillin, law 5).

73. Hisbodidus until nullification to the Unity of Hashem

The hisbodidus needs to be until one abnegates himself to Hashem Yisburach completely, that he nullifies all his desires to Hashem Yisburach's desire. And this is the aspect of justice, that a person needs to judge himself, and settle himself on every issue, if such is proper for him to wear away his life etc.. And the main hisbodidus and conversation needs to be in strengthening good desires for Hashem Yisburach, and he should utterly remove his thoughts from all the vanities (*hevel*) of the world, and abnegate his desire to Him blessed He, until from all four directions of the world, where his consciousness was scattered to, he will return from all of them to the *dallet* (the fourth letter of the Hebrew aleph bet, also corresponding to the four directions) of *echad* (-one. Spelled with the letter *dallet* at the end, which is the paradigm of G-d's unity, especially by the upper right protrusion which distinctly differentiates the *dallet* from the letter *resh* which would render the word, *achehr* – other, the antithesis of the One, Unity of G-d), to be included in His Unity and His Will blessed He. And usually during hisbodidus and the settling of one's mind, one sees himself as not having any place in any of the four directions of the world, to run away there, and to hide there from the physical and spiritual ravages of the world; of the body, soul, and money, in the aspect of (Psalms 139:7), "Where can I go from Your angry spirit etc.," until he sees that he has no where to escape to, except to Him blessed He, in the aspect of (*sleechoas*), "because from You I ran, and I returned to You," for Hashem Yisburach is present at all times for all who call Him, even if they strayed as they strayed, for His mercies are never ever exhausted.

And whoever merits to strengthen in this, to always have strong will for the truth, and not to let up on the good will, no matter what he undergoes, certainly in the very end, his comeuppance will be good. And those who are accustomed to doing hisbodidus are safe from any antagonist, and enemy, and adversary, for they always hide themselves in the shadow (-refuge) of His wings blessed He. And (Jeremiah 30:21), "Whom will take it upon himself (lit: make his heart collateral) to confront Hashem Yisburach?" For they conceal themselves by Him blessed He, in the aspect of (Psalms 91:9), "For You Hashem are my refuge."

And this is the aspect of (Deuteronomy 33:28), "And Israel dwelled confidently secure, alone etc.," in the aspect of (Psalms 4:9), "For You Hashem will set me alone, confidently secure." For by means of hisbodidus one dwells confidently secure, see there (in the source enumerated below) where it explains with this, the verse (Numbers 23:9), "they are a nation that will dwell alone," that they do hisbodidus very, very well between themselves privately, addressing what will amount of them and their aftermath, for this is the whole matter of the conversation between oneself and his Maker; "(continuation of the verse) and amongst the nations it does not consider {/is not considered}" – that they don't consider in their minds the enterprise of the nations who pursue money, "(verse 10) Who can count the earth of Jacob (Rashi interprets, the mitzvoas that are carried out with the earth)?" What is effected from every single step (that is traversed over the earth) of this that they go on an errand of a *mitzva*, to do hisbodidus and settle oneself well, "(continuation of the verse) and count one quarter of the encampment of Israel" - the aspect of the four flags (-the twelve tribes camped in four camps, each with a unique flag), the aspect of the *dallet* (-fourth letter, and final letter-) of the word *echad* (-one), as mentioned above. See there, all of this at length. **(Likutay Halachos, Laws of the Morning Blessings, law 5:87).**

74. Request mercy to be strengthened from above to request mercy

When one comes to express his words before Hashem Yisburach, and cannot open his mouth whatsoever, even still he needs to bolster (himself) to request mercy, that they should help him from above, and they should buttress his strength so that he will be able to ask for mercy. As Our Sages o.b.m. said (Sanhedrin 54), a person should always request mercy that all (the supernal beings) bolster his strength, and Rashi explains, that the ministering angels (*malachay hashurais*) help him to request mercy etc., see there.

(Likutay Halachoas, Laws of the Morning Blessings, law 5:97).

75. Reciting Psalms and holy speech to engage and champion the 50th level

Through the recital of Psalms, which encompasses all the 49 gates of repentance, which are the aspect of the forty nine letters of (the names of) the tribes, as was brought down above (article 1), and was founded by David King of Israel, who is the aspect of Messiah, so that he would merit to attain the 50th gate of holiness, as is brought down (see Sefer HaLikutim of the Ariza"l, Torah portion of Vu'Eschanan, on the verse Va'Yisabbehr), and through hisbodidus and conversation between oneself and his Maker, which is also an aspect of Psalms, as is explained elsewhere (Likutay Moharan vol. 1, torah 156), there is drawn a radiance of the sparkling (*hisnoatzitzus* - glimmer) of Messiah, which through this, one is enabled to express his words concerning everything, and request from Hashem Yisburach regarding this itself, that he should be able to request of Him: "Return us Hashem to You in truth," until this itself will be considered as our arousal from below, and through this there will also be drawn upon us a great illumination of inspiration to repent, from above, in the aspect of (Malachi 3:7), "Return to Me and

I will return to you (plural)." For in truth, the entire purpose of Hashem Yisburach's scream that He screams at us, "Return to Me etc.," His intent is this itself, that we should scream to Him constantly: "Return us etc.," and this will be considered as our (own) arousal, as if we are returning to Him on our own right, except we don't understand His holy intention. And through the recital of Psalms and hisbodidus, illumination is drawn from the fiftieth gate of holiness, which is this wondrous intellect mentioned above, which encompasses everything, from below to above, and from above to below, for our Rabbis o.b.m. said (Brachos 7b), 'A song of David' (28 Psalms begin with these words, which place the word '*mizmor*' – a song, before '*liDuvid*' – of David), 'Of David a song' (7 Psalms begin with these words, where '*liDuvid*' precedes '*mizmor*'); sometimes he said *sheera* (song of praise to Hashem) and afterwards was imbued with Divine Inspiration (*ruach hakodesh*), and sometimes the opposite (t.n. which one is which is seemingly conflicted between the Talmud and the Zohar, the Rama of Pano offers a resolution), that is as was mentioned above, that the songs (-chapters) of the Psalms encompass both aspects: of arousal initiating from below (-from the person on his own accord – *issaroosa dillisata*) first, and of arousal which was initiated from above (*issaroosa dillaila*) first. And therefore, through the recital of Psalms and hisbodidus everything is rectified, that we can request of Him: "Return us," etc..

It comes out that everything is from Him blessed He, and even still it will be considered as our own arousal since we arouse nonetheless to request Him for this, and through this we will certainly merit to repent completely.

And certainly it is a great and easy *aitza* (remedy), that everyone can merit to repentance and life of the world to come, through speech alone. However, also upon this there is huge deterrence, because the *baal duvur* (-litigator – Satan) set himself upon this very much, to preoccupy every person with the burden of making a livelihood, which incurs the main falling of *Kinnessess Yisroel* (-the Congregation of Israel) to the fiftieth gate of impurity, to the extent that it doesn't allow him to engage in even an easy *aitza* such as this, to scream to Hashem Yisburach appropriately. But in reality, this also is not an impediment whatsoever, for one needs to remind himself that it is impossible in any way to procure for himself his livelihood by means of his efforts and toil, because it is heretical to say, Heaven forbid (Deuteronomy 8:17), "My strength and the might of my hand made etc.," only, it is necessary to believe that all sustenance is drawn only from Him blessed He, with the salvation of Hashem and with His kindness, and through this even the laborer and the businessman can find several hours a day for his soul, in which to engage in reciting Psalms, and hisbodidus, to express his words before Him blessed He as mentioned above, and through this he will certainly merit to complete repentance in the aspect of (Hosea 14:3), "Take with you (plural) words and return to Hashem;" and our Rabbis o.b.m. said (Shemoas Rabba 38:4): "I do not ask of you (plural), just words." For through this, that at any rate he arouses with holy words to request Him: "Return us etc." as mentioned above, this will be recognized as our (-human) arousal, and through this we will merit to complete repentance, and understand this well, for without any arousal whatsoever it is certainly impossible to draw close.

Also, through reciting Psalms one merits to receive illumination from the holy *aitzoas* (-advice, remedies) which emanate from the sparkling (*hisnoatzitzus* - glimmer) of Messiah, from the fiftieth gate of holiness; and the mass of the *aitzoas* are incorporated in the Book of Pslams (which are the "faithful kindnesses of David (Isaiah 55:3)," which are the aspect of (the *sfeeroas* – Divine Emanations/Attributes of) *Netzach* (victory/eternity) and *Hoad* (splendor), an aspect of very holy and wondrous *aitzoas*, as is known (see Likutay Moharan vol. 1, torah 41; Keheeloas Yaakov, entry of *aitza*) that the 'kindnesses of David' are the aspect of *Netzach* and *Hoad*, the aspect of *aitzoas*), namely to scream to Hashem Yisburach always, no matter what may be, as mentioned above. And through this it is possible to leave and rise from all the falls and descents of the world, even from the paradigm of the fiftieth gate of impurity, that the *baal duvur* (-litigator – Satan) burdens every person all the days of their life, with desire for money and the burdens of making a livelihood, to the extent that he has no time whatsoever even to scream to Hashem Yisburach, as mentioned above.

And this is the aspect of the prominence of the Psalm (145) "*Teheela* <An exaltation> *LiDavid* <of David>" which our Rabbis o.b.m. said (Brachos 4b), anyone who says it three time every day is guaranteed that he is a beneficiary (/member) of the future world, and it concludes there, because it incorporates the Aleph Bet (each letter of the Aleph Bet, alphabetically, begins a verse, except for the letter Nun, see below) and addresses livelihood (verse 15): "All eyes are directed at you with hopeful expectation" (the Talmud actually cites the next verse, "You open Your hand and satiate etc.", which is the culmination of this verse, see below). And their intention is, because both aspects mentioned above are amalgamated together in this Psalm, that is, because through these two aspects which are together in this Psalm, we will certainly merit to complete repentance and to life of the future world, for through the aggregate of the twenty two letters, which encompass all the words in existence, one will draw upon himself holiness, so that he sanctifies the (-his) speech very much, to abound in (the recital of) Psalms and hisbodidus to Hashem Yisburach, and through this he will certainly merit to rectify all the mutilation of all the sins, which (they) are also from the aspect of the twenty two letters, that he drew, Heaven forbid, the letters which are in that matter that he transgressed, to the *other side* (realm of evil), as is known and understood from his words o.b.m. in the torah "*Unoachee*" ("I"), chapter four in Likutay Moharan volume one; except the burden of making a livelihood restrains a person from this, as mentioned above, but behold this Psalm reminds the person, that all sustenance – (is) just from Him blessed He, as it is written (Psalms 145:15-6), "The eyes of everyone hope (-look with hopeful expectation) to You, and You etc. You open etc. and satiate etc.. And certainly through this one with certainly merit to strengthen in holy speech, and he will merit through this to complete repentance and life of the future world.

And this is what our Rabbis o.b.m. said (Brachoas 4b): Why is the (letter) *Nuen* not mentioned (-as the the first letter of a verse) in "*Ashrei*" ("fortunate" - referring to Psalm 145 which we preface with the last verse of Psalm 144 – Fortunate...)? Because inherent in it, is the fall of the enemies of Israel (-this is a euphemism for Israel itself), as it says (Amos 5:2), "She fell etc.," and even still, David, with Divine inspiration (*ruach hakodesh*) returned and supported it ('*sumcha*' – the letter after *Nuen* is the *Samech*), as it says (Psalms 145:14), "*Soamaich* Hashem <Hashem supports – *Soamaich* – with the letter

165

Samech> all those who fall *<'Noaflim'* – starts with the letter *Nuen*, which was skipped, and mentioned with the following letter in this supportive fashion>. That is, because he did not want to mention the *Nuen* explicitly, for it alludes to the fiftieth gate of holiness (the numerical value of the letter *Nuen* is fifty), through which is afforded the main hope, because included in it is the fall of *Kinnesses Yisroel* (the Congregation of Israel), because the main fall of *Kinnesses Yisroel* is also through the fiftieth gate of impurity, which is the desire of money and the burden of making a livelihood as mentioned above, and therefore it is not viable to mention the *Nuen* explicitly, because the opposition will intensify overwhelmingly, just by allusion, it is intimated in the succeeding verse: "*Soamaich* Hashem <Hashem supports – *Soamaich* – with the letter *Samech>* all those who fall *<'Noaflim'* – starts with the letter *Nuen>* etc.." And this entails that one casts his burden on Hashem (Psalms 55:23, in contradistinction to the person discussed in Psalm 52:9), and trust that Hashem Yisburach will certainly provide for him, even if he engages several hours of the day in holy speech of prayer and Torah. For all the sustenance, even of the laborers and businessmen, is only from Him blessed He. And this is what is adjoined to this (Psalm 145:15 – verse beginning with the next letter from the Aleph Bet: *Eye'in*, here presented in plural, meaning: eyes), "The eyes of everyone hope expectantly to You," exactly as explained above.

And this is what we see that this (person) has vast wealth, and this (other person) is poor and very poverty stricken – all is from Him blessed He according to the *becheera* (free choice) of each and every one, as is known (Words of Rabbi

Nachman, article 300; Life of Rabbi Nachman, article 519; see also Rabbi Nachman's Legendary Stories, the beginning of the story of the Prayer Leader), and (Psalm 145:17 – verse starting with the letter *Tzadi* – righteous (verse 16, which begins with the letter Peh, is a culmination of verse 15, expressing how Hashem actually satiates willfully)), "Righteous is Hashem in all His ways, and benevolent (/pious) in all His conduct," for everything that He does with a person, is all great kindness from Him blessed He. And the ultimate hope of every person is to merit to the eternal life of the future world. And by what means does one merit this, through (verse 18, beginning with the letter *Koof*), "Close is Hashem to all His callers," distinctly 'to all who call to Him', no matter what may be. And this is (final verse – 21, beginning with the letter *Tuv*), "The praise of Hashem, my mouth will speak, and all flesh will bless His holy Name forever and ever," to express one's words before Hashem Yisburach at all times, and through this, certainly he will rectify everything, and he will merit through this to life of the future world.

Therefore one who says this Psalm three times a day (-this has already been instituted and incorporated in the body of the daily prayers, twice in the morning prayer of Shacharis, and once in the afternoon prayer of Mincha) is guaranteed to be a beneficiary (/member) of the future world, for through the two aspects coalesced in this Psalm, certainly he will merit to return to Hashem Yisburach, and to life of the future world, as mentioned above. **(Likutay Halachos, Laws of Reciting (*Kreyas*) Shema. Law 5).**

76. Prayer of the night and exile - when one is beyond compulsion – just from strong good desires and yearning

Our father Jacob, when he met up with that place (Genesis 28:11, beginning of Torah portion Va'Yaitzay where Jacob leaves his parents to journey to Laban), which was brought about through his taking heart to return to the site of the Temple, and immediately the land sprang to him (the phenomenon of 'kefeetzas haderech'), as our Rabbis o.b.m. said (Sanhedrin 95b), through this he merited to attain the utter virtue of arousal initiated from below (-of one's own accord – issaroosa dillisata), through which immediately help came to him from above, in the aspect of (Sabbath 104a), one who comes to purify himself – he is helped, and therefore he established then the evening prayer (Arvis), which is (prayed) when it is completely dark, because he merited with the great magnitude of his holiness to lower himself to the depth of the falls of all of Israel, in general and in particular, of every single generation until the approaching (-'heels' – ikvussa dimmesheecha) of Messiah, and shines in the heart of Israel that even in the darkness of night, and even utterly (devoid) materialistically and spiritually, it is necessary to strengthen and to arouse in arousal from below (-of one's own accord – issaroosa dillissata) with screaming and prayer to Him blessed, in the aspect of (Jonah 2:3), "from the belly of Scheol I screamed," and there is no good will that goes lost (Zohar, Shemos 150b), and like our master, leader, and rabbi o.b.m. said in the awesome discourse (see Words of Rabbi Nachman articles 2-3), when he extolled fantastically the greatness of the Creator blessed He, that people no nothing whatsoever (-in reality of G-d's true greatness, even those with great conceptions of G-d, cannot be considered to have any knowledge of G-d whatsoever, see there), and he concluded then with these words: *Afeeloo a'yir zach* <even your (plural) thing> *vee ahin itlichehr iz gifallin* <where each one has fallen> *abbee meh iz zich nit mi'ya'ish fin shra'yen* <the main thing is not to despair from screaming> *meh shreyet* <one screams> *meh bet* <one begs> etc.. There is a concept (/scheme) that everything is turned around for the good, for Hashem Yisburach is great, and people know nothing (of this) whatsoever etc., and it is precious and very significant by Hashem Yisburach every single arousing of every person, wherever he is. And immediately when a person arouses in *issaroossa dillisata* (-arousal from below – on his own accord) in any prayer or devotion whatsoever, immediately there is aroused plentiful *issaroossa dillaila* (-arousal from above), and through this he has strength to arouse further, and accordingly there will be drawn more *issaroossa dillaila* (-arousal from above) etc..

And this is the aspect of the prayer of arvis (night) not being obligatory (Brachos 27b), because at times the darkness and absence of mind so much overwhelms a person, to the extent that he is in the aspect of deprived of speech, the aspect of (Psalm 56:1) a mute dove (see Me'oaray Ohr: the Malchus is called a complete (-healthy) dove, and in exile it is called a mute <*eellaim*> dove, with the letters Yud-Hey of (G-d's Name of five letters – not to be pronounced) Eloa'H'I'm distanced and removed, remaining (just with the three letters that spell) *eellaim* (mute)), for he is entirely unable to open his mouth to pray, and do hisbodidus, and to express his words as would be proper for him, in the aspect of (Psalms 39:10), "I was rendered inarticulate, I will not open my mouth," and it says (verse 3), "I was rendered inarticulate, silent etc.." And in reality, if not for the power of the great tzaddikim, they would then completely despair of praying and returning to Hashem. And this is the main rectification of the true tzaddikim, for they are in the aspect of our father Jacob, for they arouse and strengthen us, and instill in the heart of Israel that also in the utter bitterness of the exile, physically and spiritually, which is the aspect of the utter darkness of night, one should pray and return to Hashem, and never despair of screaming and prayer, as mentioned above. And even though he is then in the aspect of deprived of speech, as mentioned above, even still, each one should look upon the point of the stark truth, until each one strengthens, from wherever he is, at any rate, with strong desires and good yearning for Hashem Yisburach, in the aspect of (Psalms 119:55), "I remembered at night Your name Hashem," and in the aspect of (Song of Songs 3:1), "On my bed in the nights I sought he whom my soul loves etc.;" That also in the utter darkness of the night we will seek and search for Hashem Yisburach with very strong desires, because ultimately what will be the *tachlis* (end, purpose, destiny) of us? Until through this, on his own accord, he will strengthen to open his mouth with words of prayer, also then, in the aspect of (Psalms 39:3), "I was rendered inarticulate, silent, I was mum (even) from (saying) good, and (-even though) my pain is debilitating." And afterwards, through this itself, that even still he yearns and longs very much for Hashem Yisburach, and is pained by this, that he is in the aspect of deprived of speech, through this (verse 4), "My heart is feverish inside of me etc. I spoke with my tongue," that he merits afterwards through this, to speak holy words with great emotion, with holiness, since the words came about through good desires and great yearning for Hashem Yisburach.

And in truth this is always the main perfection of the prayer, and this is the essential *aitza* (advice, remedy) for prayer, and conversing, and hisbodidus, that the matter should not be upon him as an obligation, like he needs to fulfill his obligation, which is the aspect of (Ethics of Our Fathers 2:18), "Do not make your prayer routine, rather (pray) compassionately and entreatingly," that first he should arouse his heart with very good desires and yearning for Hashem Yisburach, for then he will pray and beseech afterwards truthfully, from the walls of his heart, of his own volition and good will, not as a perfunctory ordeal and out of obligation alone. And this is the aspect of 'the prayer of *arvis* (night) is not obligatory', that is, as mentioned above. Just that even still our Rabbis o.b.m. established for us an obligatory prayer (at night) for the masses, because otherwise they wouldn't pray at all. But the main perfection of these prayers themselves – (is) to pray them compassionately and entreatingly not in a routine fashion. And therefore the prayers of the day; Shacharis (-morning) and Mincha (-afternoon) which are in the daytime, that is, when the intellect (/higher consciousness) still shines, therefore they are in the aspect of mandatory. And Jacob established the prayer of arvis (night), namely to pray also in the utter darkness of night, when the intellect (/higher consciousness) has completely departed, at which time it is impossible to establish a mandatory prayer, that is to place upon him an obligation to pray then, since he is then in the aspect of absence of mind and deprived of speech, and is utterly unable to open his mouth. And therefore, then the essential establishment of prayer is by means of the aspect of 'the prayer of *arvis* (night) is not obligatory', that our father Jacob r.i.p. established, to draw upon himself, also then, the illumination of the truth from the light of the countenance of the true tzaddikim whom are in the aspect of Jacob, which is the aspect of (Micah 7:20), "Give truth to Jacob," and he merited to the light of the countenance, the aspect of which our Rabbis o.b.m. said (Bava Metziah 84a), the exquisiteness of Jacob etc.. And the light of the countenance mentioned above is the aspect of desire, as brought down in his words o.b.m. (Likutay Moharan vol. 2, 4:8), as it is written (Psalms 44:4), "and the light of Your countenance for You have desired them." And through this he will merit to strengthen himself at any rate with good desires and yearning, and then of its own accord his mouth will open with holy words, and he will pour out his heart like water before Hashem as a result of the strong force of the good desire and yearning, which is always the essential perfection of the prayer. And this is the aspect of (Genesis 28:11), "And he stayed the night there because the sun had set," which alludes to the darkness of the exile, of body and soul, as is brought in the words of our Rabbis o.b.m. (Biraishis Rabba 68:19), and then (first words of the verse), "And he met up with (-arrived at) the place," and he merited then to attain the utter height of issaroossa dillissata (-arousal from below – of one's own accord), and established the prayer of arvis (night), exactly as explained above. **(Likutay Halachos, Laws of the Prayer of Mincha, law 7).**

77. Never ever stop screaming to Hashem

Whoever desires to have mercy on his soul, so that he doesn't destroy his world Heaven forbid, needs to search and investigate very much after the truth in order to truly return to Hashem Yisburach, because perhaps his mind is misguiding him in some no good way Heaven forbid, since he did not merit to configure the light of the Torah properly, because the mechanisms of his intellect are not honed because of defection of the *bris* (circumcision – covenant). And the main rectification for all this is screaming, and prayer, and words, and hisbodidus between one and his Maker, for it is necessary to scream a lot to Hashem Yisburach that He should always lead him in the straight (/just) and true way, like King David r.i.p. screamed copiously for this (Psalms 27:12), "Teach me Hashem Your way, (so that) I will go in Your truth," "Teach me Hashem Your way and lead me in the just past (Psalms 27:11)," "Teach me Hashem the way of Your statutes etc. (Psalm 119:33)," "Send Your light and Your truth they will lead me (Psalm 43:3)," and so forth many numerous more (verses). For one needs great merit, and salvation, and great mercy, and effort (*hishtadlus*), and great exertion all the days of his life, that he should merit to go at all times absolute truly in the holy way, and it is necessary to scream profusely to Hashem Yisburach for this with *meseeras nefesh* (-self sacrifice), until one's soul actually just about departs Heaven forbid, as our Rabbis o.b.m. said (Taanis 8a): The prayer of a person isn't heard unless he puts his soul in his palm. For the main rectification of the *bris* (circumcision – covenant), to merit to leave the exile of this desire completely, is through screaming abundantly to

Hashem Yisburach, for it necessary to scream at least seventy calls, and in these seventy calls are included infinitely numerous calls, and screams, and prayers, and entreaties, all the days of a person's life. For the seventy years of a person correlate the seventy facets of the Torah that one needs to merit (to them). And everyone can understand in his soul (-for himself) how distant he is still, even from the aspect of one facet of the Torah, all the more so from all of them.

Therefore even if he didn't vitiate very much, and even if he already screamed a lot to Hashem Yisburach and engaged copiously in Torah and *mitzvos*, even still, since he still did not attain conception of even one facet of the Torah, and not even a thousandth or ten-thousandth of this, how plentifully he certainly still needs to scream to Hashem Yisburach all the days of his life. And it is already known that it is forbidden to ever despair oneself of screaming, for even if one vitiated very, very much, and even if he is still the way he is, if he does not despair himself of screaming, and prayer, and entreaty, he can merit to a true revelation of a facet of the Torah, and even to all the seventy facets, for Hashem Yisburach is good to all, just that some *issaroosa dillissata* (-arousal from below – from the person's own accord) is necessary. And the main thing is – to scream abundantly to Hashem Yisburach, until one merits to break all the desires, and primarily the desire mentioned above, and then he will merit to a revelation of the Torah in the aspect of the seventy facets of the Torah.

(Likutay Halachos, Laws of Wine Libation, law 4).

174

78. Binding one's point to his heart according to the moment

It is necessary to always strengthen to abound in prayer, and entreaty, and conversation between oneself and his Maker, in order to arouse every time his good point, so that it shines to his heart, until all the ignominy and bad loves which impose on his heart, which are the aspect of the foreskin of the heart, are nullified from him through this, as mentioned previously in article 50. However, since the ignominies of the heart are rallying all the time to hide and conceal the light of his holy point which is pertinent to his heart at that time, therefore the usual tendency of a person who desires to engage in this, to express his words between himself and his Maker, is to be beset each time with the impression that now he cannot speak, and he does not know what to say whatsoever, and his heart is very sealed etc., as is known. And all of this is drawn from the ignominies of the heart, the uncircumcision of the heart mentioned above. But in truth, it is utter falsehood and the work of the *baal duvur* (-litigator – Satan). For if one were to say so, then it would always seem to him so, that now he does not have heart and he cannot speak, and he will never speak Heaven forbid. And through this itself the ignominies of the heart, the foreskin of the heart, will surge over him each time exceedingly more, for the essential abnegation of the foreskin of the heart mentioned above, is through binding one's heart to his holy point through the speech of his mouth, that he pours out his words before Hashem Yisburach and arouses his good point.

Therefore it is necessary to strengthen in this, to know and to believe that certainly there is no time in the world that one cannot bind himself then to the point pertinent to his heart at that time, and to hype oneself up to the utmost to speak in this as best as he can, to seek and search with his words, the light of his holy point. And even though it is certainly impossible for a person to know all this precisely, what the point pertinent to his heart is at this exact time and instant, even still he needs to always believe that certainly there is now the aspect of the good point which is pertinent to his heart at this exact time, and to bind himself to it, for through this he will be rectified from wherever he is. And in truth this necessitates abundant prayers and entreaties to merit to find the point pertinent to his heart at that specific time. And this is the aspect of (Psalms 32:6), "For this every *hassid* (devote, pious Jew) should pray to You *li-ais* <for the time> *mitzoh* <find/found> {-when G-d is to be found accessible/for a time when G-d will be accessible/to find what is pertinent to that time}," distinctly "*li-ais mitzoh* <to find for the time>," that he should always merit to find the point relevant to the time and moment, this being the aspect of the construct of hisbodidus and conversation between oneself and his Maker, through which one merits for himself at all times to the point pertinent to his heart at this moment. And all this is the aspect of *mishpat* (judicial justice), that he judges and adjudicates himself, and admonishes himself to fulfill all the words of the Torah. And it is necessary to synchronize the *mishpat* (judgment), to judge himself every time and every day according to the time and the moment. And this is the aspect of (Kings I:8:59), "And these words of mine which I entreated before

Hashem etc.," the aspect of the entreaties and hisbodidus discussed above (further in the verse), "to do *mishpat* (justice/what is necessary) for His servant etc.," for through this one draws the aspect of the *mishpat* discussed above, "(further in the verse) the matter of the day on its day," appropriately suited in accordance to this time, and day, and hour. **(Likutay Halachos, Laws of Teachers, law 3).**

79. No matter the distance be tenacious to prepare to speak to Hashem and He will create the words

A person needs to know of his utter distance from Hashem Yisburach, and even still know and believe that in the vantage of His Mercies blessed He, He is extremely close to each and everyone, even to the very distant, and primarily – through speech, because through speech we can call to Him from very far, and He draws close to us through this, as it is written (Psalms 145:18), "Close Hashem is to all who call Him, to all who call Him in truth," and it is written (Deuteronomy 4:8), "And who is a great nation that it has G-d close to it like Hashem our G-d in all our calling to Him." And this is the aspect of (Isaiah 57:19), "[I will] create [for him – he who was abnegated to G-d] expression of the lips (-speech)," the aspect of speech, which specifically through this one merits to the aspect of (continuation of the verse), "peace to the distant and to the close," the aspect of the distance and the proximity discussed above, that he should know truthfully the distance on his part, and the propinquity from the vantage of His Mercies blessed He.

And whoever puts his heart to examine closely and to understand the meaning of the words of this verse, "[I will] create [for him] expression of the lips," can understand from this *aitzoas* (advice, remedies) how to strengthen in the undertaking of conversation between himself and his Maker, for this is the essential rectification in the matter of 'distant and close' discussed above.

For through the conversation discussed above, he can express and converse everything before Hashem Yisburach, to explain in his talk, his utter estrangement from Hashem Yisburach, and even still, precisely through this he will draw close to Hashem Yisburach, through the recollection of His utterly profuse Mercies blessed He, beyond measure, like our fathers and rabbis o.b.m. revealed to us. However, predominantly, the conversation mentioned above, itself, is extremely difficult, because due to his utter alienation he doesn't have any words to say, as is known to whoever desires to accustom himself in this. However, our Rabbis o.b.m. have already warned us to strengthen in all types of strengthening to practice this practice every day, because the preparation and the desire alone, that one prepares himself and desires to speak, just that he is not able to speak, this also is extremely precious by Him blessed He (like it is written above, article 2). And if he is very tenacious at this, certainly Hashem Yisburach will help him, and will create words for him in the aspect of (Isaiah 57:19), "[I will] create [for him] expression of the lips," actual creation! For the words that come to a person are the aspect of an actual new creation, for certainly he is very distant from words due to his estrangement from Hashem Yisburach, but when he is strong in this devotion and prepares himself to speak and converse between himself and his Maker, and he is tenacious at this for some hours with strong desires and yearning, then Hashem Yisburach helps him, and sends him words into his mouth, which are the aspect of an actually new creation, that Hashem Yisburach in His Mercies created for him words, and ushered them into his mouth, in the aspect of "[I will] create [for him] expression of the lips," distinctly "create," and specifically through this he merits to the aspect of "peace to the distant and to the close," as mentioned above.

This is like it is written (Proverbs 16:1), "It is up to a person to arrange his heart (-thoughts and words) and from Hashem the (actual) rhetoric is (provided/on the tongue)," for the person must arrange his heart (-thoughts and words), that is the aspect of preparation discussed above, and then Hashem Yisburach sends him words into his mouth in the aspect of "and from Hashem the (actual) rhetoric (is provided)." And this is like it is written (Psalms 51:17, said before the 18 benedictions), "G-d open my lips etc.," that Hashem Yisburach Himself, so to speak, opens his lips for him to speak and converse what is in his heart, for everything is from Him blessed He, just, the person needs to prepare himself with holy desires and yearning, and Hashem helps him to speak and express his words properly, with perfection. **(Likutay Halachos, Laws of Sending From The Nest, law 5).**

In addition, see the book "Ullim LiTrufah" (Leaves for Healing, letter 286) concerning encouragement for hisbodidus, to long and yearn with good yearning and desires of holiness, and to verbalize them (lit: release them from the mouth), to scream every time for His abundant Mercy, like our master, leader and rabbi *zatza"l* warned us. And it is written there in these words: My children, my friends, and my comrades. My innards rejoice (-Bava Metzia 83b) as I see that thank G-d the words of our supreme rabbi *zatzvka"l* are making an impression in your hearts etc.. For although in fact they are words of simplicity and *temeemus* (wholesomeness, unfeigned, straightforward), but it is very difficult and arduous (lit: heavy) to accept them due to the many barriers which separate, and the confusions of the mind of each and everyone, and the follies of each one which the world refers to as "*chuchmos*" ('wisdoms', paralogism, contrivances, over-thinking and sophistication), which encircle (/turn) and twist the heart very much in many perplexing ways, and primarily with what it weakens a person's resolve, and he makes himself out as if he is a man of truth, to the extent that many such wise people say in their hearts: "What will these words help me; behold even still I know myself the truth, what I do and what is going on with me etc. etc.," until he begins to distance himself from screaming and entreating. And it is written (Jerusalem Talmud, end of Brachos): 'a day you leave Him, two days I will leave you', until Heaven forbid days or years pass by that he is very alienated. Fortunate is the man who listens to him, to apply himself diligently upon the doors of his torah, and his holy words, day after day (Proverbs 8:34), to begin every time anew, to quest, and to yearn with new yearning and desires of holiness, and to verbalize (lit: release from his mouth) the yearning with words of conversation, and entreaty, and screaming, and yelling, and sighing, and to express his words before Him blessed He every day, like a son before his father, be what might be. And he should focus himself each time on screaming and entreating however he can, for there is no scream that is lost Heaven forbid, even an arbitrary desire isn't lost, for (Zohar, Torah portion of Trumah, 150b) there is no good desire that is lost. Fortunate are you my son if you strengthen yourself to go in this way that you wrote to me etc., see there.

80. Open discussions with Hashem with thanksgiving for the past and then scream for the future

Sometimes the suffering and impediments are so overwhelming, to the extent that one cannot even open his mouth to express his words before Him blessed He. Therefore it is necessary to be careful, that every time he comes to express his words before Hashem Yisburach, he should remind himself of the abundant favors and kindness that Hashem Yisburach did with him from his inception till this day, and he should give acknowledgment and thanks to His Name blessed He for all the kindness of Hashem and the goodness He did with him until now. For every person, the way he is, since he is in the class of the Israelite, and dons a *tallis* and *tefillin* every single day, and unifies His Name blessed He twice every single day, certainly it is fitting for him to give thanks and express his gratitude to Hashem Yisburach every single day for His utter Kindness and Goodness blessed He to him, that he merited to be part of Israel, the receivers of the Torah, and all the more so being that everyone knows for himself (-in their soul) numerous specific wondrous favors that Hashem Yisburach did for him from his inception till that very day. And so too, sometimes the heart is sealed, and he cannot express his words before Him blessed He due to the abundant physical hardships, especially now in the lengthy exile, that there is hardly a day whose hardships don't surpass it's predecessor, and livelihood is very stinting, and a person needs to take stock of his ways, to search and to find the expansions (-relief, respite, ease, prosperity – opposite of hardship), which Hashem Yisburach expands for him in the midst of the hardships, and to thank Hashem Yisburach for them, and through this his heart will be reinforced to trust in Hashem, that He will hear his prayer now as well, and certainly through this, his mouth will open and he will be able to express his words before Him blessed He, properly. And this is the aspect of (See Brachos 54a), a person should always give thanks for the past and scream for the future, that is, because when one doesn't express gratitude for the past, it is very difficult to scream to Him blessed He due to extreme sealing of the heart, which is impervious due to abundant hardships and from being discouraged due to everything that he is undergoing spiritually. Therefore it is necessary to be very vigilant every time he comes to express his words before Him blessed He, to go in this way: to give thanks for the past, and through this he can scream for the future.

And this is the matter of: "A song of David when he ran from before Absalom his son (Psalm 3)," and our Rabbis o.b.m. asked (Brachos 7b): It should be "A lamentation of David," and they answered: Since he saw that it was his son, he rejoiced. He said, "A typical son has mercy on his father." And he found expansion (-respite) also in the midst of his hardship, with what he saw that his counsel held up, that the *Sanhedrin* (-leading Sages the makeup of the Supreme Court) etc. stand with him. And at first glance this is difficult, for behold the beginning of the Psalm doesn't speak in the language of song, rather in the language of a great outcry, like it is written there, "Hashem, how numerous are my oppressors, many etc.." However, this is all the aforementioned construct, that he turned over the incident and found expansions (-respite) in the midst of this utter calamity, and over all this he began to say "A song of David." And immediately upon his beginning to sing and thank Hashem Yisburach for the good things, immediately his heart and mind expanded, and specifically then his mouth opened and he began to pray and scream appropriately: "Hashem, how numerous are my oppressors, many rise against me etc.." Therefore his book, which is predominantly filled with great screams, and entreaties, and supplications, is called by name *Tihillim* (-Psalms), which is an expression of *tiheela* <praise> and thankful acknowledgment, because all of his screaming and entreaties were specifically by way of expressing gratitude and *tiheela* <praise>. Go ahead and check, and you will find in many Psalms that follow this pattern of praising Hashem Yisburach for the past and screaming for the future, and in the midst of the plea he is screaming and entreating, he returns and gives thanks and screams. For only thankful acknowledgment and praise are the conduit through which one is capable of screaming to Hashem Yisburach, as mentioned above. **(Likutay Halachos, Laws of Cross-breeding Animals, law 4).**

[**And** see in the book "Nachas Hashulchan" (- Felicity of the Table) from the holy Rav of Tchehrin *zatza"l* (In the Laws of *Lulav*, Chapter 648), where it is written: And this is what we are shaking (the *four species*, during the recital of *Hallel* - Psalms 113-8) by (the verses of) "Give praise to Hashem" beginning and end (-this verse appears twice in *Hallel*, (Psalms 118:1, 29) and at both instances the four species are waved and shaken), and by (the verse – 118:25) "Please Hashem bring salvation now (/please)," for when one merits to win the battle with the weapons, which are the aspect of the *four species* of the *Lulav*, as brought down in the holy Zohar (Tikunay Zohar 13, page 29a): "Who was victorious? He who holds the weapons in his hands," certainly he needs to give thanks to Hashem, for (Kidushin 30b) "if the Holy One Blessed He does not help him, he would not be able to prevail (over the evil inclination)." But even still, in the very midst of this itself, in the midst of the blessings and thanksgiving for the past, it is necessary in the middle of this to scream profusely for the future: "Please Hashem bring salvation now (/please)." For the battle is continuous, and (Kidushin 30b), every single day a person's evil inclination surges, and renews against him, and contrives against him with his cunning contrivances, to ensnare him in his trap, and like our Rabbis o.b.m. said (Shoachehr Tov, Psalms 34) if he doesn't get (lit: find) him at twenty years of age, he knocks him down at thirty etc.; if he doesn't get him at seventy, he knocks him down at eighty etc.. Therefore it is necessary to scream constantly to Him blessed He.

And also, because the salvation itself, what they merited to win the battle, is also still not with completion according to the greatness of the eminent holiness of each one of Israel, and according to the *tachlis* (-ultimate) perfection that every one of Israel needs to attain. Therefore it is necessary to scream abundantly to Hashem Yisburach at all times, but nevertheless it is necessary to conclude with thanksgiving (which is the aspect of the shaking-waving (of the four species) an additional time, at the end of *Hallel*, at (the verse of *Hoadoo-*) "Give thanks to Hashem"). For according to the utter danger that is prevalent in this world, how great are the kindnesses of Hashem for every single detail of every minute salvation and victory that each one of Israel merits every time, and like their saying o.b.m. (Yuma 69b; Yalkut Shimoni, Nechemia 1071), these themselves are His might etc. (-to allow and withstand the prevalence of evil). And therefore, immediately after the conclusion of Hallel, we scream again the "*Hoashanoas*" (-liturgy interjected between repeated supplications of "Bring salvation now/please") with bitter calls and screams, and great crying, for on the contrary, according to what we merited to receive such numerous salvations, hence, also now "May Your right (hand) bring salvation, and answer us," for complete and true salvation is still distant from us. And this is what the prayer concludes (Kings I:8:59), "And may these words of mine which I entreated etc.," that is, that the prayer should be accepted with such completion, to the extent that there will be a revelation of "*daas*" (-

realization of the knowledge) to all the nations of world, so that they know that Hashem is G-d, there is no other (verse 60).

81. Holy words eventually reverse sins to be considered unintentional and even good.

Even though a person is the way he is, even still he should be resolute (in his mind) in the place where he is, to speak words of prayer and hisbodidus which (/for they) are the aspect of the perfection of the Holy Tongue, through which the all encompassing evil of the lust for promiscuity is subdued, as mentioned above, article 68. And his intention should be, in order that he merit through this to subdue and break his evil, in order that he return to Hashem Yisburach. Certainly this will be beneficial for him, for certainly not a single utterance will be lost, and over time Hashem Yisburach will have mercy on him, and all the holy words that he released from his mouth will be gathered, and through this he will subdue and nullify the all encompassing evil of the lust for promiscuity, and then inherently he will easily be able to nullify afterwards all the other desires as well. And the essential thing is that he should be very strong in this, days and years, no matter what transpires over him, and through this he will merit to repentance, and the sins will first be reversed into unintentional sins (see inside), and then afterwards the tzaddikim who already merited to the summit of the perfection of the Holy Tongue will raise and clarify his holy words, and through this he will be able, with their power, to be inverted to be completely good.

And this is (Hosea 14:2), "Return Israel (up) to Hashem your G-d for you have stumbled in your sins," namely, that through repentance the sins will be reversed to (be considered) unintentional, in the aspect of stumbling. But through what means will they merit to this? Addressing this the verse concludes (verse 3), "Take with you (plural) words and return to Hashem," and through this the sins will be turned around to be unintentional, and afterwards they can be raised with ease to be completely good, with the power of the great tzaddikim, as mentioned above. And this is (continuation of the verse), "Say to Him, bear all the iniquity, and take good," that He should completely forgive the sins, to the extent that they be inverted to be completely good. **(Likutay Halachos, Laws of New-produce, law 4).**

82. Prayer is the fiftieth gate transcending even the angels and is thus the vehicle of final redemption from utter defilement

Against the present lengthy exile, which is called the exile of *Edoam*, the aspect of the strengthening of the *klipa* (- husk, evil force) of *Amulaik*, which distances a person from Hashem Yisburach as it does, there is no *aitza* (-remedy, advice), and no wisdom, and no approach (Proverbs 21:30), just, to abound in prayer, and entreaty, and screaming, and yelling, and crying out for salvation to Hashem Yisburach, without measure and limit, until Hashem looks and sees from the heavens. For prayer is – above everything, and encompasses all the fifty gates of holiness. For prayer is the aspect of (Brachos 34b), Eden, no I has beheld it (Isaiah 64:3), for it is the root of the Torah, for from there stem all the springs of the wisdom of the holy Torah. For prayer is the aspect of (Job 28:7), "a path unknown to the vulture," the aspect of the fiftieth gate, of which no one attained perception. That is, someone who engages in prayer, and strengthens with all (his) might to profuse in prayers and conversations between himself and his Maker, (he) arouses the supernal eye, which is the aspect of the fiftieth gate, the aspect of "a path unknown to the vulture." For there is no intellect that can attain conception and understand how far reaching the power of the prayers of Israel is, even of the lowest of the low, especially what each one prays concerning the suffering of his soul, of his distance from Hashem Yisburach. For even the holy angel which receives the Israelite's prayer and fastens from them crowns for his Maker, doesn't know where to raise this awesome crown, he just swears it that it should ascend on its own accord, and sit on the head of its Maker, as our Rabbis o.b.m. said (Zohar, Exodus 58a; Chagiga 13b, and see there Tosfos entitled "And fastens"). And therefore in the final redemption it says (Jeremiah 31:9), "with crying they will come, and with entreaty I will bring them." For this exile is in the aspect of (Lamentations 1:9), "And she descended astonishingly," the aspect of the domineering of the fiftieth gate of impurity. Therefore the main complete redemption of the future is just through prayer, which is also of the aspect of the fiftieth gate, as mentioned above. **(Likutay Halachos, Laws of One Who Makes a Messenger to Collect a Debt, law 3).**

83. Prayer at the very least acts as a protest which dispels the evil's assertion of ownership

Regarding protest (*'machu-u'*), what is explained in the law of asserting possession of (*'chezkas'*) land (Choshen Mishpat 140:7), that as long as he (-the original owner) protests, then the holding (*'chazaka'*) of the occupier (*'machzik'*) has no import at all (t.n. if three years of occupation transpire without protest, a claim from the occupier that he bought the property will be accepted) — it is very well understood how a person needs to strengthen every time in prayer, and entreaty, and hisbodidus, and screaming to Hashem Yisburach, be what may (be), no matter what transpires over him. For even if he sees that he is not accomplishing Heaven forbid with his prayers, and on the contrary, the evil is overbearing upon him even more, even still he should know and believe that he is achieving plenty with his prayer and his screaming, for at any rate his screaming and his prayer is the aspect of protest mentioned above, because the holiness of each one of Israel is the aspect of the holiness of the Land of Israel, and when the evil overbears upon a person with desires and bad *meedoas* (-character traits), and this is the aspect that they want to banish him, Heaven forbid, from living indigenous in the heritage of Hashem (Samuel I:26:19), which is the Land of Israel, and all that he tunnels to return to his holiness, they do not let up on him from the utter pressure assaulting him, (and) he doesn't strengthen himself against them accordingly. Therefore when he exploits even still, with prayer and screaming to Hashem Yisburach, then they cannot banish and conquer his portion in the Land of Israel,

Heaven forbid, in any way, for his prayer and screaming is the device of protest (*'mechu-u'*), through which the Other Side (-realm of evil, Satan) cannot have a holding (*'lihachzik'*) on his estate Heaven forbid, in any way, for a *chazaka* (-a holding and claim by means of occupation) does not avail when it was contested with a protest (*mechu-u*). **(Likutay Halachos, Laws of Holdings On Moveable Property, law 5).**

84. Making prayers out of holy teachings

The prominence of the virtue of making from the holy teaching (*toaroas*) – prayers, as mentioned earlier in article 2: For the main defect of all the transgressions is in the permutations of the letters of holy Torah which are the composite of this matter which one transgressed and defected. And through the prayer which he makes from the Torah, he will rectify everything, for he will revert, and rectify, and make the permutations, and restore them to their positions with enhanced empowerment. For the essential root of all the holy permutations come about through the prayer, because prayer is the root of the Torah. For all of prayer is included in the ten types of melody with which King David r.i.p. founded the Book of Psalms which is a composite of all the prayers. And the ten types of melody are the aspect of *taamim* <musical cantillation notes which embellish the words and verses of the Torah, which kabbalistically correlate to the other meanings of *taamim* – reasons and tastes – the most esoteric secrets of the Torah>, the aspect of the melody of the *taamim*. And the *taamim* are the pinnacle of the supernal root of all the aspects of *taamim, nikoodoas* <the dots and dashes which serve as vowels>, *tagim* <crowns –

vertical lines on top of the letters>, letters, which are in the holy Torah, as is understood from the Tikunay Zohar (Tikun 69, page 105, where it explains that the *taamim* are from the construct of the *Kesser* – crown), that is that all the permutations of the letters of the Torah which are brought about through the *nikoodoas* <dots-vowels>, everything is done by the *taamim*, for they are the root of everything, and the *taamim* are the aspect of melody, the aspect of the ten types of melody, the aspect of prayer, as mentioned above. It comes out, that the essential genesis of all the holy permutations from which the whole Torah was woven, is through prayer, as mentioned above, and therefore it is impossible to attain any perception of the Torah except by means of prayer. And therefore it is necessary to make from the teachings (torahs) – prayers, that is, to pray to merit to fulfill all the words of the Torah (-holy teaching) that one is learning. All the more so, when a person knows of himself that he transgressed the words of the Torah, he certainly needs to pray profusely to Hashem Yisburach, that He should forgive him for the past, and that he should merit at any rate, from now on to fulfill everything as it is written in the ("this") Torah, for through prayer he will rectify everything, as mentioned above. **(Likutay Halachos, Laws of Damage to Neighbors, law 4).**

85. One who is resolute in prayer and repentance will ultimately succeed because they are highest

The main repentance is prayer, for repentance is an aspect higher than the Torah (see Words of Rabbi Nachman article 3, reference 6), for there, everything is turned around to the good, and intentional transgressions are inverted to merits, and one merits to this through prayer, for it is also an aspect higher than the Torah, as is explained inside and mentioned above (see Words of Rabbi Nachman, article 75, and reference 3 there). And therefore whoever wants to truly return to Hashem Yisburach, the essential consummate repentance is by means of prayer, that is, that he should constantly pray to Hashem Yisburach that He should pardon and forgive him for what he defected, and He should have compassion on him from now on and He should save him from sin. For in actuality every person is in great dire danger in this world, and especially the *baal-teshuva* (-one who returned in repentance), who already blundered in what he blundered, and every day a person's (evil) inclination overbears upon him etc. (Kedushin 30b), and how will he merit to return (-repent), for immediately when he wants to overcome what he needs to overcome, they overbear upon exceedingly?

Therefore the main thing is prayer and hisbodidus, that one needs to accustom himself to do hisbodidus everyday between himself and his Maker, and to cast his plea before Hashem Yisburach, Who is full of mercy at all times, that He should merit him to return in true complete repentance. And even if he sees that he still does not accomplish with his prayer, for they still overbear upon him exceedingly, even still he should do his part and he should pray constantly to Hashem Yisburach, perhaps He will have mercy, perhaps He will have compassion, as it is written (Psalms 27:14): "Hope to Hashem etc.," and our Rabbis o.b.m. exposited (Brachos 32b): and if your prayer wasn't

192

received, return and hope. And as long as a person isn't firm in his mind that he will always hope to Hashem, and implore Him, no matter what transpires over him, his repentance is still incomplete, for who knows what the day will bring, perhaps he will be confronted with a test or a pitfall etc., and who knows if he will hold up in the intensity of the battle. However, if the person is resolute that even if Heaven forbid he does not withstand the test, and even if it will be Heaven forbid what will be, even still he will always hope to Hashem Yisburach in the aspect of (Psalms 139:8), "and (if) I lie in scheol (-hell) behold You are here," then he is certainly assured, that he will certainly merit to repent completely, for at the very end he will return to Hashem Yisburach, since he is strong in his mind that he will not fall from anything in the world. **(Likutay Halachos, Laws of Overpricing, law 1).**

86. The first redemption correlated to Torah, came to cessation. The final redemption correlates to prayer and will not cease.

Our rabbis o.b.m. said (Medrash Tanchuma, Torah portion of Shoftim, and Yalkut Shimoni, Isaiah 499): the first redemption had an end, but the final redemption will not have an end. Because the first redemption is the aspect of Torah, for Israel merited then to receive the Torah, and the final redemption is the aspect of prayer, which is the essential aspect of David and Messiah, and this is the whole construct of the five books of the Psalms which correlate the five *chumashim* (-fifths, volumes, books) of the Torah. For all the prayers of David, which are the Book of Psalms, which is replete with all the prayers of Israel, it is all just in order to merit to fulfill the Torah completely, and only through this we will merit the complete redemption which is not succeeded with exile. **(Likutay Halachos, Laws of Overpricing, law 1).**

87. Prayer is a person's main anchor, even when he falls from the Torah

As long as a person doesn't merit to prayer in its completion, then he still has no place for Hashem, and he is still transient and vagabond. And even if he engages in Torah, he is still has no assurance that he will retain his stance, for who knows what will transpire over him. Just as we see many people that engaged in Torah with great diligence for many years, and afterwards they became estranged from the Torah, and they fell to what they fell, may the Merciful One save us. Therefore the main place and station of holiness is prayer, for through prayer they merit to remain enduring upright in their capacity always, come what may. For if one doesn't merit, only, to Torah alone, even though this is certainly extremely good, and this is the main *tachlis* (-ultimate purpose), "for they (-the words of Torah) are our life and length of our days," even still, afterwards, when he falls Heaven forbid from the Torah, then he doesn't have with what to vivify himself; but when he merits to prayer, he has hope eternally, no matter what transpires over him.

For through prayer it is possible to draw close to Hashem Yisburach always, even if one is the way he is, because even though he is distant from all holiness and from the whole Torah, and he cannot vivify himself from anything, even still if he raises his eyes to Heaven, and he prays to Hashem Yisburach from the place where he is at, he still has hope, in the aspect of what King David r.i.p. said (Psalms 69:3), "I sunk in deep quagmire and there is no foothold etc.," and he concludes afterwards (verse 14), "And I, my prayer is to You Hashem, may it be a time of grace," for through prayer and entreaty to Hashem Yisburach it is possible to strengthen oneself always, because prayer is the aspect of a standing and place, even in deep quagmire Heaven forbid, where there is no foothold. And this is the aspect of what our Rabbis o.b.m. said (Brachos 6b): Standing refers only to prayer, because prayer is the main stance of every person. And therefore whoever desires to be a true Israelite, needs to espouse both of them; Torah and prayer, for both of them as a cohesive one, are good, so that if one of them fails Heaven forbid, its partner will uphold him, as mentioned above.

(Likutay Halachos, Laws of Overpricing, law 1).

88. The critical standing (station for existence) is prayer

The evil inclination and the *sitra-achra* (-other side – realm of evil – Satan) are the aspect of fraud, for they deceive and mislead the people in various sorts of deceit and error without measure and computation, until they exchange a lasting world with a transient world Heaven forbid, and cozen the person from the eternal good life to go after them, like sheep brought to slaughter, to the ways of scheol (-hell), more bitter than death even in this world, all the more so in the world to come, and there is no extortion in the world so great like the extortion of the evil inclination. And the main *aitza* (advice, remedy) and the strategy to escape fully from this great bitter extortion is just through prayer and entreaty. For if the person is strong and resolute in his mind, that he will always pray to Hashem Yisburach that He should draw him close to His service in truth, come what may, then certainly the evil inclination will not be able to extort him and delude him further in any way.

And this is the aspect of (the rule; Kesuvos 99b) land does not have overpricing, because land is the aspect of prayer, which is the aspect of faith, which is called land, as it is written (Psalms 37:3), "Dwell the land and feed on faith," as is brought down in the words of Rabbainu o.b.m. (Likutay Moharan 129 and 155). And this is also the aspect of conjugating redemption to prayer (Brachos 4b, 9b and elsewhere -primarily manifested in the daily prayers where the blessing of "Who redeemed Israel" is immediately followed by the eighteen benedictions - which is the main prayer), because our essential hope and reliance in the complete redemption, may it be soon in our days, for the generalities and the particulars, is just through prayer, as mentioned above. For even if a person is caught in what he is caught Heaven forbid, there is still hope, and support, and a standing through prayer, and entreaty, and supplication, even in the quagmire without foothold, as it is

written (Psalms 40:2-3), "Hope, I have hoped to Hashem, and
He inclined (His ear) to me, and He heard my cry. And He
raised me from the dark pit, from the muck of the
quagmire, and He stood my feet up on rock, made my
footsteps firm etc.;" for through this that I cried to Hashem
Yisburach constantly, with hope after hope, through this I
merited, "And He raised me from the dark pit, from the
muck of the quagmire, and He stood my feet up on rock,"
because the essential fundament, and the standing, and the
support is upon prayer to Hashem Yisburach, as it is written
(Psalms 122:2), "Our feet stood in your gates Jerusalem,"
because Jerusalem – the Temple is there, which is The
House of Prayer, (over) there is the main standing, as
mentioned above.

(Likutay Halachos, Laws of Overpricing, law 1).

89. Pray to attain and fulfill the Torah still beyond your grasp, inculcate, and pray for yet higher Torah

The integral aspect of prayer is strong desires and longing
for Hashem Yisburach with *divaikus* (clinging) and complete
nullification to the light of the *Ain Sof* (-Infinite One), until
one comes to words, that Hashem Yisburach has mercy on
him and opens his mouth to express his words before Him.
And this is the aspect of (Proverbs 16:1), "It is up to a person
to arrange his heart (-thoughts and words) and from Hashem
the (actual) rhetoric is (provided/on the tongue)." And the main
thing is to make from the Torahs (-holy teachings) – prayers,

as is explained elsewhere (Likutay Moharan vol. 2, Torah 25, see above article 2 and 84), namely that one should pray before Hashem Yisburach that he should merit to attain and fulfill what is hidden from him, that is, what he still did not merit to attain and fulfill. And then, when he merits to accomplish his request, to attain and fulfill this aspect as well, this is the aspect of making from prayer – Torah, namely to make from prayer (which is divaikus (clinging) to the *Ain Sof* (Infinite One), of whom there is no grasp, for this is the aspect of hidden, for also in this he still has no grasp) – Torah (that is, what is revealed), and then it is necessary to pray so as to attain another level higher than this, in the conception of the Torah, and the main thing is – in the fulfillment of the Torah, and so forth from level to level, until the *Ain Sof* (the Infinte One), because through prayer it is possible to ascend from the utter nadir of the lowest level to the pinnacle of the highest level, until the *Ain Sof* (the Infinite One). **(Likutay Halachos, Laws of Gifts, law 5).**

90. Confront heightened tribulations with intensified prayer and hisbodidus

The more a person sees that the *dinim* (-judgements – tribulations), which are the root of the aspect of the overbearing of the (evil) inclination, are overly overbearing upon him, he specifically, needs to rally to the utmost to profuse and implore in prayer and importune more and more, in order to draw the supernal charity and kindness, and to sweeten (-mitigate) and nullify the harshness of the *dinim* (-judgments – tribulations). And therefore the essential hisbodidus, which is conversation between one and his Maker, is mentioned distinctly by Isaac, as it is written (Genesis 24:63), "And Isaac went out to converse in the field," since he is from the aspect of *din* (-judgment), and of him it is said (Genesis 25:21), "And Isaac importuned to Hashem." And therefore our Rabbis o.b.m. warned exceedingly (Brachos 6b) to be overly attentive with the prayer of *Mincha* (-evening) specifically, for it correlates to Isaac. **(Likutay Halachos, Laws of Gifts, law 5).**

91. Two layers of foreskin correlate to utter lack of prayer – faulting to the left, and insufficient prayer – faulting to the right

It is explained in the words of our master, leader, and Rabbi o.b.m. (Likutay Moharan, torah 2), that the main weapon of the Israelite is prayer; and whoever merited to the sword of prayer, as it is written (Genesis 28:22), "with my sword and with my bow *<bikashtee>*," and Rashi explains: "with my prayer and with my supplication *<bakashussee>*," needs to know how to fight with the sword, hurling with precise marksmanship to a thread without missing, so that he doesn't waver to the right or to the left, see there (Likutay Moharan 2), that is, that he shouldn't be mistaken Heaven forbid that the prayers are in vain Heaven forbid, since they have been screaming for so long and haven't been saved, for this is wavering to the left. And so too, he shouldn't be mistaken to say: "Why should we abound in prayer, since the main salvation is just with His kindness alone, so in that case let us rely solely on His kindness," for this is the aspect of wavering improperly to the right, for in truth it is necessary to abound profusely in prayer constantly, and to know the truth, that we are not worthy to accomplish with our prayers, just with His kindness, and even still we need to do our part, to abound in prayer constantly, and Hashem Yisburach will do His part, and He will extend to us His kindness for His sake, and He will save us quickly, for the sake of His name (and see above, article 47). And behold it is explained there (Likutay Moharan 2), that through *tikun habris* (-rectification of the bris/circumcision/covenant) one merits to prayer, and therefore Josef, who guarded the *bris* (- circumcision/covenant), merited (the role of) the first-born, which is the aspect of the service of prayer, because the first-born takes two-fold *<pea shna'yim>*, which is the aspect of the sword of prayer, which has *pea shna'yim* (-two-fold/mouths), two aspects: praise of Hashem ("*Hamakoam*" -"the Place", for all space exists only in G-d, and not vice-versa), and the requesting of one's needs, the aspect of a two-edged (two mouths- in the Holy Tongue the blade of the sword is called its mouth, just as destruction is referred to as being consumed and eaten) sword, two mouths, and it was taken from Reuben through his desecrating the bed of his father (Genesis 49:4), because whoever defects in the *bris* (circumcision/covenant), prayer is taken away from him, see there.

And this is the aspect of the *mitzva* of circumcision, the aspect of the cutting and the revealing (removal of a thin secondary membrane, this part of the circumcision is called *preeyah*), and it is brought down that the husk *<kleepa>* of the foreskin and the *preeyah* are the aspects of Esau and Ishmael (see Zohar, Torah portion Emor, page 91b; and see Me'Oaray Ohr – Esau

has the numerical value of "live snake." And in the Siddur Kol Yaakov,
in the Secret of Circumcision it brings down that through severing the
foreskin the snake descends down to lick the dust etc., and there
remains just the membrane of the *preeyah* etc., and through *preeyah*
etc. the *Kindness of Abraham* is revealed (which is in contradistinction to
the husk of Ishmael), and understand. See also Adir BaMuroam pages 10-
11), that is, because they are the aspect of defection of the
bris, and they are two types of husks <*kleepoas*>, which
confound the *daas* (-intellect) of a person (deterring him) from
strengthening in prayer. Because Esau *Amulaik* is the aspect
of the husk of the (*kleepas*) foreskin out-and-out, because he
was a heretic (*kuffar bi'eekar* - "renounced/denied the integral"),
and does not acknowledge prayer whatsoever, and it
deludes the person's heart (to consider) that all the prayers are
for nothing, and they are of no benefit Heaven forbid. And
therefore it is said of him (Genesis 25:34), "And Esau
disparaged the (rights of the) first-born," which is the aspect
of the service of prayer, as mentioned above, and by cutting
off the foreskin which covers the *bris*, through this his evil
husk (*kleepa*) is nullified, and the aspect of *tikun habris*
(rectification of the *bris*/circumcision/covenant) is drawn, through
which one merits to constantly strengthen in prayer. But
there is still a second husk (*kleepa*), which is the husk of the
membrane of the *preeyha*, which is the aspect of the husk
of (*kleepas*) Ishmael from where is drawn a different mistake
in the heart, to be indolent in prayer Heaven forbid, since it
seems to him that certainly Hashem Yisburach already
heard his prayer, especially when he sees some sort of
burgeoning of a beacon (/force) of salvation, for then it
seems to him that his prayer has already been answered,
and he is lax from praying further. And this stems from the
aspect of the husk of (*kleepas*) Ishmael, who was so named

on account of (Genesis 16:11), "because Hashem hearkened <*shumma-E"l*> to your suffering," and the *Targum* (Aramaic translation of Unkellus) is, "since Hashem accepted your prayer." And through the *mitzva* of *preeyah*, this *kleepa* (husk) is also nullified, and one merits to strengthen in prayer constantly, and to be thanking for the past, for the burgeoning beacon (/force) of salvation which he saw, and to scream for the future, because the salvation has still not finished, and we still need a very great deal of salvations all the days of our life, until we merit to come to what we need to come to, for that which we came to this world, and therefore it is necessary to pray copiously always.

And this is the aspect of (Esther 6:12), "And Mordechai returned," and our Rabbis o.b.m. exposited (Megila 16a) that he returned to his sackcloth and his fasting. For even though he already saw such a wondrous salvation, that they rode him on the king's horse and they proclaimed before him etc., even still he was not slack on account of this from his prayer. And so too by Esther it is written (Esther 8:3), "And Esther continued (additionally) and she spoke before the king etc. and she entreated him to remove the evil of Haman etc.." This alludes to the entire general Congregation of Israel (*Kinnesses Yisroel*), for they are the aspect of Esther, who, even when she sees great and wondrous salvations and miracles, that the *sitra-achra* (other side – realm of evil) the aspect of Haman Amulaik has already fallen dramatically, and they have hung him and his sons on the gallows-tree, even still they do not suffice with this, and they still stand and pray, and cry, and entreat before Him blessed He, like a son who pleads disarmingly before his father, to remove the evil of Haman, who is the *sitra-achra* (other side – realm of evil), completely, so that they merit to complete purity and holiness. And in truth, when a person is remiss in prayer because it seems to him that he already accomplished plenty with his prayer, which is the aspect of *kleepas* (the husk of) Ishmael, the *kleepa* of the *preeyah* mentioned above, on account of this his complete salvation is held back, and his exile will be lengthened Heaven forbid, since he was indolent in prayer, and then the aspect of the kleepa of Esau will return and be aroused, which is the aspect of the *kleepa* of the foreskin, and it will utterly seal and confound his heart from strengthening in prayer. And therefore, in truth (Shabbos 137b): "one who circumcises but does not lay it bare (-do the *preeyah*) – is as if he has not circumcised," because through this Heaven forbid, the aforementioned *kleepa* of the foreskin also returns and arouses. Therefore it is necessary to remove both of them in order to merit to strengthen in prayer always, as mentioned above. **(Likutay Halachos, Laws of Inheritance, law 4).**

92. Prayer begins with praising G-d which establishes faith in oneself, like the realization of having a first-born who gets two portions.

It is necessary (for a person) to strongly reinforce with complete faith, to believe in himself, that he has the capability to accomplish every matter with his prayer and his conversation between himself and his Maker. For there are all types of (hang-ups, inhibitions, and) lack of resolve in a person's heart regarding this, as each one knows in his soul, and most people are under the impression, that they don't have the strength for this, and subsequently they don't strengthen in prayer, and hence it is necessary to toil with very great exertion and devotion in this matter. And the main exertion is at the beginning, in the aspect of (Rashi on Yisro 19:5 from the Mechilta), "all beginnings are difficult," that is, when one begins to pray and do hisbodidus, for then he still has not seen any effect brought about through his prayer and his hisbodidus. However, when he merits to rise up with all his strength to pray with *kavana* (-concentration, intention) and to do hisbodidus, until he merits to accomplish something with his prayer, for example, that he prayed for something and was answered, then he is bolstered by this to believe in himself, that he has the power to accomplish with his prayer, since he sees that his prayer also, Hashem Yisburach heard, and he was answered. And then there is established by him a complete vessel to receive the *shefa* (-bounty) through the words of the prayer, because the essential materialization of the vessel is – through faith, that is, by that which he has faith in himself, that Hashem Yisburach listens to his prayer as well.

And this is the aspect of what the first-born takes *pea-shna'yim* (double portion). And it is brought down in the writings of the Arizal (Likutay Torah, Va'yaira, page 28a, paragraph beginning with the word "vinachzor"- and let us return), that in all the (subsequent) offspring there is a component of the birth of the first-born in them, that is, because all the offspring and all the bounty are drawn through prayer, and the birth of the first-born is drawn from the aspect of the first accomplishment, that the Israelite accomplishes through his prayer, through which his faith is fortified to always pray, and a vessel is made by him etc. as mentioned above, and therefore the first-born takes (Deuteronomy 21:17), "*pea-shna'yim* (double portion) of everything that is to be found of him (the deceased father)," because in everything that is found, and was begotten, and provisioned to him by means of prayer, there is in it a component of the first action that he accomplished with his prayer, which is the aspect of the birth of the first-born, and therefore he has a portion in lieu of each and everyone; and therefore Rabbainu o.b.m. explained that the (role of the) first-born is prayer. And the concept of *pea-shna'yim* (double portion) that the first-born takes, is the concept of the two aspects that prayer has; praise of Hashem ('*mukoam*' - "the Place", as explained above), and the request of one's needs, as mentioned above. For the order of setting out the praise of Hashem first, and the request of one's needs afterwards, is also this concept, because through the recollection of His praises blessed He, that He is the "G-d of our fathers" etc., "Who bestows beneficial kindnesses," that He did with them kindness, and listened to their prayers always, which through this His name was Unified in the world, through this our belief in ourselves is strengthened by us, that He will have mercy on us as well, and He will hear our prayers when we request our needs.

And this is what is written (Psalms 44:2), "the action which You did in their days, in the days of yore etc. (verse 5) command (for) the salvations of Jacob etc.," that is, just like

You did in the days of our forefathers, and You made great miracles and salvations for them, so too "command (for) the salvations of Jacob"- now as well. However, sometimes the *baal duvur* (-litigator – Satan) can weaken a person's resolve, that even though our fathers and rabbis accomplished so much with their prayers, (but) an inferior person such as yourself, how is it possible that you will achieve results with your prayer? However the reality is not so, for Hashem Yisburach hears the prayer of every mouth, and every one of Israel has the power to achieve his request mercifully by Him blessed He, if he truly prays to Him. And therefore a person needs to take to heart and remind himself of the many times he called out from the midst of hardship to Hashem, and He answered him and saved him, and through this he will strengthen now as well in prayer, and Hashem will save him, as mentioned above.

(Likutay Halachos, Laws of Inheritance, law 4).

93. The Divine constraining Itself empowers an evil that can only be overcome through prayer which is faith.

A person has the ability and must choose this faith over using his intellect.

At first glance there is a problem with the construct of hisbodidus and conversation between oneself and his Maker, that every person needs to pour out his words before Hashem Yisburach everyday, that He should merit him to draw him close to His service blessed He, as explained above many times. And so we find that all the early tzaddikim also engaged in this, and they founded many prayers for this, to merit to be saved from the evil inclination (*yetzehr hurra*), and that they merit to draw close to Hashem Yisburach, and to fear and love Him blessed He, and all of the Book of Psalms is filled with this. And so too the prayers of the Men of the Great Assembly (*Anshay Kinnesses Hagedoala*), like: "*Hasheevainoo*" (-Return us in repentance) and so forth. At first glance there is a difficulty with this: Behold our Rabbis o.b.m. said (Brachos 33b), "Everything is in the hands of Heaven except for fear of Heaven," and if so, how is it possible to pray for this, considering that Hashem Yisburach gave the choice to us alone? However, in reality, this itself is the essential *becheera* (-choice afforded) of a person, for it is impossible to merit completely to detest evil and choose good, and to come to what a person needs to come to in this world through his choice, except by means of abounding in prayer, and entreaties, and conversations between himself and his Maker, very, very profusely to Hashem Yisburach, that He should merit him, to draw him close to His service blessed He.

And this is the main prayer, because (Psalms 32:6), "For this every *chussid* (-pious, devout person) will (/should) pray at an opportune time (- when G-d is to be found), just that the torrent of copious water doesn't reach him," that he shouldn't be swept away by the torrent of malicious copious water, which are the bad desires of this world which cascade powerfully at all times. And a very great many have already been swept away by them, may the Merciful One save us, and there is no wisdom, and no understanding, and no *aitza* (-remedy, advice) to stand up against them (Proverbs 21:30, above article 82), just through prayer and entreaty to Hashem Yisburach, that He should save him from them. For even though a person has the ability to choose (his course), even still the main thing is prayer and entreaty to Hashem Yisburach for this. Because the *becheera* (choice) is intellectual, that one has the power to choose good and despise evil, but a person's intellect does not have power, except to subdue and nullify the desires and the husks (*kleepoas*) that are of the aspect of the heresy which comes from the aspect of the *breaking of the vessels* (t.n. before the creation of this world, the supernal vessels were not able to hold the Divine emanations, and they broke, the broken pieces are holy sparks), for there are there many holy sparks which are sparks of intellect, because all (the sparks) are selected with (the supernal) thought. However there are confusions, and realms of evil, and obstacles from the holiness, which come from the aspect of the *challal hapunoy* ('vacated space' – in the Divine omnipresence, to allow for the semblance of creation and existence independent of G-d), where it is impossible to find His Divinity by means of any ruse or wisdom, just through faith alone (as is explained in Likutay Moharan vol. 1, Torah 64), which is the aspect of prayer, and entreaty, and screaming to Hashem Yisburach, that He should save him from the *kleepoas* (husks) and the evil inclination (*yetzehr hurra*) which stem from there.

And regarding this our Rabbis said (Kedushin 30b), "everyday a person's (evil) inclination overbears upon him, and if the Holy One Blessed He would not help him, he would fall into its hand," because from this evil inclination which originates in its root from there, from the aspect of the *vacated space*, it is impossible to be saved in any way through the power of choice a person has with his own intellect alone, just with help from Heaven. And therefore it is necessary to abound very profusely in prayer and entreaty to be saved from it, because there no intellect is effective, on the contrary, through intellect and wisdom one is sunken all the more, Heaven forbid (as is explained there in his words o.b.m., in Torah 64), just, the main thing is faith, which is the aspect of prayer. And in reality this itself is the essential foundation of the power of *becheera* (-choice), namely, what a person has the power of *becheera* (decision) to abnegate his intellect completely, and rely on faith alone, and to abound in prayer and entreaty to Hashem Yisburach, because the evil inclination (*yetzer hurra*) twists a person's heart so much, until this is also cumbersome on a person, even though in reality it is a very easy thing to converse, all the time, everything that is with (/upon) his heart, before Hashem Yisburach, and to plead before Him for his soul, even still the *baal duvur* (-litigator – Satan) confuses and twists a persons mind so much, to the extent that for the most part, this matter of prayer and hisbodidus is harder for a person to carry out, more than all the difficult devotions. And this is all due to lack of faith, that he doesn't have complete faith, which is the main foundation of everything, as the adage of our Rabbis o.b.m. (Makos 24a), "Habakkuk came and based them (-all the commandments) on one (Habakkuk 2:4), 'and a tzaddik with his faith will live'."

And therefore in this itself lies a person's main power of choice, for someone who merits to choose true life, he will choose what is integral to the way of faith and prayer, in the aspect of (Psalms 119:30), "The way of faith I have chosen." And then, when he has complete faith, and abounds in prayers and words before Hashem Yisburach, that He should merit him to truly return to Him, which through this all the *kleepoas* (husks) and *sitra-achra* (-other side – realm of evil) which originate in their root from the aspect of the *tzimtzum* (-constrain of the Divine Omnipresence to allow for the semblance) of the *challal hapanoy* (vacated space), are mitigated and nullified, (and) then Hashem Yisburach helps him so that he merits to serve Him blessed He, with the Torah and *mitzvoas* (-commandments), and illuminates his eyes in His Torah, until he merits to understand in the Torah and devotion what is possible to understand with human intellect, and through this he subdues and nullifies all the *kleepoas* (husks) and *sitra-achra* (realm of evil) which originate in their root from the aspect of the *breaking of vessels*, and raises from there all the holy sparks. And because the aspect of the *breaking of vessels* itself also stems in its root from the severity of the *tzimtzum* (constraint) of the aspect of the *vacated space*, as is explained inside, and it has already been explained that it is impossible to completely mitigate this *tzimtzum* (constraint) of the *vacated space* (until these *kleepoas* and barriers etc. which nourish from there, are also nullified) just, through prayer, which is the aspect of faith, therefore the main foundation of the entire Torah and the mitzvoas (commandments), which are the aspect of intellect, is also just through prayer and faith, the aspect of (Psalms 119:86), "all Your commandments are faith." And therefore this is the essential foundation of the entire power of *becheera* (choice), as mentioned above. **(Likutay Halachos, Laws of a Deposited Item, law 3).**

94. First one is silent, and can only yearn, and then Hashem provides the words

Whoever desires to approach the holy (Numbers 8:19), to merit to draw close to Hashem Yisburach, it is essential to pray copiously between himself and his Maker, as has been explained already many times. However, this itself is also very heavy on a person, and it seems to him that he has no words, and he doesn't know what to start speaking about, and most of the times he is under the impression that his heart is not with him, and if he does say some words, they are also without any arousal of the heart; so therefore it is necessary at the beginning to stand like a mute, (and) just yearn, and hope, and raise his eyes to Heaven, that He should confer him words, passionate like burning coals, and he should settle his mind well; where is he in the world, and to where has he strayed, and the utter magnitude of the pity on his soul, that has become so distanced from his Father Whom is Heaven. Only, even still he needs to search and find in himself also the good points that he still has nonetheless, and the power and merit of the true tzaddikim that he leans upon, in order that his badness should not make him fall into despairing of himself completely Heaven forbid. However, before Hashem Yisburach he should stand like a poor man, and like a pauper, and like a mute not opening his mouth, and stand, and hope, and yearn, that Hashem Yisburach will confer him passionate words, so that he can draw upon himself the holiness of the Torah, so that he merits from hereon to accept and fulfill the words of the Torah, until through this itself he subsequently merits to great arousal and speaks with holy passion, in the aspect of (Psalms 39:3), "I was mute with silence, quiescent (even) from (saying) good etc.," and specifically through this (verse 4), "my heart is impassioned inside of me, when I speak it burns (like) fire, I spoke with my tongue."

And this is the aspect of "*chashmal*" (-a spiritual force described in the first chapter of Ezekiel), and our Rabbis o.b.m. exposited (Chagiga 13b): at times quiet <*chushoas* – based on the first syllable>, at times speaking <*mimahliloas* – based on the last syllable>, and they further exposited (elongating the word in a function known as *noatreekun*, taking the word to be an abbreviation): '*cha'yoas* (-angels of the realm of '*yetzira*' which correlates to speech) *aish* (-fire) *mimahliloas* (-speak, cut)', that is, that the main rectification of speech is through first being silent and quiet like a mute not opening his mouth, just yearning with strong desire for Hashem Yisburach, and having pity on himself with great mercy, as everyone knows in his soul the great pity that there is upon him at all times, and specifically through this the mercy of Hashem Yisburach is aroused, until he begins to speak weakly (lit: chirp) and to speak a little, in the aspect of (Isaiah 29:4), "and from the dirt you words will speak out weakly," until he merits subsequently to words passionate like burning coals, the aspect of '*cha'yoas* (-angels) *aish* (-fire) *mimahliloas* (-speak, cut)'. And through this he merits afterwards to draw close to the holiness and to the aspect of receiving the Torah consummately. And this is the aspect of what our Rabbis o.b.m. said (Shabbos 104a): 'MaNTzPaCh (-these are the five Hebrew letters that are doubles, their counterparts function in the beginning and middle of a word only, and they function only as the last letter) the seers said them', because MaNTzPaCh are the aspect of the five *gevooroas* (-mights – in contradistinction to kindnesses, these are spiritual forces that have harshness and or constraint) which are the aspect of fire, and they are the root of the five *moatza'oas* (stations of enunciation, from which all vocalized sounds emanate) of the mouth, which is the aspect of words passionate like burning coals, which one merits to this through keeping silent at first, and hoping, and yearning, and waiting for the kindness of Hashem, in the aspect of (Mica 7:7), "And I put my hope in Hashem, I yearn for the G-d of my salvation;" the aspect of (Lamentation 3:26), "It is good for one to yearn and *doomam* (hope/wait expectantly/be silent) for the salvation of Hashem;" through this specifically one merits to perfection of speech as mentioned above. And this is also the aspect of (Psalms 19:4), "There is nothing said, and no words etc.," the aspect of the silence and absence of speech, just through hope and yearning, which is the aspect of (verse 5), "Throughout the whole world went (/go) out their rays" - (the word for rays is the same as that) denoting hope and yearning for the kindness of Hashem, and through this (continuation of the verse), "and their words (go out) to the end of the world." And this is also the aspect of what the darkness and the night proceed the light in the order of creation, because the darkness is the aspect of murkiness of the mind and the deficiency of speech, which is the aspect of the silence which proceeds the speech, the aspect of *chashmal* mentioned above, because

213

at night, it is then the aspect of yearning and longing for Hashem Yisburach, in the aspect of (Song of Songs 3:1), "On my bed in the nights, I sought whom my soul loves etc.," and it says (Psalms 77:7), "I remember my melody at night, with my heart I converse etc.," and afterwards one merits through this to the light of day, which is perfection of the words, for they are the main light, in the aspect of (Psalms 119:130), "The opening of your words illuminate."

And the general concept is that one cannot force the hour (-bring something about before its time) whatsoever, for immediately when one desires to truly draw close to Hashem Yisburach, then it is necessary to be very careful from destruction, not to force the hour Heaven forbid, because most of the troubles Heaven forbid are only by means of this, for this is the aspect of the warning (Exodus 19:21), "lest they break rank (-'destroy')," that He warned Israel at the time of the giving of the Torah. Just, it is necessary to wait and await abundantly for the salvation of Hashem, which is the aspect of (Avoada Zura 55a), "He who comes to be purified, they (-from above) help him (etc.) they tell him wait," - distinctly. And it is necessary to abound, just in prayer and entreaty to Hashem Yisburach, and in this as well it is forbidden to force the hour, to desire to achieve what he seeks immediately, for this is the aspect of (Ethics of Our Fathers 2:18), "Do not make your prayers a device to steal (see above article 65), just, invoking mercy and entreaty before G-d ("the Place" - because all of space exists in G-d and not vice versa);" and if Hashem Yisburach gives – He gives; and if not – wait longer and continue to entreat copiously before Him. And like our Rabbis o.b.m. said (Brachos 32b) concerning the bolstering of prayer (Psalms 27:14), "Hope to Hashem," and if your player wasn't accepted, return "and hope" (continuation of the verse). However, even in the (expression of the) words of the prayer itself one cannot force the hour, which is the aspect of what everyone would like, that immediately upon entering hisbodidus and expressing his words before Hashem Yisburach, when he so opens his mouth, immediately and instantly he will speak abundant words before Hashem Yisburach, perfect words and passionate like burning coals, and with great arousal. And because not every person merits this, and each time it seems to the person that he does not have words, and he does not have any arousal whatsoever, due to this he is completely negligent (also) from prayer and entreaty. Therefore it is necessary to know this well, that this as well is the aspect of forcing the hour (Brachos 64a, Airuven 13b), because it is not possible to draw consummate words, mentioned above, except through the silence and hoping which proceeds speech, because it is necessary first to be silent (expectantly) and quiet, just, to wait, and to yearn, and to long, and to hanker for the kindness of Hashem, that He should provide him with consummate words, and afterwards he will merit through this itself to express his words before Hashem Yisburach with great arousal, with the entire sentiments of his heart, this being the aspect of "chash-mal", the aspect of 'at times quiet <chash> at times speaking <mal>', 'cha'yoas (-angels) aish (-fire) mimahliloas (-speak, cut)', as mentioned above. (Likutay Halachos, Laws of Robbery, law 5).

And see in the book "Ullim LiTrufah" (Letters for Healing, letter 162), where it is written, in these words: That everyone needs to follow, to begin each and every time to fulfill the procedure of the aspect of *chashmal* mentioned above, that is, to begin by being silent and quiet before Hashem Yisburach, with great longing for Him blessed He, and with great pity on himself, "that I have become so distant, to the extent that I have no idea where to begin to talk, in the aspect of (Psalms 139:4), 'When there is no word on my tongue, behold Hashem You know everything', (Psalms 39:10) 'I have been mute, I will not open my mouth etc.', because it seems to me already, that I have started many times and yet I am still so very distant etc.," as everyone knows in his soul. And Hashem Yisburach is always full of abundant mercy, and will usually have mercy upon you and will open (-give words to) the mouth of a mute such as yourself, *mamash mamash* (-really, literally, exactly) like a mute who begins to speak. And like we spoke (see above, article 79) about the verse (Isaiah 57:19), "Creator of the utterances of the lips," that Hashem Yisburach *mamash* (-literally) creates from new the utterances of the lips, so that we can express our words (even) in the utter alienation, however it is, even if it was thousands of times (more) so, because to His greatness there is no reckon, and especially since in truth we believe, and can even slightly discern and understand, that even still, however it is, certainly not a word or scream is lost, even from the very depth of scheol (-hell), as was heard from the mouth of our master, leader and holy Rabbi, many times, and we must believe this with complete faith.

Especially [so,] since everyone can understand for himself, that if he would not strengthen in these screams and good yearning etc., certainly it would be very much worse, infinitely so, for there is no limit to the incitement of the *baal duvur* (-litigator – evil inclination – Satan), who desires to destroy and uproot the person completely Heaven forbid, like many souls have already sunk due to this, and principally – through not strengthening in all that was mentioned above. And blessed is our G-d who had compassion on us in this orphaned generation, and in this new generation, upon these generations it is said emphatically (Lamentation 1:9), "And she went down terribly, and there is no one to help her," which was said regarding these generation of this bitter exile, like we see and understand from a distance, what is going on in the world, the evil conduct which is conducted under the sun, if not for Hashem who was with us, and sent us our master, leader and holy rabbi, such an awesome, august, new light, who did and does with us what he does, and in his mercy holds us strong with "seven responders (-restorations) of reason (Proverbs 26:16)." Therefore it is upon us to give thanks and praise to Hashem Yisburach always, and to go in his holy ways, to begin every time from new, to fulfill everything mentioned above, and Hashem is great, and to His greatness there is no reckon, and everything will be turned around to the good, see there.

95. Victory of Singing and Holy Words

The main power of the *Malchus* (-kingdom) of holiness, which is the aspect of the *Malchus* (-kingdom) of Messiah, is through speech – '*Malchus peh*' (-the Zohar says that the attribute of *Malchus* – kingdom – is manifested in the '*peh*' – mouth, spoken words), because the king rules his entire kingdom just by means of speech, and the entire victory of the *Malchus* of holiness, which is the *Malchus* of Messiah, is through speech. And this is the aspect of the whole Book of Psalms which was constituted by King David r.i.p., who is the root of the *Malchus* of Messiah, and he fought the battles of Hashem all his life, physically and spiritually, and he won all of them through the speech of mouth, that is, through copious prayers, and entreaties, and songs, and praises without measure, until he included them all, with his Divine Inspiration (-*ruach hakodesh*) in the holy Book of Psalms, and therefore he truly merited to eternal *Malchus*, which is the *Malchus* of Messiah. And therefore the majority of the chapters (-*mizmorim* – of the word '*zemmehr*'-song) of Psalms begin with "*Lamnatzayach*", which Rashi explains (Psalm 4:1) that he composed a Psalm (-*mizmor*) for the Leviites to say (- in the Temple that was to be built), for they are '*menatzchim*' (-performing, prevailing, victorious) with song etc.. And likewise, his explanation also applies plainly to everyone of Israel, like a warning, saying to anyone who desires to enter to fight the battle of Hashem, which every person must do, because he was created just for this, and he wants to win the battle completely, he should say this (-such and such) Psalm, or this Psalm with a full mouth (-saying the words out loud), and understand this well.

And this is the same case regarding hisbodidus, which is also an aspect of reciting Psalms, as is explained elsewhere (Likutay Moharan, Torah 156), because by means of the holy

218

words he will certainly be victorious. Also, David said "*Lamnatzayach*" (-to prevail, be victorious) on himself, to uplift and encourage himself saying, "Lamnatzayach mizmor lidovid" - that is, "To David <*lidovid*>," who wins <*minatzayach*> all the battles through his speech, say now this Psalm <*mizmor* – from the word *zemmehr* – song>. And so too very person, even in his lowly level, needs to know and believe that certainly he is abundantly victorious with every single word of conversing and hisbodidus etc. that he says, for this is eternal victory which remains forever and ever and for all eternity. And if he will be strong at this, to engage in this until his soul literally departs, be what might, no matter what transpires over him, certainly he will vanquish the battle with His great kindness. And like in a physical battle the essential thing is the strength of heart of the soldiers, that they don't lose their heart, and for this there are many lessons to strengthen the hearts of the army's men going out to wage war, in this very similarity this matter is as well, that it is necessary to strengthen oneself very much at all times, and to know, and believe, and also to remind this to oneself with a full mouth (-out loud), that however he is, speech has enormous power to win all the holy battles, this being the aspect of "*Lamnatzayach*" that he mentions each time, because it is necessary to strengthen himself abundantly when he desires to engage in prayer, and conversation, and words between himself and his Maker, and to believe that certainly through this he will be victorious if he will be tenacious to engage in this his whole life, as mentioned above. And be what may, even if he doesn't merit to vanquish the battle completely Heaven forbid, even still he already vanquished plenty with the holy words themselves which he spoke and requested from Hashem Yisburach to draw him close to him, because everything that is done for the victory of holiness remains forever, even if he didn't merit Heaven forbid to finish his endeavor completely, because there is no good desire which is lost (Zohar, Shemos 150b), especially words and callings of prayer, which are more precious than everything.

(Likutay Halachos, Laws of Blessings on Sitings, law 5).

96. The commanding power of speech

Words of the mouth have enormous power, as we can see by what our Sages o.b.m. constituted for us, that whoever dreamed a not good dream, should better it <*yitteyvennue*> in front of three people, saying to them: "a good dream I saw," several times, and with this we see the wondrous potency of speech, that even though in reality he dreamed a bad dream, even still through the *mayteevim* (-those who make it better) saying to him verbally, "a good dream you saw," several times, with this they have the power (to effect) that the dream will be in fact good, (and) to turn around from bad to good. It comes out, that it can be seen from this how great the power of holy speech is, because speech has enormous power to turn around the person himself from bad to good, because the main victory of the battle is through speech which is the main weapon of Israel, because our strength is only with our mouth (see Bamidbar Rabba, 20:4), as mentioned above. And this is the main weapon of Messiah (as explained in Likutay Moharan, Torah 2) and of all the

220

true tzaddikim, for their arsenal is just (armed) with prayer and holy speech. And likewise the essential nullification of the forgetfulness, and to merit to holy memory, to bind one's mind to the future world, generally and particularly, consummately, is only by means of speech, as our Rabbis o.b.m. said (Megila 18a), "*Zuchor* (- that which the Torah commands to "remember" the Sabbath, is meant to be fulfilled) – with the mouth." And as can be seen empirically also with regard to regular study, that through reviewing one's studies (*mishna*) many times out loud (see Eruvin 53b-54a), through this he always remembers what he learned.

And likewise, this is also the case regarding remembering (-consciousness of) the future world, as mentioned above, that the main *aitza* (-advice, remedy) to merit to this is to review (the mention of) this remembrance (-consciousness) with word of mouth, to frequently speak aloud about it everyday: "What will be the *tachlis* (-ultimate end – What will I amount to) of me in the future world? What will be my end? For did I come here to situate myself permanently Heaven forbid in this world? Behold everyone knows that there is no permanence in this world which is transitory, and speeds by, and is very ephemeral, and I didn't come here except to prepare myself for the future world etc.." And therefore it is necessary to learn a great deal of books of *mussar* (-moral, morale, and ethics) which are built upon the foundations of our holy faith, because the holy books of *mussar* remind well of the *tachlis* (-ultimate purpose) of the future world. And similarly it is necessary to do a lot of hisbodidus everyday, and to speak with oneself aloud of the *tachlis* (-ultimate purpose) of the future world, as mentioned above, because speech has great power to bring remembrance (-higher consciousness) to a person. And this is the aspect of (Jeremiah 31:20, and see above article 62), "because as I speak of him, I strongly remember him ever more."

97. The Pauper's Prayer, from the most dire abject destitution, is unfathomably precious to Hashem

In the words of our Rabbis o.b.m. (Menuchos 104b, Vayikra Rabba 4:11) it is elucidated how very dramatically they regarded the prominence of the *Mincha* Offering, which is the Offering of the Poor, that even though he cannot bring a cow, or a ram, or a lamb etc., even still Hashem Yisburach found a solution for him, that he should bring a tenth of an *ayfah* (an *ayfah* is a measure of 432 *bayah*-eggs divided by 10 = 43 and a fifth) of flour, which is very dear in the eyes of Hashem Yisburach, because it is said of it (Leviticus 2:1), "And a soul when she brings a *Mincha* Offering," which hints that the Scripture gives him credit for this, considering it as though he offered his soul (-the verse suggests that the soul brings itself as the offering). And in the Medrash Rabba (Leviticus 8:4) they said regarding the prominence of the *Mincha* Offering: and not only this, but (also-even more:) all the offerings are not brought (partially) in halves, and this is brought in half, half of it in the morning and half of it in the afternoon; and not only this but (also-even more:) whoever brings it for an offering, the Scripture credits him, considering it has if he is bringing an offering from one end of the world to the other etc., see there. They also said in the Medrash Rabba,

(Torah portion of) Lech Licha (43:14): all the offerings the Holy One Blessed He revealed to our Father Abraham (Genesis 15:9); three calves, and three goats, and a dove, and a pigeon, which are the aspect of cows etc. and birds, except for the tenth of the *ayfa*. And there is one who says there that He also revealed to him the offering of the tenth of the *ayfa*, just by allusion. And all of this alludes to the matter of the prayer of the pauper, which is elucidated in the holy Zohar (Torah portion of Bulak, page 195), that it is extremely precious in the eyes of Hashem Yisburach, see there. For the essential sacrifice now is prayer, because through this is the main repentance, the aspect of (Hosea 14:3), "Take with you (plural) words and return to Hashem;" And our Rabbis o.b.m. said (Shemos Rabba 38:4): He does not ask of you (anything), only words. For a person needs to know, when he feels his poverty and lowliness, physically and spiritually, even when he is unable to pray and express his words before Him blessed He with proper thoroughness, even still, when he surmounts to pray and converse before Him blessed He however he can, from the midst of his extremely bitter poverty and exile, physically and spiritually, in the aspect of (Psalms 102:1), "A prayer of the pauper when he is overwhelmed and before Hashem he pours out his words," like one who pours out water, in the aspect of (Lamentation 2:19), "Let your heart pour out like water," even if it seems to him that it is without proper sense and *kavana* (-intention, concentration), even still he (should) pour out all the sentiments of his heart in words before Him blessed He, and even if this prayer itself is jumbled with abundant rubbish and wayward thoughts, which are certainly not befitting to think of Heaven forbid, even still His mercy is so very abundant that even however he is, since he surmounts to pray from the midst of his extremely bitter poverty and lowliness, the Holy One Blessed He has compassion on him, and accepts it, and not only that, but (moreover) the rectification of this prayer specifically reaches infinitely, from one end of the world to the other (end), because distinctly a prayer such as this, is extremely precious by Hashem Yisburach, and it is a secret which is utterly impossible to comprehend, how far His mercy reaches, as long as a person doesn't despair (of himself) from screaming and prayer.

And the entire final redemption is contingent on this, because the essential rectification of repentance is dependent on this, not to despair of oneself even in the most abject lowliness etc., and therefore this secret was not revealed even to our Father Abraham, just by allusion, because it is impossible to reveal this secret explicitly, how far His mercy and His abundant pardon reaches, which is the aspect of (Isaiah 55:7), "And to our G-d for He is abundant(ly magnanimous) to forgive," which they explicated in the Medrash Vayikra (Rabba 3:3): this is the tenth of the *ayfa*, that is, as mentioned above. Only, everyone needs to understand for himself, that he should have mercy on himself, and not despair himself ever from mercy, because (Lamentation 3:22), "The kindness of Hashem do not finish, and His mercy do not exhaust. And this utter kindness is revealed in every generation by the *tzaddikim*, who draw the aspect of the *hisnoatzitzus* (-sparkling) of Messiah, who always make himself poor and needy, the aspect of (Psalms 40:18, 70:6), "And I am poor and needy,"

224

that David said; the aspect of (Zechariah 9:9, and see Sanhedrin 98a), "a pauper and riding upon the donkey," and he works to rectify and save all the poor, in the aspect of (Pslams 72:13), "he will have mercy on the weak and destitute etc.." And they hint to us the preciousness of the prayer of the pauper when he is overwhelmed by his hardship, even if this pauper's prayer isn't complete, how far its rectification reaches. And this is the aspect of the *Mincha* Offering which is brought in half (namely, the prayer of the pauper which isn't complete, and is mixed with a great deal of improper thoughts, even still the Holy One Blessed He accepts it, as mentioned above), and whoever brings it as an offering, the Scripture credits him (considering it) as if he is bringing from one end of the world to the other (end), that is as mentioned above. (**Likutay Halachos, Laws of the Prayer of Mincha, law 7**).

98. Holy Words Are the Vessels For the Divine Light

The main safeguarding of the memory, that is, to remember well His Divinity and Lordship blessed He, and not forget Him ever, is through holy words, because the words are vessels through which to receive the *hisnoatzitzus* (- sparkling, flare) of the light of *Ain Sof* <the Unlimited> blessed He, and all that one abounds to speak more holy words, he draws more revelation of His Divinity, and merits to remember Him more (/exceedingly). And therefore it is necessary to speak a great deal of words of Torah and prayer, and not be quiet, and not be silent, and not to let Him be silent (-unresponsive), because a very large amount of holy words are required in order to merit to receive this huge awesome light of the *hisnoatzitzus* (-sparkling, glimmer, flare) of His Divinity blessed He, and to bind it well in one's mind and heart, and not to forget Him ever.

(Likutay Halachos, Laws of the Arvis Prayer, law 4).

99. The main binding to Hashem is through music

In Likutay Moharan, volume 1, torah 237, it is explained: The essential conjugation of two thing that are like two opposites, is through melody. And this is the aspect of what Leah said when Levi, who is the aspect of the realm of melody, was born (Genesis 29:34), "This time my husband will accompany me." And this is the secret (behind) what music is played on musical instruments for a wedding, see there. And therefore the main connection and *divaikus* (binding) to Hashem Yisburach, who is extremely lofty and exalted from this very inferior, coarse, and lowly world, even for someone who sinned and became very estranged from his Father in Heaven, is just through the Book of Psalms which was constituted by King David r.i.p., of which our Rabbis o.b.m. said (Buva Basra 14a) that it is replete with all the ten types of melody. And so it can be seen empirically, that even a person who is extremely alienated from Hashem Yisburach, and is stuck in a very low level, usually, by singing (/playing) a melody for the sake of Heaven, one will be aroused to Hashem Yisburach, and will remind himself where he is in the world, because the main connection of two seemingly opposite things is through melody as mentioned above. Thus, through the recital of Psalms, which is a composite of all the ten types of melody, certainly one is able to bind and connect to Hashem Yisburach from any place he may be, as mentioned above. And this is also the aspect of *pihsukay dizimra* ('verses of song' – the second section of the morning prayers which consists of Psalms and similar Scripture) which are the aspect of melody, which are said before *Kreyas Shema* (the reading of the Shema – Hear Oh Israel) and the prayer (-18 benedictions), because through this he can bind himself to Hashem Yisburach at the time of *Kreyas Shema* and the prayer, for the primary *divaikus* (binding) is then, as is known (see Likutay Moharan, vol. 2, torah 84). **(Likutay Halachos, Laws of Nisseyas Kapahyim – Blessing of the Kohanim-priests, law 5).**

100. All is for the good, but prayer is necessary for this beneficence itself to be good

There is a seeming difficulty; since the reality is that all of a person's suffering and lackings, it is all for his benefit; either so that he merits on their account to eternal life, or in order that he be saved from hardships much greater, as is known (Likutay Moharan 65:3), and like our Rabbis o.b.m. said (Brachos 60b) that a person is required to say: "All that the Merciful One does, He does for the good," if so, why did our Sages o.b.m. warn us to pray for necessities and lackings. However, in truth, even still, a person needs to pray for all that he is lacking, because before a person prays, certainly everything that occurs to a person, even suffering Heaven forbid, is greatly beneficial, because he still does not have vessels and conduit by which to receive the *shefa* (-bounty) of kindness, and if the kindness descends before the establishment of vessels, it will be the aspect of too much oil which causes the flame to extinguish (Tzaida Laderech 12), and then the kindness is turned around to be harsh *din* (-judgment) Heaven forbid, and it is possible that as a result of this he will experience harm and loss Heaven forbid, from somewhere else. And therefore, as long as a person doesn't pray for his lackings, then they are greatly beneficial to him, but through prayer he sweetens (-mitigates) the *dinim* (-judgments), and renders vessels and conduit by which to receive the *shefa* (bounty) of kindness, because the main rectification of vessels is through prayer (see inside). And specifically then, after he prayed properly, the *shefa* (bounty) will come to him: children, life, and sustenance, and health, without any lacking, just beneficial and for blessing, in such a way that the *shefa* (bounty) will not harm him at all, since vessels and conduit were already fixed through the prayer, to receive through them the *shefa* (bounty) of kindness. **(Likutay Halachos, Laws of Circumcision, law 5).**

101. The words said in hisbodidus become agents of redemption

[**Sefer** Hameedos (The Book of the Traits - Character) of our master, leader, and holy rabbi, the rav, Rabbi Nachman *za.tz.vka.l.*, entry of Salvation, article 3: Through hisbodidus comes salvation. And see there also the entry of

Hisbodidus: The words that a person converses between himself and his Maker, this conversation becomes afterwards a redemption and salvation for his children. (And see Biraishis Rabba, Torah portion of Va'Yaitzay, section 70, where it is written regarding the prayer of our Father Jacob r.i.p., "If G-d will be with me etc.": The Holy One Blessed He took the words of the fathers and made them the key to the redemption of the children.)

102. The Supernal Collective *Pidyon* (redemption) of the True Tzaddik Is Aided By One's Hisbodidus

In Likutay Moharan volume 1, torah 215, the following is explained: Know, that there are twenty four courts (see Idra Rabba, Zohar Torah portion of Nusso, page 136, and Idra Zutta, page 293), and correlating each and every court there is a unique *pidyon* (-redemption, ransom) to sweeten (-mitigate) the *din* (-judgment) that is there. Therefore sometimes a *pidyon* (-redemption, ransom) that is done doesn't help, because not everyone knows all the twenty four *pidyonos*; and even if he does know them, he doesn't do all of them, and therefore, when he doesn't do the *pidyon* designated for that judgment, on account of this it doesn't help. But know, that there is one *pidyon*, which (is a gestalt which) includes that of all twenty four courts, and can sweeten (-mitigate) all the twenty four courts, and this *pidyon* needs an *ais rutzon* (-auspicious time, "time of desire"), the aspect of the revelation of the *forehead of desire* (*maitzach hurutzon*), like at *mincha* (-afternoon) of Sabbath, the aspect of (Psalms 69:14), "And I, my

229

prayer etc. *ais rutzon* (-auspicious time, "time of desire"). However, even the tzaddikim, not just any one knows this *pidyon*, and there is not to be found but one in a generation that knows this *pidyon*. And sometimes even when this tzaddik does the *pidyon*, even still it doesn't help, and this is because also above they very much desire this *pidyon*, because it is not every time (-common) that there comes to them from below such a *pidyon*, which can sweeten all the twenty four courts simultaneously. And therefore, when this sweetening (-mitigation) comes to them, they use it for a different necessity, namely, through this *pidyon* and sweetening are made proselytes, because as long as there is idolatry in the world - there is (Divine) wrath in the world (Sifrey, Ri'ay 13:18), and when the din (judgment) and wrath is sweetened, the idolatry is mitigated, and proselytes are made.

And this was the *avoada* (service of G-d) of Moses r.i.p. all the days of his life and also after his death, for he endeavored to draw close the *ayrev rav* (-'mixed multitude' – the gentiles who joined Israel when they left Egypt) in order to make proselytes, and also in his death, he was buried opposite the House of Pi'or (Deuteronomy 34:6 – idolatry of the worst defilement), in order to mitigate the idolatry, so that proselytes would be made. And therefore he passed away on Sabbath at *mincha* (afternoon), for then it is an *ais rutzon* (-auspicious time, "time of desire"), in order to sweeten all the twenty four courts, as mentioned above, in order to make proselytes, because the entire *avoada* (service of G-d) of Moses was – to sweeten the wrath of idolatry (so much so that it would turn) into *rutzon* (-desirable). And therefore the numerical value of "Moshe" (-Moses) <345> is the mean between the numerical value of "*shmad*" (-apostasy) <344> and the numerical value of "*rutzon*" (-desire) <346>, because he stands always to sweeten the *shmad* (-apostasy) and turn it around to *rutzon* (-desire), as mentioned above etc.. And see also in Likutay Moharan, volume 1, torah 10, where it is brought that "Moshe" (-Moses) has the numerical value (*gimatreya*) of "*charon af*" (wrath – Supernal wrath), which is also understandable with this article.

And in Likutay Halachos (Laws of the Morning Blessings, 5:22) based on this article it is explained the utter preciousness of hisbodidus, that through a person presenting argumentation, and conversing, and pouring out his heart before Him blessed He, and revealing his sentiments and desire, that he deeply desires to do His will blessed He, just, what can he do, "the leaven of the dough (-the evil inclination which sours our hearts) obstructs," like the words of the *Tana* (-sage of the Mishna; Brachos 17a): "It is revealed and known before You that our will is to do Your will, and who prevents (this)? The leaven of the dough obstructs"; and beseeches and entreats before Him blessed He, that he should merit to abnegate and subdue the evil inclination (-*yetzehr hurra*), which is the leaven in the dough – through this he gives additional might and daring to the true tzaddik, who is always engaged by means of the supernal *pidyon* mentioned above, which is drawn from the supernal *forehead of desire*, to sweeten the wrath (*charon af*), through which the distant are brought close, so that they return in complete repentance, and he raises them from apostasy (*shmad*-344) to desire (*ratzon*-346). And through the

231

conversation between one and his Maker, mentioned above, a person merits to strengthening of the *ratzon* (-desire, will), and also draws upon himself radiance of the *forehead of desire* mentioned above, to abnegate from himself the leaven that is in the dough, as mentioned above. And if he will be very strong at this, then certainly in the end he will rectify everything through the power of the great tzaddik who is engaged in the supernal collective *pidyon* mentioned above, in his life and after his death, because everything is rectified there.

And see there further (#65): that therefore Heaven forbid the one who brings the *pidyon* should doubt ("have thoughts concerning") the great tzaddik who performs the supernal collective *pidyon* mentioned above, even though his salvation has yet to reach him, because certainly it is wondrously beneficial for him, because *baaley teshuva* (-people who return in repentance) are made, as mentioned above, and every person needs this, because this is the main salvation and mercy – to merit to return to Hashem Yisburach and be saved from sin. And also, behold the reality is that every person needs a very great deal of salvations, and certainly in this great sweetening (-mitigation), through which *baaley teshuva* (-people who return in repentance) are made, are included all the salvations, physical and spiritual, because all the hardships Heaven forbid, are from the *hastuhras punim* (-hiddeness of the Countenance), from the aspect of *charon af* (-wrath – Supernal wrath) mentioned above, like it is written (Deuteronomy 31:17), "Behold, because my G-d is not in my midst" - which is the aspect of idolatry and wrath (*charon af*) - "these evils have found me," and through the *pidyon* mentioned above, everything is sweetened, and through this there will naturally be drawn, with the progression of time, all the salvations which he needs, with all sorts of expansions, and eternal completion, except they will need to tarry; and "the believer will not demand it's immediate arrival (Isaiah 28:16)."

And this is (Psalms 130:7): "Hope (oh) Israel to Hashem, for with Hashem is the kindness," that is, that certainly He will do kindness, however (continuation of the verse): "and abundant redemption is with Him," that is, that there is with Him abundant redemption and salvations which are needed to save a person, therefore his lackings cannot be filled immediately, and he needs to just sit tight and hope for the salvation of Hashem, until He redeems him from the greater adversity, and afterwards He will save him from this as well. And the main thing is what He blessed He redeems Israel from all their sins (verse 8) – through the supernal *pidyon* mentioned above, and this is the aspect of (verse 8), "And He will redeem Israel from all its iniquity," which is the aspect of the making of proselytes which is effected by the supernal *pidyon* mentioned above, which (is a gestalt which) includes all the *pidyonos* of all the twenty four courts. And therefore it is necessary to wait and hope to Hashem, and the more that he strengthens to hope to Hashem and not to force the hour, the salvation will come closer (/sooner), because through the hope and trust itself, his salvation will sprout shortly etc., see there further.

And so it is readily understood that a person needs to abound in conversation between himself and his Maker, as mentioned above, in order to give more power and fortitude to the true tzaddik who engages in this supernal *pidyon* gestalt mentioned above, through which everything is sweetened and rectified, as mentioned above. And it seems to the weak mind of the transcriber (-R' Alter of Teplik), that from all of this can be understood the root of the matter of what I brought above in the previous article (101) from Sefer Hameedos (The Book of the Traits - Character), that the words that a person converses between himself and his Maker become afterwards a redemption and salvation for his children, because (while) it is certainly possible to merit through this that his salvation will come with time to him himself as well, as mentioned above, however, even if he does not merit to this himself, certainly through this the redemption and salvation will come through for his children.

Na Nach Nachma Nachman MeUman

Making Prayers From Holy Teachings

a synopsis of

Likutay Halachos
Laws of the First of the Month #5

The transcriber (R' Alter of Teplik) said: I saw fit to connect the end of the book with its beginning, and to transcribe a synopsis of what comes out of the wondrous discourse from the book Likutay Halachos (Orach Chaim, Laws of the First of the Month, law 5), which is based on the homily "Psalms are conducive (*mesugal*) for repentance," in Likutay Moharan volume 2 (torah 73), which is copied out in the beginning of this book (article 1), and on the homily "Hisbodidus is a very lofty virtue," in Likutay Moharan volume 2 (torah 25), which is copied out in this book (article 2), which speaks a great deal about the greatness of the prominence of one who merits to express his words before Hashem Yisburach, to ask Him that He should draw him close to His service blessed He, and of the greatness of the enterprise of making from torahs (-holy teachings) – prayers. And this is a summation of his holy words in that law mentioned above:

1.

Based on the these articles mentioned above an explanation is presented for the theme of Rosh Hashanah (Jewish New Years), Yom Kippur, Succos, the four species, Hoshana Rabba (-7th day of Succos), and Shmeeney Atzeres etc.. Because all our devotions during these days that are from Rosh Hashanah until Shmeeney Atzeres (the 22nd of the month of Tishri), (it) is all for the sake of the *Malchus* (kingdom) of Holiness, to build her as a complete *partzuf* (-countenance; a full Divine structure of ten *sfeeroas*), and unite her with *Zi'ehr Anpin* (-the Small Face, referring to the full set of attributes which govern this world), as explained in the Kavanos (-the Arizal's kabalistic intentions and meditations for the prayers and holidays), namely, that all our *kavana* (-intention, concentration) in these days is – to build the prayer, to stand her up from her fall, because now the prayer, which is the aspect of the Kingdom of David, is very fallen, as our Rabbis o.b.m. expressed (Brachos 6b, brought as well, below, articles 6 and 11): "with the rise <*kiroom* – the Talmud also explains this word to connote the colors of a person's face when shamed> of the dregs <*zooloos* - scorned> of society (Psalms 12:9)," - these (-there is an allusion here) are things that stand in the lofty height of the world <*biroom*> and the people denigrate <*mizalzail* – same root as *zooloos*> them, and what are they? Prayer. And this is the entire essence of our devotions in these days – to erect the prayer, the aspect of *malchus* (kingdom), and build her up as a complete structure.

Now, there are two aspects – two prayers: There is prayer which is lower than Torah, and it is subordinate to the Torah, and there is prayer which is an aspect *mamash* (-very much so) with the Torah, and it is also higher than the Torah. That is, because there is prayer, that is prayed for one's needs, that is, for livelihood, and children, and life, and healing etc., and this prayer is called "life of the hour" (*cha'yay shu'u*, see Sabbath 10a, opposing views whether one can engage at length in such prayer at the expense of time spent in Torah study), and it is below the Torah and subordinate to her, because certainly someone who prays for his body's concerns and doesn't have any intention for the Torah, he just prays that Hashem Yisburach gives him children, life, and sustenance etc., for his pleasure and the needs of his body – this prayer certainly does not have any perfection, because whoever doesn't look at the final true *tachlis* (- ultimate purpose), what does he live for, and what contentment (*nachas-ruach*) does Hashem Yisburach have from his prayer, that he prays that Hashem Yisburach gives him livelihood and money for him to fill his stomach's desire, and it could turn out to be that it will be the aspect of (Ecclesiastes 5:12), "wealth guarded for its owner for his detriment," and therefore the holy Zohar cries foul on these prayers (Tikunay Zohar, tikun 6k, page 22a): shrieking like dogs: "Give us life, give us sustenance etc.,"

(*) The transcriber (R' Alter of Teplik) said: With this we can explain straightforwardly what our Rabbis o.b.m. said (Yuma 11b), "and you should speak in them (-in Torah; Deuteronomy 6:7)," and not in prayer. That is, referring to prayers such as these, see there in the commentary of Rashi and Tosfos (A.P. points out that "in them" - *bum*, spelled out: bais mem, has the numerical value of Na Nach Nachma Nachman MeUman with the inclusive!).

Because Hashem Yisburach derives no *nachas* (enjoyment, appreciation) from prayer which is for the body's needs, only when the one praying intends his prayer for the sake of fulfilling the Torah, that he should have children, life, and sustenance in order that he can co His will blessed He, and to truly fulfill His Torah and *mitzvos*. And if his intention is truly for this, certainly Hashem Yisburach has *nachas-ruach* (pleasure, satisfaction) from this prayer, just, even still, a prayer such as this, is below the Torah and secondary to it, for behold the main thing is the Torah, just that he prays for bodily needs in order that through this he will be able to fulfill the Torah, and therefore this type of prayer is secondary to the Torah and below it.

And regarding someone who protracts in this type of prayer, our Rabbi o.b.m. said (Shabbos 10a): forsaking eternal life <*cha'yay oalum*> and engaging in life of the hour <*cha'yay shu'ah*>, for behold, irregardless (of his good intentions), for the time being, this prayer is for bodily needs, which is life of the hour, just that it is necessary for the sake of the Torah, which is eternal life. Therefore, certainly actual engagement in Torah is definitely greater than this prayer; and this type of prayer needs great protection that the *cheetzoanim* (the outsiders, a reference to evil forces that are superficial and have no integral basis), that is, since he prays for bodily needs, just that his intention is for the sake of the Torah, therefore the *sitra-achra* ('other side' – realm of evil) can easily grasp him, and veer his intention for the bodily needs themselves. And therefore when the prayer, which is the aspect of *Malchus* (-kingdom), is in this aspect, this is the aspect of what is explained in the *Kavanos* (-Lurianic intentions and meditations for the prayers and times; see Otzros Chaim, Shaar Hanikudim, chapter 6) that the *Malchus* (-kingdom- of female character) is attached, so to speak, to *Zehr Anpin* (-the Small Countenance- husband of *Malchus*) back to back, so that the *cheetzoanim* (-outsiders) don't take nourishment from her (- because they can only access and siphon from the aspect of the back, which is vulnerable, therefore by going back to back with her husband, protection is afforded), because the aspect of *Zehr Anpin* is the aspect of the holy Torah, as is understood from the *Kavanos* for *Kreyas Hatorah* (-reading the Torah scroll in a quorum) and in other places, that is, for then the *Malchus*, which is the aspect of prayer, does not have her own unique *partzuf* (-countenance), she is just attached with the Torah, which is the aspect of Zehr Anpin, and without the Torah she has no role and significance whatsoever as mentioned above, and also she needs protections so that the *cheetzoanim* don't latch on to her, as mentioned above.

However, the main completion of the structure of the prayer is when a person prays just for the concerns of his soul alone, namely, that all his prayers are – to merit to fear of Heaven, and to His service blessed He, and to merit to fulfill the Torah that he learned, because (Ethics of Our Fathers 1:17), "The main thing is not study, but action." And this type of prayer is not secondary to learning the Torah; on the contrary, it is the main fulfillment of the Torah, since he is asking just to fulfill the Torah, which is the main completion of the Torah. And this prayer is equal to the Torah and higher than it, so to speak, for behold the main intention of studying the Torah is in order to fulfill the Torah, and this is all his intention in his prayer, that he asks just to fear Hashem and fulfill the Torah, like King David r.i.p. said (Psalms 27:4), "One thing I asked from Hashem etc.," It comes out, that the Torah and the prayer, both of them are equal in their standing, and also prayer is even higher, in the aspect of (Proverbs 12:4), "A woman of valor is the crown of her husband," and in the aspect of (Psalms

111:10), "The primary (/beginnings of) wisdom is fear of Hashem," namely this type of prayer, which is the aspect of (Proverbs 31:30) "a Heaven fearing woman," she is primary, and above wisdom, which is the Torah, because through her one merits to fulfill the Torah, which is the main thing.

And this is the aspect of all the intention of the *nessira* (-cutting apart, removal) that we are engaged in on Rosh Hashana (-Jewish New Years), to sweeten (-mitigate) the *dinim* (-judgments), and to nullify the grasp of the *cheetzoanim* (-outsiders) who draw their nourishment from the austerity of the dinim (-judgments) Heaven forbid, in order to sever (*nassehr*) the *Malchus*, so that she shouldn't be in the aspect of back to back, rather she should be a unique complete *partzuf* (-countenance), and she should unite (with *Zehr Anpin*) in the aspect of face to face, as is explained in the writings of the Arizal (Shaar Hakavanos, Rosh Hashana, Drush 1, 6:3), that is as was mentioned above, that we engage then to draw complete rectification of the prayer in the world, that the main prayer of every single person will be just for the fear (of Heaven), "to fear Hashem ("the Name"), the glorious and awesome (Deuteronomy 28:58)," and to fulfill his commandments perfectly. And therefore we begin (in the first blessing of the body of the Shmoaneh Esreh – the standing prayer) on Rosh Hashana: "And so, put Your fear etc.," for this is the essential perfection of the prayer, as mentioned above.

2.

Now behold, Rosh Hashana (the Jewish New Years) is the first of the ten days of repentance (*assehres yimay teshuva*), and it is necessary then to draw the way of repentance in the world, so that all that traverse the world will merit to return to Hashem Yisburach. And this is drawn by engaging in the building of the stature of the prayer, to completion, that is, that we should merit to do a great deal of hisbodidus, and to pray constantly to Hashem Yisburach that we should merit to fulfill the Torah as mentioned above, for this is the main consummation of prayer, to make from the holy teachings – prayers, that is, to pray for the fulfillment of the Torah, because specifically through this one merits to repentance, because through prayer it is possible to accomplish everything, because even though he is the way he is, and has already been caught up in his bad desires, to the extent that it seems to him that it impossible to get out of there, even still he has the ability of speech, and if he abounds to speak words of prayer and entreaty, and he prays copiously to Hashem Yisburach that he should merit to return and to fulfill all the words of the Torah, certainly he will arouse the mercy of Hashem Yisburach on himself, until Hashem Yisburach will open for him the gates of repentance, and he will at long last, finally merit to return to Hashem Yisburach, and He will have mercy on him (Isaiah 55:7). And therefore it is explained in that torah (-holy teaching) mentioned above, in the first article, that the recital of Psalms is conducive (*mesugal*) for repentance. Because the entire Book of Psalms was founded just on this method. And like King David himself said (Psalms 27:4), "One thing I requested from Hashem etc. to see the pleasantness of Hashem," and it is written (Psalms 86:11), "Show (/teach) me Hashem Your ways, I will go in Your truth," and similarly many verses. And even all the prayers that he prayed to be saved from his enemies, his entire intention was to be saved from the enemies of his soul, who are the evil inclination (*yetzehr hura*) and his legions, because all the foes and enemies also stem from them.

The general rule is, that the whole intention of King David r.i.p. with the Book of Psalms is to beseech from Hashem Yisburach that we should merit to fulfill the Torah and to be saved from all the enemies ('haters'), and those who prevent and hold (us) back from serving Hashem Yisburach, physically and/or spiritually, because the entire Book of Psalms is from the hisbodidus of King David r.i.p., and therefore they are five books of Psalms (-the Psalms is divided into 5 sections, which are called books) correlating the five books (*chumashing* – fifths) of the Torah, that is, he made from the toaroas (-holy teachings) – prayers, this being the main completion of prayer, which itself is the aspect of David, as it is written (Psalms 109:4), "And I am prayer." And therefore the main arousal of repentance is through the recital of Psalms, because the main repentance is merited by making from toaroas (-holy teachings) – prayers, which is the aspect of Psalms, as mentioned above.

However this way of making from the toaroas (-holy teachings)- prayers, needs to be drawn from a very high place, from the aspect of *cheedooshay* (-original ideas, developments, innovations etc. on the) Torah which are drawn from the Torah of *Atteeka Siseemah* (-Atteeka can mean many things, but primarily it is: Old, meaning extremely supreme, sublime, and esoteric. Siseemah, means sealed. This is a *partzuf* – a Divine Countenance which is pure goodness remote from this world), just like an expert doctor, when he wants to heal the sickness in a person, it is not possible to know completely the nature of the malady, only if he is very proficient in the field of dissection, and knows all the details of the structure of a person, and the characteristics of all his limbs, and veins, and arteries, completely, and how the inner and outer organs are arranged and in order one next to the other, and the characteristics of their parts, connections, and attachments, how every limb and bone etc. is connected and attached to each other through the connection of the veins and arteries etc., and how the blood runs in them, and all the other characteristics of the body which are included in the knowledge of dissection, and specifically then, when the doctor is thoroughly proficient in all this, then he can undertake to understand the nature of the illness, and work at healing it. Similarly the true tzaddikim of the generation who are engaged in healing the sicknesses of the souls of Israel, it is not possible for them to engage in their healing except when they are fully knowledgeable of the nature of the maladies of the soul, and this is through the knowledge of the characteristics of the stature of the supernal man, which is the aspect of the characteristics of the stature of the Torah, which is called man ("*adam*", Numbers 19:14), because the Torah is the aspect of the stature of man, which is 248 positive commandments (-the dos) and 365 negative (-do nots) commandments, which correlate the 248 limbs and 365 blood vessels that are in the structure of man, and just like the limbs and blood vessels that are in person are arranged, and in order, and connected to each other, as mentioned above, so too it is necessary to know in the aspect of the structure of the Torah the order of connection and attachment of all the 248 positive commandments and 365 negative commandments, and all the rabbinical commandments which are included in them, to know well how they are arranged, and ordered, and connected this to that, and this to that, and then it is possible to know the *segula* (-quality) of each and every *mitzva* (-commandment), and each and every attribute (-*meeda*), to which healing it is most conducive, and how to heal the sickness of the soul.

And specifically then, when one draws *cheedooshay* (novelties of) Torah such as these, which through them the nature of the structure of the Torah is knows, as mentioned above, then it is possible to draw the holy way of making from the *toaroas* (-holy teachings) – prayers, that is, that we can pour out our hearts like water directly before the countenance of Hashem to (merit to) fulfill this (-a certain) *mitzva* in order that we merit through this to this (-a certain) good attribute (-*meeda*), and through this we will merit to come to rectify this (-a certain) matter, and to this (-a certain) level. Take for example, when someone wants to ask from Hashem Yisburach that he should merit to fulfill the *mitzva* of *tzitzis* (-fringes on a four cornered garment) consummately, if he doesn't know the *segula* (-quality) of (the) *tzitzis*, which vice (trait-*meeda*) he will merit to break through the *tzitzis* and to which virtue (/height) he will merit on its account etc., then certainly he is unable to pray at length until he breaks his heart, until he arouses the mercy of Hashem Yisburach, because he is unable to ask, just: "Master of the World, let me merit to fulfill the *mitzva* of *tzitzis* consummately," even though this as well is certainly very good; fortunate is one who is adherent to this, to request regarding every *mitzva* from Hashem Yisburach, even still, he still does not merit to make his prayer mercy (invoking) and entreaty, which is this (- is the case with prayer) that one merits to conjure some innovation.

But the main, complete prayer which is made from Torah, is from *cheedooshay* (novelties of the) Torah, which through them one merits to know the *seguloas* (-qualities) of the *mitzvos*, like in the example of the *tzitzis* which we mentioned, when a person knows that *tzitzis* is *mesugal* (-conducive) to breaking sexual desire, and to merit through it to the *aitza* (-advice) of the tzaddikim, and to perfect faith, and to prayer, and to the Land of Israel, and to make miracles etc., as is explained in the book Likutay Moharan, torah 7, behold by means of this way, certainly he can set in order many prayers with wondrous length pertaining the *mitzva* of *tzitzis*, because every person, according to what he knows in his soul how distant he is from rectification of the *bris* (-covenant, circumcision), and everything that he undergoes in this matter, every time, how very much he needs to implore Hashem Yisburach that He should bring him salvation – to fulfill the *mitzva* of *tzitzis* as it is configured, in order to be saved from sexual desire which stands over him every day to wipe him out Heaven forbid, to distance him from the Life of Life. And so too when he remembers how far he is from complete faith, which is the foundation of the entire Torah etc., and so too how far he is from prayer etc., and so too (how) many of the evil *aitzos* (-rationales, ideas, courses) of the reversers of the truth etc. set out to overcome him, and how much salvation and mercy he needs to merit to true *aitzos* (-advice, remedies), which are the *aitzos* of the tzaddikim; decidedly on all of these, he certainly can pour out his words in his prayer, to make from this torah (-holy teaching #7 of Likutay Moharan) which speaks of the *segula* (quality) of the *mitzva* of *tzitzis*, to express through this, all that is in his heart , and similarly with the rest of the *mitzvos* of the Torah.

And *cheedooshay* (novelties of the) Torah such as these, are drawn from the aspect of Torah of *Atteeka* <old, sublime> *Sisseema* <sealed>, which is the aspect of the root of the holy Torah, and over there is the root of the thirteen methods (*meedoas*) that the Torah is extrapolated with, which are the collective entirety of all the *cheedooshay* (novelties of the) Torah which the tzaddikim draw, and over there is also the root of the Thirteen Attributes of Mercy which are the root collective entirety of the whole order of prayer, which is mercy (invoking) and entreaty. And therefore through the true tzaddikim who draw their *cheedooshay* (novelties of the) Torah from there, through this they draw this way, to make from their *cheedooshay* (novelties of the) Torah – prayers, for this is the main consummation of prayer, and through this one merits to repentance, as mentioned above. And for this the *shofar* (-ritual horn) is sounded on Rosh Hashana (-Jewish New Years), because by means of the *shofar* we draw such *cheedooshay* (novelties of the) Torah, with which we can merit to erect the prayer, to make from the *toaroas* (-holy teachings) – prayers, through which is the main repentance, because the Torah was given with the calling of the *shofar* (Exodus 19:16), and also *shofar* is the aspect of fear (of Heaven), the aspect of prayer, as it is written (Proverbs 31:30), "fear of Hashem it is (to be) praise(d)" [-praise being a term of prayer]. And for this the Torah was given with the calling of the *shofar*, to show that the main completion of the Torah is when one merits to make from the Torah – prayer, which is the aspect of fear (of Heaven), which is revealed through the *shofar*, as mentioned above.

And behold it is known, when one wants to ascend from level to level, it is necessary to remove the previous *moachin* (-mind, consciousness), as we find in the Talmud (Buva Metziah 85a): Rabbi Zairu, when he went up to the Land of Israel, he would fast in order to forget the Torah of the lands outside of Israel, and to merit to receive the *moachin* (-mind, consciousness) of the Land of Israel. And this is the aspect of what is explained in the writings of the Arizal (Shaar Hakavanos, Rosh Hashana, drush 1, 6:3) of the slumber and deep sleep (*durmeeta*) which falls upon *Zehr Anpin* (-Small Countenance), who is the Torah, as mentioned above, and afterwards he is aroused through the *shofar*, which through this the *Malchus* (-Kingdom, female mate of *Zehr Anpin*) is detached (-*nesseera* from the back of *Zehr Anpin*) and constructed, because on Rosh Hashana, when it is necessary to merit to repentance by means of meriting to make from *toaroas* (-holy teachings) – prayers, and it is necessary to draw this way from an extremely lofty place, from the aspect of *cheedooshay* (novelties of the) Torah of *Ateeka Sisseemuh*, as mentioned above, therefore *Zehr Anpin* is cast into slumber and deep sleep (*durmeeta*), which is the aspect of removal of the previous *moachin* (-mind, consciousness) in order to merit to more lofty *moachin* by means of the *shofar*, that is, to draw *cheedooshay* (novelties of the) Torah of the aspect of *Atteek*, in order that we merit through them to build the structure of the *Malchus*, which is the aspect of prayer, to make from *toaroas* (-holy teachings) – prayers, through which the main way of repentance is in the world, which is necessary to draw now on Rosh Hashana, as mentioned above.

And also, because the first tablets were broken on account of the golden calf, and then Moses ascended to appease Hashem Yisburach, and then Hashem Yisburach revealed to him the Thirteen Attributes of Mercy, which are the Thirteen Methods (*meedoas*) with which the Torah is extrapolated. That is, Hashem Yisburach revealed to him that through the Thirteen Attributes of Mercy which are drawn from the Thirteen *Meedoas* (-methods) of the Torah, namely, the making from Torah – prayer, through this there is merit to institute in (the Children of) Israel fulfillment of the Torah, to return all of them to Hashem Yiburach in complete repentance, as mentioned above. And therefore on Rosh Hashana, which is the first day of the Ten Days of Repentance (*A'ssehress Yimay Teshuva*), which culminate on Yom Kippur, which are the last ten days of the final forty days (-Moses went up to the Heavens for forty days, three times) in which Hashem Yisburach restored his favor to Moses, as our Rabbis of blessed memory said (Medrash Tanchuma, Key Seesa 31), we sound the *shofar* then, for it is also to draw the aforementioned *tikun* (-rectification), to make from toaroas (-holy teachings), prayers, as mentioned above.

3.

And this is the aspect of (the three sections of prayer, which are called:) *Malcheyos* (-kingships), *Zichroanos* (-remembrances), (and) *Shoafros* (-ritual horns), which are said in the prayer of *Mussaf* (-additional standing prayer for the holidays) of Rosh Hashana, which incorporate many verses from the Torah, Prophets (*niveyim*), and Writings (*kesuvim*), namely that the verses of TaNaCh (-acronym for: Torah, Prophets, and Writings) are made then into prayer, which is the aspect of making from Torah – prayer, and therefore they are said in the prayer of Mussaf, because the entire concept of the prayer of *Mussaf* is based on this construct, the making from *toaroas* – prayers. That it, because due to our inability to actually offer the sacrifices, that we need to offer, therefore we pray to Hashem Yisburach, "That the *Bais Hamidkdush* (-Temple) should be built, soon, in our days," "and we will offer before You the sacrifices we are obligated, as we are commanded in the holy Torah," this being the aspect of making from Torah, prayer, namely, from the commandment of bringing the *Mussaf* (-additional) offering, that we do not merit to fulfill now, we make from this a prayer, and with this we draw the way of making from *toaroas*, prayers, that is, that each and everyone, according to how how distant he is from fulfilling a certain *mitzva*, be it a positive commandment or a negative commandment, needs to pray to Hashem Yisburach that he merits to fulfill it.

And just like, through that which we pray that we merit to bring the *Mussaf* offering, through this we will merit to eventually finally return to our land and bring there the sacrifices we are obligated in real actuality, and for the time being this prayer itself is considered in place of the sacrifice, similarly with regard to this way, mentioned above, to make from *toaroas*, prayers, through this we will certainly merit in the end, finally, to return to Hashem Yisburach completely. And also, as long as we still do not merit to complete redemption of the soul, even still, the prayer itself that we prayer for the fulfillment of the Torah, this also is very important and acceptable by Hashem Yisburach, and is considered as if we did what was required of us. And therefore the main *mitzva* of sounding the *shofar*, which is to draw this way of making from *toaroas*, prayers, as mentioned above, is during the prayer of *Mussaf*.

And therefore every day that has extra holiness: on Sabbath, and *Rosh Chodesh* (the first of the month), and Yom Tov (-holidays), and Rosh Hashanan, and Yom Kippur, we pray *Mussaf*, because all these days are days of repentance, and Sabbath is the aspect of an inkling of the future world (*mayain oalam habu*), for then it will be a day that is completely Sabbath (Zohar, Teruma 138a, and various prayers), a day that is completely repentance, as is brought down in his words o.b.m., Likutay Moharan, volume 1, torah 6 (article 3). And Sabbath is the aspect of (Deuteronomy 30:2), "And you will return to (lit: until) Hashem Your G-d," as so too all the holidays are days of judgment, as our Rabbis o.b.m. said (Rosh Hashana 16a): On Passover (*Pesach*) there is judgment on the crops, on *Atzeress* (*Shavuos*) there is judgment etc., on *Chag* (*Succos*) there is judgment etc.; and days of judgment are days of repentance, as is explained in his words o.b.m., Likutay Moharan, volume 1, torah 30 (article 6, and torah 135). And *Rosh Chodesh* (-the first of the month) is the root of repentance, as is explained in his words o.b.m., Likutay Moharan, volume 1, torah 10 (article 9), that from this (Shavuos 9a), that Hashem Yisburach said, "Bring atonement for Me, for that which I shrunk the moon," from this evolved repentance to all creation on *Rosh Chodesh* (- when the shrinkage of the moon is predominantly manifested). And Rosh Hashana and Yom Kippur are certainly days of repentance. And the essential drawing of the way of repentance is through making from *toaroas*, prayers, which is the aspect of the prayer of *Mussaf*, as mentioned above, and therefore, on all these days we pray the *Mussaf* prayer.

4.

And this is the aspect of *Rosh Chodesh* (-the first of the month). And the main *tikun* (-rectification) of *Rosh Chodesh* is to fill the slighting of the moon, that they should both (-the sun and moon) be equal in their stature, in the aspect of (Isaiah

30:26), "And the light of the moon will be like the light of the sun." And this is merited through making from *toaroas*, prayers, that is, by praying just for the fulfillment of the Torah, and through this Torah and prayer are incorporated together, for they are the aspect of Moses and David, the aspect of the sun and moon, as is known (see Zohar vol. 3, page 181b – Moses is the sun; and there page 262a – David merited to rectify the third support of the chariot (the secret of the kingdom, the moon)); both of them equal in stature, and both of them utilizing one (-the same) crown, because the purpose of both of them is one (-the same), because the purpose of the Torah is – repentance and good deeds (Brachos 17a). And this is the purpose of prayer, since his entire prayer is to merit to fulfill the Torah, to come to fruition, which is the main thing, and the purpose (*tachlis*).

And therefore Rosh Hashana is set on Rosh Chodesh, because this is the aspect of the combining of the sun and moon together, because the years are determined (lit: counted) by the sun, and the months are determined (lit: counted) by the moon, as is brought down (see Zohar, Beraishis 236b), because then, on Rosh Hashana, which is the first of the ten days of repentance, that we begin (them) with arousal for repentance, through engaging to erect the structure of the prayer, to make from the Torah, prayer, therefore the sun and moon are combined together then, because both of them are equal, because all this is merited through making from the *toaroas*, prayers, as mentioned above.

And behold it is already explained (-inside the source of this excerpt from Likutay Halachos, article 7; above article 2), that this is the aspect of the five books of Psalms which correlate the five *chumashim* (-books – fifths) of the Torah, that the essential arousal to repentance is through this. And it is explained in the torah mentioned above in article 1, that the 49 gates of repentance are the aspect of the 49 letters which comprise the names of the twelve tribes of Y-ah, because everything is one, because the root of repentance is *Rosh Chodesh*, as mentioned above, because Rosh Chodesh is the aspect of the Kingdom of David, that is, the aspect of Psalms which David constituted, through which one merits to repentance, and therefore there are twelve *Roshey Chudushim* (-firsts of the months) corresponding to the twelve tribes which are comprised of 49 letters, which are the aspect of the 49 gates of repentance, which one merits to come to (them) through Psalms, which is the aspect of David, all of this being the aspect of Rosh Chodesh, as mentioned above.

And this is (Psalms 122:4), "the tribes of Y-ah, a testimony to (the Children of) Israel, to give praise to the Name of Hashem," - specifically "to give praise," the aspect of Psalms, which is the aspect of thanking and singing praise to Hashem Yiburach, all of this being the aspect of *Rosh Chodesh*, as mentioned above. And the essence of this *tikun* (-rectification) of Rosh Chodesh, the aspect of Psalms and the letters of the tribes of Y-ah, happens on Rosh Hashana, which is set on Rosh Chodesh, as mentioned above. And this is what the Scripture writes adjacent (verse 5), "Because over there sat the seats of justice," that is the aspect of Rosh Hashana, for then they sit, the seats of justice, and then it is necessary to engage in this *tikun* (-rectification). And this is (continuation of the verse), "the seats of the House of David," for the *tikun* (-rectification) of Rosh Hashana is accomplished through the aspect of the Kingdom of David, namely, through Psalms; and therefore all of Israel is engaged then in the recital of Psalms, as is explained in the aforementioned torah, because the main *tikun* (-rectification) of *Rosh Hashana* and the ten days of repentance is – to erect the prayer and to merit to repentance, and this is merited to through Psalms, which is the aspect of hisbodidus, and to make from the *toaroas*, prayers, as mentioned above.

5.

And this is the aspect of Yom Kippur, for then the high priest (*kohen gadol*) enters the innermost sanctuary where there are positioned the ark and the tablets which are the entire Torah in its root, and there it is also the essential location of the ascension of the prayer in its root, because all the prayers ascend by way of there, as is known (see Brachos, Chapter 4, Mishna 5). And there, in the Holy of Holies, is the essential pinnacle of complete holiness, because this is the essential complete holiness, when Torah and prayer are combined together, which is merited through making from *toaroas* (-holy teachings), prayers, as mentioned above. And therefore, there, in the place of the ark, there, is the superlative Unity, as is known (see Yuma 54b), because there Torah and prayer unite in consummate union, and therefore the high priest (*kohen gadol*) draws from there the supernal intellect to make from the *toaroas*, prayers, through which is the main repentance and main forgiveness and pardon; and therefore on Yom Kippur (-Day of Atonement) the last tablets were given, and then Hashem Yisburach acquiesced to Moses, and his prayer was accepted, and He said to him (Numbers 14:20), "I have forgiven according to your word," because then the Torah and prayer connected and united together, because it is meritorious then to draw the *tikun* (-

rectification) of making from *toaroas*, prayer, through which everything is rectified, as mentioned above.

And this is the aspect of the confessions of Yom Kippur, that we specify in the confession all the sins, and have remorse over them, and request of Hashem Yisburach, "May it will be the will before You (*yihee rutzon milfunnecha*) that I do not sin anymore." It comes out that we make from the Torah, prayer, namely, from all the commandments of the Torah that one transgressed, he prayers over them to Hashem Yisburach that He should save him in the future, and forgive him for the past, all this being the aspect of prayer which is made from the Torah. It comes out, that the entire day of Yom Kippur, we are engaged it making from the Torah, prayer, through the many confessions that are said then, because that is what is necessary then, because then it is the last day of the final forty days, when the essential completion of the rectification of the sin of the (golden) calf, that they transgressed the Torah (occurred). For the main rectification is – through making from the *toaroas*, prayers, which is the aspect of the Thirteen Attributes of Mercy which were revealed to Moses then, which are drawn from the Thirteen Meedoas (methods) With Which the Torah is Extrapolated, for the sake of the rectification, as mentioned above. (And therefore we pray on Yom Kippur five prayers (evening, morning, *mussaf*, mincha, *ni-eela*) correlating the five books (*chumashim*) of the Torah, which is the aspect of the five books of Psalms, corresponding the five books of the Torah, as mentioned above.)

And therefore, at the end of the prayer of *Ni-eela* (-closing-final prayer of Yom Kippur) we say seven times: Hashem is the

G-d, that is, that Hashem (Y-HVH) and G-d (E-lohim), which are the aspects of Zehr Anpin (Small Countenance) and Malchus (Kingdom), the aspects of Torah and prayer, as is known (see Me-oaray Ohr, category of the letter Tuv, items 15 and 42), are entirely one, as mentioned above. And therefore we say this seven times, this is the aspect of prayer, the aspect of (Psalms 119:164), "seven (times) a day I sang Your praise," and so too the Torah is the aspect of seven, as it is written (Proverbs 9:1), "She carved out her pillars, seven." And this is (Psalms 119:164), "Seven (times) a day I sang Your praise for the laws of Your righteousness," which is the Torah; because prayer, which is "seven (times) a day I sang Your praise," is made from the Torah, which is, "the laws of Your righteousness." And this is the aspect of (Psalms 12:7), "refined sevenfold," seven times seven (see Rashi on Isaiah 30:26, and Zechariah 4:3), the aspect of forty nine gates of repentance, forty nine letters of the (names of the) tribes, which are the aspect of Psalms, the aspect of prayers which are made from the Torah. And then it will be fulfilled (Isaiah 30:26), "And the light of the moon will be like the light of the sun, and the light of the sun will be sevenfold," as mentioned above. (And therefore upon the departure of Yom Kippur we sanctify the moon, and pray, "and the light of the moon will be etc.," as mentioned above.) And all of this is merited on Yom Kippur, the secret of the great Jubilee, the fiftieth gate, where the aspect of the great *shofar* is (Isaiah 27:13), which is the aspect of highest gate of the fifty gates of understanding (*beena*), which Messiah will attain, for he will attain conception of the Torah of *Atteeka* <old, venerable superlative Divine countenance> *Sisseemuh* <sealed>, from where is drawn this true intellect of making from the *toaroas* (-holy teachings), prayers, as mentioned

above, which through this, all of Israel will return to
Hashem Yisburach forever and ever.

6.

And this is the aspect of the *succuh* (-ritual hut for the holiday
of Succos which begins four days after Yom Kippur), because the
succuh is the aspect of (Amos 9:11) erecting the fallen
succuh of David, and to merit to the complete *succuh*. And
the essential fallen *succuh* of David is the aspect of prayer,
which has fallen due to our many sins, because the entire
occupation of King David r.i.p. was prayer, as it is written
(Psalms 109), "and I am prayer," that is, to erect the prayer
from its fall, because now the prayer is the aspect of (Psalms
12:9), "with the rise *<kiroom>* of the dregs *<zooloos - scorned>*
of society," - these are (-there is an allusion here to) things that
stand in the lofty height of the world *<biroom>*, and what are
they? Prayer (i.e. the aspect of these prayers that are made from
the *toaroas*, which produce great delights above, as is explained
there in Likutay Moharan, volume 2, torah 25), and the people
denigrate *<mizalzail –* same root as *zooloos>* them (Brachos 6b).
And therefore prayer is now the aspect of the fallen *succuh*
of David, and on Succos we engage in erecting it. And this
is the aspect of what our Rabbis o.b.m. said regarding the
mitzva of *succuh* (Succuh 2a): Go out from a permanent
dwelling and reside in a temporary dwelling, this is the
aspect of (Ethics of Our Fathers 2:18), "Do not make your
prayer routine, rather (pray) compassionately and
entreatingly;" and our Rabbis o.b.m. said (Brachos 29b), this
means that he knows to make some sort of innovation to it.
And one merits to this specifically when making from
toaroas (-holy teachings), prayers, for then one certainly

merits to come up with something new in his prayer every time.

(**And** see in the letters of our Rabbi, the Rav, Rabbi Nussun za.tza.l., in the year 5595, Rosh Chodesh (the first of the month of) Cheshvon (03/11/1834), that this is the aspect of a new *succuh* (ritual hut), for it is specifically necessary that the *succuh* be new, because there are those that rule out an old *succuh*; and this is the aspect of a new prayer, see there.)

And this is the aspect of *succas shulaim* (-the *succah* of completion), that is, to make peace and complete unity between Torah and prayer, which are the aspects of *Zehr Anpin* (-Small Countenance) and *Malchus* (-Kingdom), for that is where the main Unity and peace is, and there in the *succuh* enter all the seven shepherds, from Abraham to David, all for the sake of this aspect, because the beginning is from prayer and the end is prayer, because the devotion of the forefathers began from prayer, because there had yet to be any Torah, and therefore Abraham established *Shacharis* (-morning prayer) etc. (Brachos 26b), but it still was not the ultimate perfection, since the Torah had not been given yet, to make from it prayer. And Moses and Aron are the Torah, and Josef is the one who brings the Torah to the aspect of David, to make from it prayer to produce (lit: give birth to) good deeds, because Josef is the aspect of the tzaddik foundation of the world (Proverbs 10:25 – the *sefira* – Divine Attribute – of *Yesod* – foundation - by anthropomorphism, the male reproductive member), tzaddik the life of the world (Zohar, introduction 4b, and throughout the entire Zohar; "life" has the numerical value of 18 which signifies the reach of the Attribute of Yesod which is the 9th sefira, from the top and to the top), the eighteen blessings of the prayer (see Likutay Moharan, torah 44, and Zohar, Beraishis 211a, and the introduction to the Tikunay Zohar),

257

who is the aspect that connects both of them: Moses and David, Torah and prayer, to make from the Torah prayer. And therefore "Moses Yosef David," has the numerical value (gematria) of "prayer" <515>, because the three of them specifically are the aspect of the perfection of prayer, because the essential ultimate perfection of the prayer is with the making from Torah, prayer, which is done through these three tzaddikim, as mentioned above.

And therefore the three of them departed from this world at the time of the pinnacle consummation of the ascension of prayer which is on Sabbath at *Mincha* (-time of the afternoon prayer), at the time of *raava di'raavin* (-desire of desires; Zohar, Shemos 156a), in the aspect of (Psalms 69:14), "And I, my prayer is to you Hashem (it should be) a desirable time," which is said then, and this is (end of the verse): "answer me with Your true salvation;" "true," is the aspect of the Torah, the aspect of (Malachi 2:6), "the Torah of truth," that is, through the truth, that I will merit to make from Torah, prayer, through this, certainly You will "answer me" - "and be for me a salvation" (Exodus 15:2, Psalms 118:14). And this is (beginning of the verse), "My (/the) might and the cutting <*zimras* – also term for song> of Y-ah," "My (/the) might," this is the aspect of the Torah, the aspect of (Psalms 29:11), "Hashem will give might to His nation" (Bamidbar Rabba 18:14, Tanchuma, Likutay Moharan 80); "And the cutting <*zimras* – song> of Y-ah," this is the aspect of prayer, that is, when I merit to speak Torah and prayer, meaning, to make from the Torah, prayer, then certainly, "and it will be for me a salvation." And therefore all these seven shepherds, who are the aspect of the perfection of prayer, enter into the *succuh*, because on *Succos* we are engaged in this, as mentioned above.

And also, these seven shepherds mentioned above are the root of the twelve tribes of Y-ah, because the twelve tribes are the aspect of the twelve diagonal boundaries, the aspect of twelve elemental (letters of the Hebrew Alef Bet; Sefer Yetzira – The Book of Creation 5:2) which are drawn from the seven (letters of the Alef Bet that are) doubles, from the aspect of seven days of building (-the seven lower sefiros – Divine Attributes – which correlate the seven days of creation), as is known (see Keheelos Yaakov, entry of Twelve elementals, and twelve tribes, and twelve diagonal boundaries). And therefore the names of the twelve tribes have forty nine letters, seven times seven, because their root is the aspect of the seven shepherds. And the forty nine letters of the tribes are the aspect of the forty nine days of *sifeera* (-counted from the second day of Passover till Shavuos), the aspect of the forty nine gates of repentance, which are the aspect of Psalms, which is the aspect of making from *toaroas* (-holy teachings), prayers, as mentioned above, and on *Succos* we are engaged in this, and therefore they enter the *succuh*, as mentioned above. Because the *tikun* (-rectification) of the forty nine days of *sifeera* (-counting), through which they received the Torah on the fiftieth day, on Shavuos, was marred afterwards by the sin of the (golden) calf, and then the pollution <*zoohama*> of the snake which had ceased at the Giving of the Torah, returned to be drawn, and now, every single year we are engaged in rectifying the rectification of the sin of Adam *Hureeshoan* (-the first), and the rectification culminates on Yom Kippur, for then it is the culmination of the final forty days (that Moses ascended to Heaven), when there was the revelation of the *tikun* (-rectification) of the Thirteen Attributes of Mercy, which are drawn from the thirteen methods (*meedos*) that the

Torah is extrapolated with, which is the aspect of making from *toaroas* (-holy teachings), prayers, as mentioned above.

And therefore after Yom Kippur we make seven days of Succos, and the seven shepherds enter into the *succuh*, and with this we draw anew the *tikun* (-rectification) of the seven weeks of *sifeeras hu'oamehr* (-the counting of the *Oamehr* – 49 days from the second day of Passover till Shavuos); and afterwards it is *Shimeenee Atzehress* (-the eighth day of Succos, a holiday of its own right), which corresponds to Shavuos, which is also called *Atzehress*, and we also finish (reading) the Torah then (- on *Shimeenee Atzehress*), and the *tikun* (-rectification) which we began from Rosh Hashana, which is to rectify and complete the collective aspects of the Torah and the prayer through combining them together, and making from the *toaroas*, prayers, as mentioned above, is completed then. And (Ecclesiastes 7:8), "the end of a matter is bettered from (/than) its beginning," for the *tikun* (-rectification) of the forty nine days of the *sifeera* (-counting) which ends on Shavuos, was marred, as mentioned above, since they only received then the Torah, and there was yet to be revealed the *tikun* (-rectification) of the Thirteen Attributes of Mercy, which is the aspect of making from the *toaroas*, prayers, as mentioned above. Whereas from Rosh Hashana and Yom Kippur until now we are engaged in making from the *toaroas*, prayers, and this is the main rectification, as mentioned above. And this is also the construct, that the *succuh* needs to have more shade than sun (Succa 1:1), because the sun is the aspect of the Torah, and shade is the aspect of prayer, and the succuh is comprised from a mix of sun and shade, namely from Torah and prayer. However the shade needs to be more, because the main thing is the prayer that is prayed for the fulfillment of the Torah; and prayer such as this is the aspect of action, the aspect of actually fulfilling the Torah, therefore it is the main thing, because (Ethics of Our Fathers 3:17) it is necessary for ones actions to be more than his wisdom, which is the aspect of its (-the *succuh's*) shade more than its sun, as mentioned above.

7.

And therefore on Hoshana Rabba (the 7th day of Succos), which is when the *tikun* (-rectification) is completed, we say then the whole Book of Psalms, for this is the primary rectification which we are engaged in from Rosh Hashana until now – to draw the recital of Psalms into the world, and to engage in hisbodidus, and to make from the *toaroas* (-holy teachings), prayers, for all of this is the aspect of Psalms, as mentioned above.

8.

And this is the aspect of the *kavanos* (-intentions – referring to the Kabbalistic meaning) of the 18 <*chay* – life...> shakings (*naanoo'im*) that are done with the *lulav* and its species (-the four species that the Torah commands to take on Succos), because they are 18 <*chay* – life...> shakings corresponding the 18 blessings of the prayer (-the standing prayer of the 18 benedictions). And it is explained in the writings of the Arizal (see Shaar Hakavanos, Succos, drush 5; Likutay Moharan, torah 33), that the *kavana* (-intention – specifically Kabalastic meaning) of the shakings is in order to draw illumination from the *moachin* (-brains, consciousnesses) that are in the head, into the six extremities (-the six lower *sefiros* – Divine Attributes – the body of *Zehr Anpin* – the Small Countenance), so that the *moachin* (-minds) that are in the six extremities will have the power to illuminate into the *Malchus* (-Kingdom, the female countenance). That is, because when we make from Torah, prayer, this is the aspect of shining the *moachin* (-minds) that are in the six extremities, which is the Torah, to the *Malchus* which is the aspect of prayer, and this is even with an ordinary prayer to fulfill each and every *mitzva*. However, this sort of prayer cannot have the aspect of invoking mercy and entreaty (-as prescribed in Ethics of Our Fathers, as mentioned above), because one cannot yet elaborate with it, and pour out his heart like water directly before the presence of Hashem (Lamentation 2:19) until he comprehensively arouses His mercy blessed He through this. Therefore it is necessary to draw illumination from the *moachin* (-minds) that are in the head, namely from the aspect of *chidooshay* (-novelties in the) Torah, which are drawn from the aspect of the Torah of *Atteeka* (-the Supernal Old Venerable Divine Countenance) *Sisseema* (-sealed), which are the aspect of the roots of the Torah, and through this one knows the nature of each and every *mitzva*, what one can merit through it, and then, through *chidooshay* (-novelties of the) Torah such as these, this way of making from *toaroas* (-holy teachings), prayers, is drawn completely, so that one can pour out his heart like water before Hashem, that he may merit to fulfill every *mitzva* properly, as mentioned previously in the explanation to the concept of the *shofar* (-ritual horn), see there (above, article 5).

9.

And this is the aspect of the *hakafos* (-circling) of Simchas Torah (-the Holiday of the Rejoicing of the Torah, in Israel this is the same day as Shimeenay Atzehress, discussed above, in the diaspora it is celebrated the day after) that we circle with the Torah and say then the entreaties and supplications: "Please Hashem save now/please (Psalms 118:25);" to show that the Torah is still the aspect of *makifin* (-higher intelligence which surrounds in the periphery, encompassing the lower levels) by us, and our entire occupation is to supplicate and entreat Hashem Yisburach to bring the *makif* (higher, surrounding intelligence) inside, that is, that we make from the *toaroas* (-holy teachings), prayers, that the fulfillment of the Torah and mitzvos which we have not yet merited completely, and are in the aspect of *makif* (higher, surrounding intelligence) by us, we should merit to fulfill them perfectly; and this is our entire supplication: "Please Hashem save now/please (Psalms 118:25; the word for save, has the same root as "face", which is the internal intelligence, which is the internalization of the makif). And therefore we are extremely joyous then, because when one merits to consummate prayers such as these that are made from the *toaroas*, the main joy is from there, as is understood from Likutay Moharan, volume 1, torah 22 (article 9), that "*naaseh vinishmah* (Exodus 24:7)" (-we will do and we will listen – the Jews response in acceptance of the Torah), which are the aspect of Torah and prayer, are the main joy, the aspect of what our Rabbis o.b.m. exposited (Shabbos 88a) on the crowns (-that the Jews were crowned with immediately upon their aforementioned response. Crowns are the aspect of *makifin*) of *naaseh vinishmah*, that in future the Holy One Blessed He will return them (-they were taken away due to the sin of the golden calf) to us, regarding them it is said (Isaiah 35:10), "and eternal joy is on their heads" (-thus we see that the crowns, the *makifin*, are the aspect of joy). And the foremost perfection of joy is through *yirah* (fear – of Heaven), which is the aspect of prayer, the aspect of (Psalms 2:11), "and rejoice in trepidation (-the aspect of fear);" see there.

10.

And this is the construct of the water libations on the holiday (of Succos), because this is the aspect of (Samuel I:7:6), "And they drew water, and they poured (it) out before Hashem," which is said by Samuel; and Rashi explains, that they poured out their hearts like water, that is the aspect of the completion of prayer, which is completed on Succos, as mentioned above. And this the aspect of the rejoicing of the Bais Hashoayva (-House of the Drawing (of the water for the libations) – the Temple during Succos when the water libations were performed, every night there was tremendous celebration and rejoicing initiating the drawing of the water), which is so called based on what is written (Isaiah 12:3), "And you (plural) should draw water joyously from the springs of the salvation," and the *targum* (-aramaic translation of Yonason ben Uziel) renders this: "and you will receive a new set of teachings," namely the aspect of the *chidooshay* (-novelties in the) Torah mentioned above, that are drawn from the aspect of *Atteeka* (-the Supernal Old Venerable Divine Countenance) *Sisseema* (-sealed), and they are the aspect of actual "springs of the salvation," the aspect of (Proverbs 18:4), "gushing stream source of wisdom (-acronym NaChMaN)," because gushing out of them are endless *aitzoas* (-advice, remedies) and wondrous salvations without boundaries, which are capable of saving everyone, even be one as he may. And from *chidooshay* (-novelties of the) Torah such as these, when one merits to make from *toaroas*, prayers, through this one merits to pour out like water before Hashem, every single person according to his familiarity with the maladies of his heart and his pains, how he is distant from Hashem Yisburach, and to what evil vices, and bad desires, and vile confusions he fell to by his sins, and all that he undergoes every day, all the time, for everything can be found in these prayers that are made from these *toaroas*, as mentioned above, and to express his words before Him blessed He, invoking mercy and entreatingly over all of them, like a son pleads disarmingly before his father, all of this being the aspect of drawing water mentioned above. And this is (Isaiah 12:3), "and you should draw water joyously," because when one merits to draw this way in perfection, it is certainly a boundless joy, the aspect of (Psalms 2:11), "and rejoice with trepidation," mentioned above (end of article 9), the aspect of (Isaiah 35:10), "and eternal joy," as mentioned above regarding the joy of (the holiday of) Simchas Torah and the *hakafos* (-circling).

11.

And this is (Jeremiah 31:21), "Until when will you avoid (Me) wayward daughter, for Hashem has created a new phenomenon in the land, the female seeks out <*tissoavaiv*> the male," and Rashi explains the verse in regard to repentance, and this is Rashi's words: Avoid – hide from me, for you (feminine) are embarrassed to return to me because of your way. Behold a new phenomenon has been created in the land, that the female seeks out the male to ask him to marry her, <*tissoavaiv* – seek out, the root being: circle> an expression as in (Song of Songs 3:2), "<*assoavuvuh*> I will circle about in the city I will seek etc., here ends the quotation of Rashi. And upon first glance, what does the concept of *nekaiva tissoavaiv gehvehr* - that the female will seek the male, have to do with the matter of repentance? However, based on what was expounded above, it is very clear, because a man and a woman, a male and female, their root is above in an extremely high place, for all the supernal unifications (*yichudim*) are dependent on them, as is understood in all the books of the holy Zohar and the writings of the Arizal, and they are the aspect of the Written Torah and the Oral Torah, which are the aspects of Torah and prayer, because prayer is the aspect of the Oral Torah, because the main wholesomeness of prayer is when one makes from the Torah, prayer, and this is not possible, except through the aspect of the Oral Torah, which is the aspect of the general collective of all the *cheedushin* (-original concepts) of the Torah, which all stem from the aspect of the spirit of Messiah, who will merit to a renewal of the Torah in absolute perfection, which is the aspect of the Torah of Atteeka (-Supernal Venerable Divine Countenance) Sisseemuh (-sealed).

And through these novelties, this way of making from *toaroas* (-holy teachings), prayers, will be drawn into the world completely, as mentioned above, and then we will not be ashamed to return to Hashem Yisburach even if we did what we did, and even if we are now the way we know ourselves, each and everyone, even still, through this way of making from *toaroas*, prayers, which is drawn now from the *hisnoatzitzus* (-sparkling, flaring) of Messiah, which is *misnoatzaitz* (-sparking) to come soon in our days, for certainly he will not procrastinate any more Heaven forbid, as he hindered until now, through this way we all, however we may be, can return to Hashem Yisburach, since our entire repentance, and our hope, and our expectancy to

Hashem Yisburach is just through prayer, that we hope and supplicate, and entreat from Hashem Yisburach that He return us to Him, and help us, and save us with His great might and His wondrous kindness, to fulfill the entire Torah, from here on. Therefore, certainly we have no reason now to fall in our resolve from praying to return to Hashem Yisburach due to our improper conduct, for behold, on the contrary, this itself is our request from Hashem Yisburach, that He should help us rectify our conduct, and in this we can engage always, until He will have compassion on us from the Heavens, to fulfill our request. And in truth, whoever is strong in this way, to abound in hisbodidus and to make from *toaroas* (-holy teachings), prayers, and to abound with prayers such as these always, finally, in the end, he certainly will return to Hashem Yisburach, as I understood from the mouth of our master, leader, and holy rabbi (Nachman).

And this is what the prophet screams (Jeremiah 31:21), "Until when will you avoid (Me), wayward daughter," that is, the prophet cries foul, and screams, and shouts out, dreadful and horrific, over what we fall in our resolve every time from returning due to our many bad deeds, that we have repeatedly perpetuated in our foolishness innumerable times, as it is known that most of those that distance themselves from Hashem Yisburach, it is because of falls such as these, since they see that it has been so long that they desired to return, and each time they fell more, and the *baal duvur* (-litigator- evil inclination, Satan) incites them and overpowers them more and more, and because of this their hands are weakened (-they are disheartened) from further returning, as though there is no hope Heaven forbid. And regarding this the prophet screams, "Until when will you avoid (Me)," "until when will you hide from me, for you are ashamed to return to Me because of your way. Behold a new phenomenon has been created in the land, that the female seeks out the male," that is, that the female, "the Heaven fearing woman" (Proverbs 31:30, see above article 1), which is the aspect of prayer, chases after the Torah, which is only when one makes from the *toaroas*, prayers, for what is now the way of a man to seek the woman, this is because of her low status, because now the prayer is undeveloped (*katnus* – childhood, lower consciousness), and most of the prayers are for necessities of the body, and then (-as such) the prayer does not have cogency (lit: opening of the mouth) to pursue the Torah and make demands of it (/propose), because prayer which is for bodily needs does not have completion except by means of the Torah etc, as mentioned previously at the beginning of this discourse.

And therefore it is certainly not a good nor truthful way to say, "I will study Torah in order that I will be able to pray for my bodily needs," because this is the aspect of (Ethics of Our Father 4:5), do not make them (-the Torah) an ax to hew with (-i.e. to use the Torah for personal benefit), because his primary intention is for the necessities of his body, just, since he is embarrassed to ask for his needs, he therefore studies so that he will ask for his needs; and this is certainly very abhorrent. Therefore it is not appropriate for such a pray, that the prayer should request of the Torah, as mentioned above; but the prayer which is made from the *toaroas* (-holy teachings), which is to fulfill the Torah, then the prayer is constructed with great perfection, and then certainly there is no shame for the prayer, the aspect of the woman, to pursue after her husband, which is the Torah, in the aspect of, "the female seeks out the male," the aspect of

(Isaiah 4:1), "seven women will grasp one man etc.," because a perfect prayer such as this can certainly pursue after the Torah and request it, "Study and engage in Torah for my sake, in order that I will be able to make from the *toaroas*, these prayers, because my whole intention is to do the will of my Creator." [This is the import of the prophecy mentioned above:] "And through this way you need not be ashamed to return to Me always, be what may, because my mercies are inexhaustible, and every time you can come in prayer and entreaty to request of Me that I draw you close, from here on."

And certainly your words will be effective finally, in the end, because this way is drawn from the aspect of the final redemption, which has no cessation, for it is the aspect of "wellsprings of salvation" (see above article 10), which never ever stops, as mentioned above, for it is the way that our forefathers traversed from time immemorial: Abraham, Isaac, and Jacob, Moses, Aaron, Josef, David and all the aboriginal tzaddikim who engaged in prayer and hisbodidus plentifully to draw close to Hashem Yisburach; just that in the beginning they were still unable to merit to this completely, to make from Torah, prayer, since the Torah was still not in the world, and they were forced to engage copiously in prayer – all the forefathers until Moses, who merited with his abundant prayers, the aspect of (Psalms 90:1), "A prayer of Moses," to draw Torah. However, the time still hadn't come to return and insert the Torah into prayer and to pave this way in the world, to make from the *toaroas* (-holy teachings), prayers, and therefore there was what was, that the *airev rav* (-mixed multitude) caused the Israelites also to sin etc., until there came King David r.i.p., who completes the seven shepherds, and he was the root of the soul of Messiah, and he began to arouse this way, to make from *toaroas*, prayers, this being the aspect of Psalms etc., as mentioned above. However, the main completion will be in the days of Messiah, for then this way will be renewed entirely. And by virtue of this way we will not be embarrassed nor will be shamed ever, for however it may be, we will return to Hashem Yisburach, as mentioned above.

And this is the aspect of (Psalms 109:4), "In place of my love they bedevil me, and I am prayer," that is, "love" is the aspect of the Torah, the aspect of (Proverbs 31:26), "the Torah of Kindness," as our master, leader, and rabbi o.b.m. wrote in Likutay Moharan, volume 1, torah 33, on the verse (Psalms 42:9), "[In the] day Hashem will command His kindness," that all the *mitzvos* of the Torah are an aspect of love and kindness etc. see there. And this is, "In place of my love," that all that I merited to the aspect of love, the aspect of the *mitzvos* of the Torah; all that I desire to begin to engage in any Torah and *mitzva*, which are the aspect of love - "they bedevil me," that they incite and bedevil me, and desire to make me fall Heaven forbid, and I don't know what to do against this incitement, therefore, "and I am prayer," that is, all my occupation that I do with the Torah, which is the aspect of love, I make from it prayer, and through this I still hope for salvation, that I merit to truly return to Hashem Yisburach.

And now you will see wonders, what is brought in the holy Zohar (Tikunay Zohar, tikun 13, page 53b, and see Siddur Kol Yaakov, the *kavanos* of Succos) that on Succos it is the aspect of (Jeremiah 31:21), "the female will seek out <*tissoavaiv* - circle> the male," the aspect of (Isaiah 4:1), "seven women will grasp one man," see there. And this is the construct of the *hakafos* (circling) with the lulav (-the four species taken on Succos) around the Sefer (book – i.e. scroll) Torah, and the saying of prayers and *hoashanos* (-every supplication is sandwiched between cries for salvation) around (-while circling) the Torah, in the aspect of, "the female will circle the male," as mentioned above, namely, that we draw the Torah into the prayer, to make from the *toaroas*, prayers, because then, on Succos, the prayer ascends through that which we engage then in drawing the way of making from *toaroas*, prayers, which is the aspect of, "the female seeks out the male," the aspect of, "and seven women will grasp one man," as mentioned above. And this is, "and seven women," the aspect of prayer, which is the aspect of, "a Heaven fearing woman," the aspect of (Psalms 119:164), "seven times a day I sang out Your praise etc.." And this is what the scripture concludes (Isaiah 4:1), "we will eat our own bread and wear our own clothing," because the bread and the clothing, which is the livelihood that is drawn through regular prayers for bodily needs, (and) the main livelihood is drawn from the Torah, because this type of prayer hasn't the power to give sustenance except for what it receives from the Torah, from where everything is provided etc.. However, prayer that is made from the Torah, this prayer is itself Torah, and has by it all the provisions, since its entire endeavor is to fulfill the Torah, where all the provisions are from. And this is, "our bread" - specifically (-our, for they are the source of the provisions) - "we will eat, and our clothing we will wear."

And this is (continuation of the verse), "just may we be called by your name, gather (-remove, end) our shame," that is, to raise the prayer from the embarrassment and shaming of the degradation of exile, from the aspect of (Psalms 12:9), "the shame of degradation etc.," "these (-prayer) are the matters etc." (Brachos 6b; see above, article 1), whereas prayer such as this, is the aspect of (Proverbs 12:4), "A woman of valor is the crown of her husband," the aspect of (Proverbs 31:29), "Many daughters amassed wealth (/achieved virtue) but you are above (-surpass) all of them," the aspect of (Proverbs 31:11), "The heart of her husband trusts her," for there is a woman whose husband needs to provide for her, to bring her all the necessary sustenance, and she just fixes the food, cooking and baking etc., and this is the aspect of regular prayer for bodily needs, where all the provisions of the prayer are brought from her husband, who is the Torah, just that the main completion of the cooking (-preparation) of the provisions needs to be through prayer, in order that it can come down to provide for the world. However, there is a woman of valor (aishes cha'yil), that all of her husband's wealth and vitality is – from her, the aspect of (Proverbs 31:11), "her husband's heart has confidence in her," and this is the aspect of the prayers that are made from the toaroas, to fulfill the Torah, that the whole life of the Torah, which is the fulfillment of the Torah, is through her, that is, through the prayer, as mentioned above.

And this is what is written adjacent there in Jeremiah, after the verse, "until when will you avoid (Me) etc.," "Behold days are coming, says Hashem, and I will sow the House of Israel etc. the seed of man and the seed of animal." And Rashi explains: The good and sensible among them, I will plant all of them to be My seed. "The seed of man and the seed of animal" - Yonason translates this: I will erect them like people and make them successful like animals, who are not taken to task for their sins. That is, "man" is the aspect of Torah, the aspect of (Numbers 19:14), "This is the Torah, man," the aspect of the holy Divine Name "Mah" (-lit: what. "Mah" has the same numerical value as "adam"- man (45), and is the numerical value of the Divine Name Y'H'V'H when each letter is elongated using the letter alef for all the necessary vowels: YUD-HAy (Ay=alef)-VUV (U=alef)-HAy (Ay=alef)); "animal" is the aspect of prayer, because animal <bihaima> has the numerical value as the holy Divine Name "Ban" (referring to the elongation of the Divine Name Y'H'V'H with the numerical value of 52, in this format: YUD - HH (the letters Hay)-VV-HH), which is the aspect of Malchus (-Kingdom, the final, feminine *sefira* – Divine Attribute), as is brought down (Aitz Chaim, Shaar 48, Drush 2), because the essence of the prayer is that one should set himself like an animal (see Chulin 5b), as if he doesn't have any intellect to figure things out for himself, (and) just supplicate and entreat for mercy, in the aspect of (Psalms 42:2), "Like a hart cries out for fountains of water," and like it is written (Joel 1:20), "Like the animals of the field I cry out to You," the aspect of (Isaiah 38:14), "Like a swallow and a crane I chirp, I moan like a dove." And through this aspect, that He sows Israel, as seed of man and seed of animal together, namely that they make from *toaroas*, prayers, through this they merit to draw salvation to all of them, even to those who are the aspect of actual animals due to their conduct, because through this way they will also merit to repentance and to forgiveness of sin, the aspect of, "I will erect them as people and make them successful as animals, who are not taken to task for their sins," because the foremost repentance and forgiveness of sin is through this, because it is the aspect of the Thirteen Attributes of Mercy, through which is afforded the primary forgiveness and *tikun* (-rectification), as mentioned above. And this is what is written adjacent there (Jeremiah 31:30/31), "Behold days are coming

and I will make a covenant with the House of Israel etc.,"
that is as mentioned above, because through this way we
will merit to fulfill the Torah, in the aspect of (verse 32),
"And I will put My Torah inside of them, and upon their
hearts I will write it." "Heart" is the aspect of prayer,
because the service of the heart is prayer (Taanis 2a), namely
that the Torah will be written inside the heart through that
which they will write from the *toaroas*, prayers, which are
the aspect of the heart, and through this we will return to
Him blessed He in truth, and He will draw us close in His
mercy, in the aspect of (continuation of the verse), "And I will
be for them G-d, and they will be for me a nation."

12.

And this is the aspect of Jacob, and Leah, and Rachel.
Rachel is the aspect of the Oral Torah, which is (Isaiah 53:7),
"like a lamb <*ruchel* – same as the Hebrew Rachel> before those
who shear it," for everyone shears and make halachic
decisions from it, as is explained in Likutay Moharan,
volume 1, torah 12 (article 1). Leah is the aspect of prayer,
the aspect of (Genesis 29:17), "And Leah's eyes were tender,"
for she would cry that she shouldn't fall into Esau's portion
(Buva Basra 123a), in the aspect of (Jeremiah 21:9), "with crying
they will come, and with entreaties I will transport them."
Jacob is the aspect of the collective entirety of the Torah,
the aspect of (Deuteronomy 33:4), "The Torah, Moses
commanded to us, an inheritance to the Congregation of
Jacob," namely the aspect of the Written Torah. Because
the Written Torah and the Oral Torah are the aspect of man
and woman, the aspect of Jacob and Rachel, as is known
(Aitz Chaim, Shaar 37, Chapter 1). And we already explained (in

Likutay Halachos, article 16) that the essential prayer which is made from Torah is through the Oral Torah, which is the aspect of *Cheedushim* (novelties) of the Torah, which are drawn for the Thirteen Methods (*meedoas*) etc., for specifically through this, one knows (how) to make from the *toaroas* (-holy teachings), prayers. And therefore Leah and Rachel are considered as one, as is brought in the holy Zohar (see Zohar, Vayikra 244b), and the writings of the Arizal (see Keheelas Yaakov, entry of Yaakov). And Jacob, who is the foundation of the Torah, all of his service was for Rachel ("in/with Rachel," Genesis 29:18,20,25), who is the aspect of the Oral Torah, because there is no completeness to the Written Torah without the Oral Torah, and it is impossible to produce any devotion, or *mitzvos*, or good deeds from the Written Torah, except by means of the Oral Torah, because from the Written Torah itself there is no complete knowledge of any *mitzva*, as all of this is explained elsewhere (in Likutay Halachos there). And therefore all of Jacob's service was for Rachel. However, in reality it is impossible to merit to completely fulfill the Torah and the *mitzvos*, which are the aspects of Jacob and Rachel, except through prayer and entreaty, as mentioned above, which are the aspect of Leah, as mentioned above.

And since Torah and prayer are dependent upon each other, for it is impossible to merit to Torah except through prayer, and it is impossible to merit to prayer except through Torah, because it is necessary to study Torah in order to know what to pray for, but to merit to study Torah, also needs prayer, like we pray everyday: "And illuminate our eyes in/with Your Torah," "and put in our hearts understanding etc., to learn and to teach etc.," and because of this, one doesn't know from where it begins. And therefore even our father Jacob r.i.p. wasn't able to figure it out, and thought that he must bond first with Rachel, who is the aspect of the Oral Torah, because it seemingly looks that way, that it is necessary to begin with the enterprise of the Torah, as mentioned above. And also because Rachel is the aspect of the revealed world (*alma di'isgalya*), as is brought down (Zohar, Genesis 54a), that is, because everyone sees the virtue of *cheedooshin* (-novelties) of the Torah which are drawn from the Oral Torah and are cherished in everyone's eyes since they have great wisdom and intellect apparent to all, and wisdom is important in everyone's eyes; whereas Leah is the aspect of the concealed world (*alma di'iscassya*) as is brought down (Zohar, Genesis 54a), because the importance and virtue of prayer is sealed and hidden from everyone's eyes, because prayer is just the aspect of faith, and it is impossible to understand the matter of prayer with any intellect whatsoever. And therefore regarding prayer it says (Psalms 12:9), "when the exalted are scorned," and our Rabbis o.b.m. explicated (Brachos 6b, above articles 1, 6, 11): these are matters etc., and people denigrate them (t.n. the beginning of this verse states that the evil people circle, which is exactly the problem – the denigration, as explained above in article 11, that the aspect of circling belongs to prayer).

And this is the aspect of (Genesis 29:17 – the verse speaks first of Leah), "And Rachel was of beautiful visage and beautiful complexion – and Leah's eyes were tender," because the beauty of the splendor of the Oral Torah everyone sees, and is important in everyone's eyes, and everyone runs to the mishna (Buvu Metziah 33b); but, "(and) the eyes of Leah are tender," for she was constantly crying to not fall into Esau's lot. And this is an allusion to *Kinnesses Yisroel* (the Congregation of Israel), regarding each and everyone of Israel,

276

that it necessary to cry so much, like Leah, to the extent that her eyes were tender, so as not to fall into the lot of the *Sammech Mem* (-Satan – referring to him by the first two letters of his name), Heaven forbid, who is Esau's [supernal] minister. Whereas the virtue and importance of this matter of prayer not everyone sees, because it is the aspect of the concealed world, as mentioned above, and therefore even the kosher (-upstanding) people do not run after it so much, and on the contrary, they denigrate it, as mentioned above, and even Jacob was not able to figure it out, and served specifically "with (-for) Rachel (Genesis 29:18,20,25)," as mentioned above.

And Laban the Aramean (Syrian) in his great deceit <*rama'os* – same as Aramean> desired to trick Jacob and switch Leah with Rachel on him, because Laban did not know whatsoever the prominence of prayer, for he certainly denigrated prayer completely, and therefore he thought that Leah has no importance at all, and he thought that he deceived Jacob deviously with what he switched Leah with Rachel on him. However, in reality everything was from Hashem, for His thoughts, blessed He, are extremely profound (Psalms 92:6), and in truth everything was for the very best, because the righteous Rachel gave over her signs (-code, to validate her identity on their wedding night) to her sister Leah so that she would not be embarrassed, because Jacob gave signs (-a code) to Rachel, the aspect of (Jeremiah 31:20/21), "Put up signs for yourself;" and our Rabbis o.b.m. explicated (Eruvin 54b), make signs (-mnemonics) for the Torah, so that you don't forget and don't mix it up, so as not to be brazen faced against the Torah distorting the *halacha* (-the given ruling). And all the signs are in the aspect of the Oral Torah, which is the aspect of Rachel, for there is the placement of all the *messoares* (lit: tradition, refers to the text of the Torah, exact to the letter, especially when this presents different perspective from the pronunciation) and the signs (-mnemonics; series of words or abbreviations, each word or letter representing a concept, ruling, or discourse); but Rachel, who is the aspect of the Oral Torah, gives over all the signs to her sister Leah, who is the aspect of prayer, and teaches her how to speak with Jacob, who is the entirety of the Torah, and how to make from the Torah, prayer, and then Rachel and Leah are truly combined together, because the Oral Torah and prayer are both the same aspect, as mentioned above, and both of them conjugate with Jacob, who is the foundation of the collective entirety of the Torah. And all of this was in order to produce the twelve tribes of Y-ah, who have in them (- their names) forty nine letters, which correlate to the forty nine gates of repentance, which is the aspect of Psalms, all of this being the aspect of making from the *toaroas* (-holy teachings), prayers, as mentioned above. Because in reality, with all the matters that it is unknown from where to start, like the aforementioned matter of Torah and prayer, it is necessary to begin with both of them, that is, to study part of the day and to engage in prayer part of the day, and then, even though at first one will not know the order of the prayer very well, and how to make from Torah, prayer, even still, Hashem Yisburach has mercy on him, and illuminates his eyes, and gives over to him the signs and ways of the Torah, and teaches him according to his aspect, how to make from Torah, prayer, and subsequently, through prayer he knows (how) to attain more Torah, and so it is each time, for each one supports its friend; prayer the Torah, Torah the prayer. And this is the secret, what first Rachel, who is the Oral Torah, gives over her signs to Leah, who is prayer, as mentioned above.

And this is the aspect of what is presented in the words of our Rabbis o.b.m. (opening to Eicha – Lamentations- Rabba 24) that Rachel herself lay under the bed, and spoke the signs with Jacob when he was conjugating with Leah, in order that Leah should not be shamed; and in the writings of the Arizal (Likutay Torah, Ke Seesa, in Taamay Hamitzvos) there is presented a great and awesome secret pertaining this, that this is a secret of what occurs in the supernal unions <yichudim>, that when the (Divine) light which is called Jacob mates with the (Divine) light called the aspect of Leah, then the aspect of Rachel is under the bed etc., see there in Aitz Chaim. And according to our theorem presented above, this secret is very in compliance with the construct of prayer mentioned above (as is known in *kavanos* (-mystical intentions) that all the supernal unifications <yichudim> are conducted in accordance to the devotion of those below, and specifically through prayer, which is the primary completion of the unification), that is, because when an Israelite enters (-begins) to pray his prayer and words before Hashem Yisburach, that he should merit to draw close to Him, and to fulfill His Torah and His *mitzvos*, and desires to make from Torah, prayer, but he still has not a word (on his tongue) to say, because he still does not know the ways and the signs of the Torah, and he doesn't know how to pray, and to speak, and converse, then the aspect of Rachel, who is the aspect of the Oral Torah, the aspect of *cheedooshin* (-novelties) of the Torah from *Atteeka* (-venerable transcending Divine Countenance) *Sisseemah* (-sealed), from Whom are drawn the ways to make from *toaroas*, prayers, as mentioned above, (then) she herself has compassion on this Israelite who is praying, which is the aspect of Leah, as mentioned above, and she (-Rachel) gives over to him the signs and the ways of the

Torah, and she herself speaks with her beloved, the aspect of Jacob, the aspect of the collective entirety, root of the Torah, in order that he can make from Torah, prayer, so that the Torah and prayer can mate together, so that they can produce (lit: give birth to) good deeds.

And this is the aspect of the words that are provided to a person when he enters to do hisbodidus and to express his words before Hashem Yisburach, for at the beginning he has no knowledge of anything to say, but when he is strong in resolve, and nonetheless forces himself to speak, then usually words come to him, which never occurred to him that he should say them, and these words are sent to him from Heaven, and are drawn from the aforementioned aspect. And therefore the main parturition is through Leah, who gave birth to six tribes, because the foremost progeny of tzaddikim, which are their good deeds (Rashi on Noah, Genesis 6:9), are by means of prayer, which is the aspect of Leah, the concealed world (*alma di'iscasya*; Zohar, Genesis 154a), as mentioned above. And also the entire parturition of Rachel was just in the merit of her giving over the signs to her sister, as our Rabbis o.b.m. explicated (Beraishes Rabba 73:4) on the verse (Genesis 30:22), "And G-d remembered Rachel," that is, that all the progeny of the tzaddikim, that they produce (lit: give birth to) good deeds through their Torah, which is the main thing, because (Ethics of Our Fathers 1:17), the explication is not the main thing, rather it is the action (-carrying out), the essential parturition is just through giving over the signs to Leah, who is prayer, namely, through this that also all their Torah learning is in order to merit to make from their Torah, prayers, as mentioned above. Because all the tzaddikim did not merit to their (high) levels in the service of Hashem, except through hisbodidus and prayers etc., as is delineated in his (Rabbi Nachman's) holy words (Words of Rabbi Nachman, article 229).

And therefore Jacob merited that his maidservants also were included in the holiness, because maidservant <shifcha - 393> has the gematria (-numerical value) of "mishna" <395> with the inclusives, as is brought down in the writings of the Arizal (see the forward of Rabbi Chaim Vital to Shaar Hakdumos), and when one doesn't study properly, to adhere, and to practice, and to fulfill, just to be haughty and to annoy, then it is said (Proverbs 30:23), "and a maidservant when she displaces her mistress." However, through proper study of the six orders (sheesha sidray) of the mishna, one selects the good from the bad, through that which one delineates (-selection – marking the boundaries) the permissible from the forbidden etc. (Tikunay Zohar 30, page 75a; Likutay Moharan 31 and 79), and then the aspect of the maidservant is included in holiness under the hand of her mistress, as it was at the splitting of the *Yam Soof* (Red Sea), the maidservant at the sea, saw etc. (- more than the Prophet Ezekiel; Mechilta, Bishalach 3). And it is impossible to produce (lit: give birth) from the Torah, holy offspring, except when one subdues the *sitra-achra* (-other side – realm of evil), until the maidservant is included in holiness. And this is the secret of the forefathers who married maidservants. However, Abraham, even though he subdued the aspect of the bad maidservant <shifcha beesha> through that which Sarah gave over to him her maidservant, and he merited to beget Isaac in holiness, even still there was not a complete reversal of bad to good, and therefore the actual parturition of the maidservant was the birth of the *sitra-achra* (-other side – realm of evil), who is Ishmael.

However, our father Jacob, by means of his having merited
to both of them; to Rachel and to Leah, and both of them
were included together, which is the aspect of making from
the Torah, prayer, which is the main vehicle of completely
subduing the bad maidservant, until she is reversed from
bad to utter good. Because the main subduing of the *sitra-
achra* (-other side – realm of evil) entirely is through prayer
which is made from the *toaroas*, which through this all the
tzaddikim merited to their (high) levels, as mentioned above.
Therefore Jacob merited to marry the maidservants in
complete holiness, to the extent that he merited to sire from
them as well holy and awesome parturition, who are the
tribes of Y-ah, because from Torah by itself, sometimes
there is nurturing to the *sitra-achra*, Heaven forbid, for it is
the aspect of the bad maidservant, which inserts in one's
mind that he should not study *lishma* (-for the sake of Heaven,
particularly the *Shechina*), as mentioned above, and then he is
the aspect of (Proverbs 30:23), "and a maidservant when she
displaces her mistress," which is the aspect of the mishna,
as is alluded in the Tikunay Zohar (Tikun 67, page 98b). And
so too, from prayer by itself the *sitra-achra* can grasp, for it
inserts in one's mind to prayer only for his bodily needs, as
mentioned above. However when Torah and prayer are
combined together, and all his prayer is – that he fulfill the
Torah, in order that he should know (how) to make prayers
from the Torah, that he should merit to guard, and do, and
fulfill, then the Torah and prayer are combined in utter
unity, and then (Psalms 92:10), "all the perpetrators of
iniquity will be scattered," and the *sitra-achra* has
absolutely no suckling, on the contrary, the bad is reversed
to good, and the maidservants are included in holiness,
which is the aspect of Jacob, for through this that he

merited to Leah and Rachel, who are the aspect of Torah and prayer together, through this he merited to sire tribes of Y-ah from the maidservants as well, as mentioned above, and through this is the primary repentance and essential forgiveness of Rosh Hashana and Yom Kippur, for then the sins are turned around to be merits, as mentioned above.

13.

And this is the aspect of Yom Tov (-holidays), during which all *milluchos* (-work) are forbidden like on Sabbath, except for preparation of food (*oachel nefesh*), which is permissible on Yom Tov. Because the main *tachlis* (-purpose) for which all of humanity was created, is Torah and prayer, for this is the main sustaining force, and vitality, and the purpose of every person, for which all the worlds were created, all of it is for the sake of this purpose, that one should merit to engage all his days in Torah and prayer, and go from level to level until the highest level that there is in Torah and prayer. And if a person would merit to this with perfection, then there would be nullified all the toil and burden of all the endeavors and work which are included in the thirty nine *milluchos* (-work; there are 39 categories of work forbidden on Sabbath), because all the exertion of the work for a livelihood, it all came about from the sin of Adam *Hurishon* (-the first), who violated the Torah and prayer, because the *mitzva* that he was commanded not to eat from the *Aitz Hadaas* (Tree of Knowledge) was the aspect of Torah, because in this was included the Torah, as is known (see Likutay Torah, portion of Beraishis, on the verse (3:23) And He etc. sent him from the Garden of Eden). And he also needed to pray then in order to complete the *tikun* (-rectification) of creation to perfection, as Rashi explained on the verse (Genesis 2:5), "And there was no man etc.: when Adam came and prayed for rain – they rained down and they grew, see there. But he ate from the Tree of Knowledge, and with this he violated the aspect of Torah, and also he couldn't pray his prayer, that he needed to pray for the *tikun* (-rectification) of the worlds. And through this there was decreed the exertion of making a livelihood and the thirty nine *milluchos* (-acts of work), the aspect of (Genesis 2:17), "in dreariness you will eat it etc.."

And therefore, now as well, every person according to what he merits to engage in Torah and prayer with more perfection, so too he merits to nullify from himself the *zoohuhma* (stench, pollution) of the snake, for from there stems the burden of the *milluchos* (-acts of work), and he merits that his work is done by others, as it will be in the future, when all of Israel will engage just in Torah and prayer, (as) it is written (Isaiah 61:5), "and strangers will stand and shepherd your sheep etc.." For this is a big principle, that the entire subsistence of the world and all the *shefa* (-provision) are drawn only through Torah and prayer, because the essential creation of the world was through the Torah, as it is written (Proverbs 8:30), "and I was *umoan* (-fostered, to foster, hidden, covered, important) by Him," and our Rabbis explicated (very beginning of the Medrash Rabba), do not read "umoan," rather "Uman" (ooman- craftsman, the tool of the creation (the name of the city where Rabbi Nachman is buried)). And now as well, the entire subsistence of the world and the entire renewal of the Act of Creation that takes place everyday, it is all just through the Torah; however, all the life and *shefa* (-provision) which are drawn through the Torah, their form is not finished completely, and they do not descend to the world, except through prayer, because prayer is the main conduit through which the form of the *shefa* (-provision) is finished for the good and is drawn into the world. And therefore, every person according to what he merits to engage in Torah and prayer, and the main thing is to make from the Torah, prayer, as mentioned above, so too he merits through this to draw all the provisions and blessings, and to nullify from himself the toils and burden of the *milluchos* (-acts of work), as mentioned above.

And this is the difference between Sabbath and Yom Tom (-holidays); that on Yom Tov, *millucha* (-work) to prepare food (*oachel nefesh*) is permissible, and on Sabbath this is also forbidden, because on Sabbath it is the aspect of the future world, when everything will be abolished, and there will only remain Torah and prayer, that the tzaddikim will merit to in the future, therefore (then) on Sabbath there is a cessation of all the thirty nine *milluchos* (-acts of work), because the world subsists just through Torah and prayer, whose holiness is drawn then from the holiness of the future, and there is completion and ascension then in the utmost ascent and perfection. And therefore Sabbath shielded Adam *Hureeshoan* (-the first) as well, as our Rabbis o.b.m. said (Zohar, Exodus 138a). Whereas the Yomim Tovim (-holidays) are a remembrance to the exodus from Egypt (*yetzias Mitzra'im*), which is the first redemption, which was through Moses, through which we merited to receive the Torah, but the aspect of perfect ascension of prayer was not delineated yet then, until the coming of the Messiah, through whom there will be the final redemption. Because in the broad scheme of the world, the first redemption and the final one are the aspect of Moses and David, which is the aspect of Torah and prayer. Therefore on Yom Tov it is still permissible to do *milleches* (-the work) of preparing of food, that is the aspect of the *milluchos* (-acts of work) which are related to man's eating, which is the aspect of the final forming of the *shefa* (-provision) to give life to man, which is done through prayer, as mentioned above. Because the *milluchos* which are still distant from preparation of food, are the aspect of subsistence and the drawing of *shefa* which is done through the Torah, as mentioned above.

And therefore on regular weekdays when the *cheetzoanim* (-externals – evil forces) have a grasp, and great toil is necessary to clarify and raise the Torah and prayer, therefore there is then the exertion of all the thirty nine *milluchos*, which prevail on weekdays, since there is no perfection then of the Torah and prayer, and it is necessary to toil to clarify them, to nullify from them the grasp of the *cheetzoanim* (-externals – evil forces). And as long as there is selection (-identifying and gathering the good from the rest – this is actually one (three) of the 39 categories of *millucha*, and is a general description of the entire function of man's service on the weekdays), *milluchos* are necessary, as is known (see the Siddur of Rabbi Yaakov Kuppel, Shaar Mikru'ay Kodesh); and on Sabbath, due to the holiness of the very day the grasp of the *cheetzoanim* is completely nullified, and the Torah and prayer ascend in great perfection, therefor all the *milluchos* are idle (/nullified) then; but on Yom Tov the holiness of the very day is only drawn in the aspect of the ascension of the Torah, that we merited to receive then after the first redemption, but prayer has yet to be clarified completely. And therefore our Rabbis o.b.m. explicated (Rashi Brachos 6b, brought above, article 12 and elsewhere) that people denigrate it, because the completion of the ascension of prayer will only be in the future by Messiah, as mentioned above.

It comes out that also on Yom Tov, even thought we have the power then to bring up the prayer as well, with more perfection, and more ascension, due to the extra holiness of the Yom Tov, nevertheless it still isn't clarified and does not ascend with perfection like on Sabbath, therefore there still is *milleches oachel nefesh* (-the work of preparation of food), which are the *milluchos* of the final formation of the *shefa* (-provision), which is drawn through prayer, for the prayer still needs clarification, as mentioned above. And in reality, since the prayer isn't perfect, therefore the Torah also isn't in the utmost perfection. And therefore, on regular weekdays the *cheetzoanim* have a grasp on the Torah as well, and it necessary to toil to clarify them, as mentioned above. And like our Rabbis o.b.m. said (Yuma 72b): one who does not merit (to study the Torah properly) – it is made into deadly poison for him, may the Merciful One save us, because Torah and prayer are both dependent on each other, just that nevertheless the violation doesn't effect the Torah so much as it does to prayer, and people do not denigrate so much. And therefore on Yom Tov when there is abundant additional holiness, consequently by the Torah there is no shortcoming and no violation reaches it, just by the prayer, and therefore all *milluchos* are forbidden on it, except for the preparation of food, as mentioned above.

And this is was is explained in the writings (of the Arizal, see at length in the Siddur of Rabbi Yaakov Kuppel, Shaar Mikru'ay Kodesh; Life of Rabbi Nachman, article 135), that on Sabbath very great additional light (-spirituality) is received (clothed) in garments, whereas on Yom Tov the additional light is smaller than (that of) Sabbath, but it is without garments, and all of this is due to what was explained above, because on Sabbath the ascension of prayer is also complete, and through prayer it is possible to receive all the great and awesome lights (clothed) in garments, which are made and finished through prayer, which is the aspect of faith. Because Sabbath is called *Kallah* (-bride) because it is *killoola* (-a composite replete) with *kul* (everything), as is brought down (see Zohar, Beraishis page 265a, and Shemos page 92a), because faith and prayer, which is the aspect of the sanctity of Sabbath, is a composite replete with all the lights of the world, because all the lights, which are impossible to receive through any knowledge, can be received through faith, the aspect of prayer, which is the aspect of Sabbath, as mentioned above. Whereas on Yom Tov, when the additional sanctity of the very day is just in the aspect of Torah, consequently the light received is not so lofty, and it is without garments, because the main garments and vessels are finished through prayer, as mentioned above.

And behold the fundamental ascensions of the prayer is (-takes place) just when one makes from Torah, prayer, and this is what we read the Torah during the prayer, and therefore every day that has more additional holiness, for then the prayer ascends in a greater ascent, therefore we call up more people to read (from the Torah), culminating with Sabbath, for then there is the main completion of the ascensions of the prayer, as mentioned above, therefore seven men read from it, for they correlate the seven shepherds, through whom the Torah and prayer ascend in completion, as mentioned above. And this is what our Rabbis o.b.m. said (Megilla 21b) the reason for the (number) of readers of the Torah is based on cessation of work (-on a day when people go to work, only three people are called up, so as not to make it difficult on the people, on a semi-holiday, four people, on a holiday, five, on Yom Kippur when work is more severely forbidden, six etc.), that on a day when there is a more severe prohibition on doing work, more men are called up to the Torah, that is as was explained above, because the prohibition of doing *millucha* (-work) on Sabbath and Yom Tov is according to the completion of the ascension of the prayer, and likewise, the number of people who go up to the Torah is also according to the ascension of the prayer, because Torah and prayer are dependent on each other, and on a day that the ascension of the prayer isn't complete, and consequently the *cheetzoanim* (-externals – evil forces) still have a grasp on it, so that it is still necessary to do *milluchos* (-work), as mentioned above, also, the Torah does not have so much completion. However, on the holy Sabbath, which is when the Torah and prayer ascend in the utmost perfection, consequently all the *milluchos* are terminated (/idle) completely, and seven men read from it (- the Torah), as mentioned above.

14.

And this is (Deuteronomy 32:2), "Listen heavens etc., my sage advice will precipitate like rain etc.," that certainly my words will enter their ears, similar to what Rashi explains there in his interpretation. And the reason (verse 3), "When I say the Name of Hashem," and I pray in the Name of Hashem, and I will make from the *toaroas* (-holy teachings), prayers, and through this, certainly, "my sage advice will precipitate like rain, my words will distil as dew," and my words will enter your hearts like rain and like dew, and you will merit to fulfill the Torah. Because the main fulfillment of the Torah is through this that one makes from the *toaroas*, prayers, as mentioned above. For the whole song of "*Ha'azeenoo*" (-"Listen" - the second to last portion of the Torah, chapter 32) was said in order to merit in the end of days to fulfill the Torah, as it is written there of the matter (Deuteronomy 31:21), "I will utterly hide My face etc., and this song will resound before him (-the Nation of Israel) as a witness, for it will not be forgotten from the mouths of his progeny," because the song of "*Ha'azeenoo*" is the aspect of prayer, which is the aspect of song and melody, the aspect of the ten types of melody from which King David r.i.p. founded the Book of Psalms, that is, that through this song, Moshe Rabbainu (- our Leader Moses) r.i.p. included the collective entirety of the Torah inside the aspect of song (*sheerah*), which is the aspect of prayer, and through this he illuminated for us this light (-awakening, inspiration, spirituality) to merit to make from the *toaroas*, prayers, through which is the fundamental fulfillment of the Torah in the end of days, the aspect of, "and this song will resonate etc. because it will not be forgotten from the mouth of his progeny etc.," as mentioned above.

And this is (Jeremiah 3:17), "In those days they will no longer say the ark of the covenant of Hashem etc., in that time they will call Jerusalem the throne of Hashem etc., and they will no longer go after the evil wanton of their hearts." Jerusalem <*Yerushalaim*> is *yira-shulaim* (fear-complete) (Beraishis Rabba 56:10), the aspect of prayer, as mentioned above (articles 1, 2, 9, 11), because that is where the Bais Hamikdush (-Temple) is, His house, the House of Prayer (Isaiah 56:7), that is, that the essential perfection of the Torah will be when it will come inside the aspect of Jerusalem, that is, inside the prayer; through which one merits to guard, and to do, and to fulfill, because it is not the explication which is fundamental, rather the conduct (Ethics of Our Fathers 1:17). And this is (Hosea 14:3), "Take with you words and return to Hashem" - "words," specifically. For certainly it is very difficult to merit to repentance, since also before he sinned and became soiled with sins and was caught in the traps of the *yetzehr hurra* (-evil inclination), he didn't have the strength to stand up against it, all the more so afterwards, how can he stand up against it, after he already caught up in what he was caught? Therefore the foremost repentance is – through the recital of Psalms, which is the aspect of hisbodidus, and most essential – when one makes from the *toaroas*, prayers, as mentioned above, for then, at least he can speak with his mouth, and request from Hashem Yisburach for all the words (/matters) of the Torah, for every single *mitzva*, that he should merit to fulfill it, and return to Him, and specifically concerning all the things that he already transgressed (them); and through this certainly one merits to repentance, in the aspect of, "take words with you, and return to Hashem," as mentioned above.

And this is the aspect of (Psalms 111:10), "The beginning (/preceding/foremost) of wisdom is fear of Hashem," namely, that it is necessary to preempt one's fear of sin to his wisdom, because the *tachlis* (-purpose, fundamental, utmost) of the Torah is – repentance and good deeds (see Brachos 17a). Except, how does one merit this? Addressing this it (-the verse) concludes, "his praise <tiheeluso> stands forever," that is, through *Tehilim* (-Psalms, same root as "praise"), which is the aspect of making from *toaroas*, prayers, he will merit to this. And this is (the middle of the verse), "good intellect to all who do them," because this is drawn from the aspect of supernal intellect, from the aspect of the Torah of *Atteeka* (-

the Old Venerable Divine Countenance) *Sisseemah* (-sealed), which is the aspect of good intellect; because certainly it is good and wondrous intellect to draw fulfillment of the Torah through the aspect of "his praise <*tiheelusso*> stands forever," which is the aspect of *Tehilim* (-Psalms), to make from the *toaroas*, prayers. And this is, "his prays stands forever," because this aspect stands forever, because through this there will be the final redemption, which will be complete redemption forever and for all eternity. For it is impossible to ever ruin this aspect, the aspect of (Jeremiah 31:30-1), "I will make a covenant with them etc. not like the covenant etc.." And this is the aspect of (Zechariah 14:7), "and it will be one day [it is] known to Hashem, not day and not night," because prayer such as this, is above time, because it is "not day," which is Torah, "and not night," which is prayer, because it is replete with both of them. And then there will be a fulfillment of what is written afterwards (verse 9), "And Hashem will be King over the entire world, it will be on that day Hashem is One and His Name is One.

CHAZAK [It is/be STRONG] CHAZAK [STRONG] ViNiSCHAZEK
[and let us STRENGTHEN ourselves]

Blessed is the Giver of strength to the tired, and to those without strength He increases power.

Finished and Complete Praise G-d Creator of the World!

Na Nach Nachma Nachman MeUman!

Rabbi Nachman

of

Breslov

Who He Was and What He Said

RABBI MOSES FEINSTEIN
455 F. D. R. DRIVE
New York, N. Y. 10002

ORegon 7-1222

משה פיינשטיין
ר"מ תפארת ירושלים
בנוא יארק

בע"ה

לכבוד אחינו בני ישראל, כברכת שלום וברכה וכט"ס,

באתי בזה להפליג על הגאון ר' ישראל דוב אדעסער שליט"א, שבא לכאן
מארצנו הקדושה, ונבצשתי עמו לפני חג הפסח, וראיתי פתק סדרי שיש
לו, דבר נפלא מאד.

הוא איש חשוב מאד, ויש לו ידיעות גדולות בחכמה הקבלה, ובדי
לקבלו נכבוד הראוי לה, ולחזכו כפי שאפשר, כפרט ברצונו להדפיס
ספרי האדמו"ר רבינו נחמן מברסלב זצ"ל, וכל אלו שיעזרו, יתברכו
בכל הברכות.

ועל זה באתי על החתום לכבוד התורה, בז' אייר שדמ"ח.

משה פיינשטיין

I am writing on behalf of a most unusual individual, Rabbi
Yisroel Dov Odesser shlita, from Israel. This individual is
a Uoan in Torah. I had the pleasure of recently meeting with
him and was inspired by a secret document which he possesses.

Rabbi Odesser is soliciting funds to enable him to print
Rabbi Nachman's seforim, and it is a great mitzvah to assist
him in this endeavor. Hashem will reward all those that so
assist him.

M. Feinstein

Rabbi Moshe Feinstein

Famous Powerful Quotations and Teachings of Rabbi Nachman

1. It's not enough to believe in G-d and His Tzadikim, you also must believe in yourself. [Words of Rabbi Nachman 140; Likutay Halachos, Laws of an Object Deposited for Safekeeping and Watchmen 5:7; Laws of the First of the Month 7:35; Outpouring of the Soul 92]

2. It is forbidden to be old – neither an old saint or an old devotee, being old is not good. One should always start living and do good deeds as if it is his/her first time. Elders of Holiness constantly lengthen their days expanding their consciousness with fear of Heaven. In this way they reveal and draw the Divine Will making it clear that the world is governed completely by Divine Providence, thus nullifying all the philosophers and scientists, their philosophies and wisdoms. Giving charity helps to open these gates of renewal and Divine Desire (The converse also holds true; leaders and rabbis who do not actively renew their devotions to G-d with new excitement, knowledge, intensity, and desire, cause the Holy Faith to be shrouded in the darkness, gloom, and depression of philosophy and science). [Likutay Moharan 60; Likutay Halachos, Laws of Tefilin 5:5; Likutay Aitzoas, Fear and Devotion 25]

3. When a person knows that everything that happens to him is for the best, this is a taste of the world to come. [Likutay Moharan 4]

4. The main job of a Jew is to wake up for midnight (which is 6 hours after nightfall). [Words of Rabbi Nachman 301]

5. Know that the primary essence of exile is only our lack of belief. [Likutay Moharan 7]

6. Gan Ayden (Eden - heaven) and Gi'henom (hell) are literally in this world. [Likutay Moharan 22]

7. A Jewish person needs to always look at the wisdom within everything in order that it will enlighten him so that he can come close to G-d through each thing. Because this wisdom is a great light and it will enlighten all his ways. [Likutay Moharan 1]

8. All the deficiencies are in reality only deficiencies of 'daas' (realization of knowledge), as the Talmud revealed, if one has daas he has everything, and if one does not have daas, he has nothing. [Likutay Moharan 21]

9. Everybody says there is this world and the coming world. Behold, the coming world -- we believe that the coming world exists; perhaps this world also exists in some world, because here it looks like hell, for everybody is full of great afflictions all the time, and he (Rabbi Nachman) said that this world does not exist at all. [Likutay Moharan vol. 2, 119]

10. Know! You need to judge every person favorably, even someone who is completely wicked, you need to search and find any little bit of good. By finding in him a little good and judging him favorably you actually bring him over to the side of merit and you can return him in teshuva (repentance). [Likutay Moharan 282]

11. A person also needs to find in himself a little bit of good. Because no matter how low a person is, how can it be that he didn't do one good thing in his entire life? [Likutay Moharan 282]

12. Every single Jew has a point in them that is uniquely precious. And it is with this point that he bestows upon, enlightens, and arouses the heart of others. We all need to accept this arousal and this unique point from each other. As it says, "And they receive one from another" (Isaiah 3). [Likutay Moharan 34]

13. Every single Jew has in him a portion of G-d above. [Likutay Moharan 35]

14. Every single Jew is a portion of G-d above, and the essence of G-dliness is in the heart. This G-dliness, which resides in the heart of a Jewish person, is infinite, for the light of its flame reaches infinity, that is, his yearnings and desires are without end or limit. [Likutay Moharan 49]

15. Just as G-d constricted His infinite light in creating the world, for due to the greatness of the light there was no room for creation, so too a person needs to constrict the infinite light of his heart in order to serve G-d in measure and in steps, for if the light would remain unconstricted it would be impossible to serve Him. So it turns out, that this "constriction" of light, of both good and bad desires, actually makes room for its own "revelation." [Likutay Moharan 49]

16. There are two concealments. When Hashem is hidden in one concealment, it is certainly very hard to find Him, but nevertheless, since it is only one concealment a person is able to exert himself and search until he finds Him, for at least he knows that Hashem is hidden. However, when Hashem is hidden in a concealment within a concealment, that is, the concealment itself is hidden from the person, in other words, he has no idea that Hashem is hidden from him, then it is extremely difficult to find Him, for he doesn't even know that Hashem is hidden. (In this

atmosphere the Kingdom of Evil prevails, encouraging people to covet and desire to amass and accumulate possessions). Even still certainly G-d is there giving life and sustenance, and when one reads aloud the Torah, which is in fact a composition of the Names of G-d, he is calling G-d to reveal Himself, and all layers of concealment are transformed to be the most profound and intimate presence of G-d! [Likutay Moharan 56]

17. There is no despair in the world whatsoever! [Likutay Moharan vol. 2, 78]

18. Wherever a person is, even in the depth of defilement and filth, G-d can be found, even in the lowest places it is G-d who is sustaining everything with the letters of the Torah. However, due to the impurity, the Torah there must be of the most secret and esoteric. Even still, when one holds on to the belief in G-d, and screams out to Him, "Where is my holiness?!" He reveals the signs of G-d, and gains profound G-d Knowledge. [Likutay Moharan vol. 2, 12]

19. A person must know that "G-d's glory fills the entire world" (Isiah 6), and "There is no place void of Him" (Tikunay Zohar), and "He fills all worlds and surrounds all worlds" (Zohar)... even in the most defiled places there is G-dliness, for He gives life to everything as it says, "And you give life to everything" (Nechemia 9). So even if a person is stuck in the lowest of places, he cannot excuse himself and say, "I cannot serve Hashem here because of all the thickness and materialism that attacks me always," for even there you can find Him and cling to Him and do complete teshuva (repentance), "For it is not far from you" (Devarim 30), only that in this place there are many garments." [Likutay Moharan 33]

20. This is the Tikun Haklali, the general rectification. Whoever destroys his sexual impulse, it will be easy for him to get rid of his other evil desires. For all other impulses stem from this one. [Likutay Moharan 36]

21. Whoever breaks free from the lust for food can become a miracle worker. But someone who is stuck in this desire it is a sign that he is a liar. Even a Tzaddik who already freed himself from all desires and then falls back into the desire for food, it must be that something false left his mouth. It also shows that there is *judgment* upon him from above, and it is a sign of poverty. [Likutay Moharan 47]

22. If you believe that you can damage, then believe that you can rectify! [Likutay Moharan vol. 2, 112]

23. It is a great good deed (mitzva) to be happy always. [Likutay Moharan vol. 2, 24]

24. Sadness is very very damaging. Sadness is from the "other side" (i.e. realm of evil). [Likutay Moharan vol. 2, 48]

25. Man has to pass through in this world on a very very narrow bridge, and the principle and main thing is not fear whatsoever. [Likutay Moharan vol. 2, 48]

26. When one enters the devotion of G-d, he must be obstinate and hold himself up no matter how he much he's thrown down. [Likutay Moharan vol. 2, 48]

27. When a person is right at the door, the very threshold of entering real holiness, the "other side" (i.e. evil) goes all out with terrible intensity to overpower him, confusing and confounding him. Know this well to be strong and do whatever it takes to break through. [Likutay Moharan vol. 2, 48]

28. Know that every movement and extraction that you remove and move every time, even the slightest amount, from the physicality to the devotion of the Blessed One, all of these gather and join and bind and come to your aid in time of need. [Likutay Moharan vol. 2, 48]

29. One should go with the practice of seeking and searching and finding in one's self any merit, any good point, and with the small good that one finds in himself, one should be happy and strengthen himself, and not leave his place even if he fell to what he fell G-d forbid, even still he should strengthen himself in the tiny miniscule good that he still finds in himself, until he will merit to return through this to the Blessed G-d, and all his sins will be turned into merits. [Likutay Moharan vol. 2, 48]

30. When a person enters into service of Hashem and sees it is so hard for Him, and it seems as if they are distancing him from above and not allowing him at all to enter, he should know that all this feeling of being "distanced" is truthfully only his being "drawn near". He must remain very very strong not to be discouraged even if many years of hard work go by and he still feels that he is very far and that he didn't even begin to enter into the gates of holiness, for he sees that he is full of materialism, evil thoughts and the like, and every time he tries to do something holy it is so hard for him and all his crying and pleading with G-d seems to be going to waste... On all this he needs great courage not to pay attention to these delusions at all. Because all this "distancing", in truth, is only his "drawing near", and all the great tzaddikim had to go through this kind of experience before they reached their level. [Likutay Moharan vol. 2, 48]

31. You need to have great stubbornness in the service of Hashem. [Likutay Moharan vol. 2, 48]

32. You need to greatly encourage yourself in His service as much as you can, even if you are the way you are, you should rely on His abundantly great mercy which is beyond limit, for certainly He will not forsake you, no matter how badly you've acted. The past doesn't exist. The main thing is that from now on you honestly resolve not to do it again. [Likutay Moharan vol. 2, 49]

33. The main thing is to be happy always, and one should make himself happy however possible, usually this is only attainable though foolish things, to act as if he is crazy and do silly funny things or to jump around and dance, in order to come to happiness which is a very great thing. [Life of Rabbi Nachman 593; Likutay Moharan 24, 48]

34. When a person falls from his level he should know that it's Heaven-sent, because going down is needed in order to go up, therefore he fell, in order that he arouses himself more to come close to Hashem. Whenever a person rises from one level to the next, it necessitates that he first has a descent before the ascent. Because the purpose of any descent is always in order to ascend. [Likutay Moharan 261]

35. There is a lot to talk about here (in the above topic). Because each person who fell to the place where he fell thinks that these words weren't spoken for him, for he imagines that these ideas are only for great people who are always climbing from one level to the next. But truthfully, you should know and believe, that all these words were also said concerning the smallest of the small and the worst of the worst, for Hashem is forever good to all. [Likutay Aitzoas, hischazkus-encouragement 5, based on Likutay Moharan 22:11]

36. It is a great thing for a person to still have an evil inclination because then he is able to serve Hashem with

the evil inclination itself. That is, to take all of the fire in his heart and channel it towards service of Hashem. For example, to pray with fiery passion of the heart, etc. For, if there is no evil inclination in a person, his service cannot be complete. [Likutay Moharan vol. 2, 49]

37. It is good to set aside a specific time everyday to be heartbroken and to speak out all ones problems before G-d (especially at midnight – 6 hours after nightfall), but the rest of the day be only happy. [Likutay Moharan vol. 2, 34]

38. The essential joy comes from good deeds. [Likutay Moharan 30:5]

39. Hisbodidus (personal private prayer and conversation with G-d) is a virtue of great height and magnitude more than everything. I.e to set a time, at least an hour (sometimes in Hebrew "an hour" can refer to a small slot of time) or more, to be alone in seclusion in a room or field, and express himself to his Creator, with argumentation and justification, with words of favor, good will, and appeasement. To ask and plead before the Blessed G-d, that He should draw him to His devotion in truth. This prayer and conversation should be in one's vernacular. [Likutay Moharan vol. 2, 25, The holy book of Outpouring of the Soul is dedicated to this subject]

40. A person needs to scream to his Father In Heaven with a powerful voice from the depths of his heart. Then G-d will listen to his voice and turn to his outcry. And it could be that from this act itself, all doubts and obstacles that are keeping him back from true service of Hashem will fall from him and be completely nullified. [Likutay Moharan vol. 2, 46]

41. Know that it's not enough to have yearnings [for G-d] in the heart alone, for a person needs to bring all his yearnings out into words. [Likutay Moharan 31]

42. When a person has a yearning for something and he brings it out into words, a soul is created. This soul flies in the air and reaches another person thereby awakening in him too a yearning. [Likutay Moharan 31]

43. Behold! Precious is the sigh (called '*krechtz*') from a Jewish person. [Likutay Moharan 8]

44. When one prays with all his energy as in "my entire essence speaks..." (Tehilim 35), the energy (*coa'ach*) that he inserts into the words are the 28 (*coa'ach*) letters which the world was created with. The 10 sayings of creation receive their energy from these 28 letters. The words that come out of this person's mouth are then actually the words of Hashem, as in the verse "I will place my words in your mouth" (Isaiah 51). [Likutay Moharan 48]

45. Prayer depends on the heart. A person should put all of his heart into it, so that it shouldn't be in the aspect of "With their lips they honor me but their hearts are far from me (Isaiah 29)." [Likutay Moharan 49]

46. Someone who wants to merit to do *teshuva* (repentance) should make it a practice to say Tihillim (Psalms). [Likutay Moharan vol. 2 73]

47. A person should find himself within the words of Psalms. Tihillim (Psalms) was written with Divine Inspiration and includes within it each individual's personal struggle, whatever he may be going through at any given time. [Likutay Moharan vol. 2, 125; Outpouring of the Soul 1]

48. Rabbi Nachman revealed that saying the following ten chapters of Psalms together serves as a Tikun Klali – a general rectification: 16, 32, 41, 42, 59, 77, 90, 105, 137, 150. [Likutay Moharan vol. 1, 205; vol. 2, 92; Sefer Hameedoas, Nocturnal Emission 5, Words of Rabbi Nachman 141; Life of Rabbi Nachman 59, 162, 184, 225. "General Rectification" - Likutay Moharan 29]. Many Jews say these every day.

49. "Even when people are serving idolatry, nevertheless, deep down, they are all submissive to G-d and serving Him, only it is taking place in a greatly concealed realm." [Likutay Moharan 56]

50. Immersion in a *mikvah* redeems a person from all hardships, and purifies from all impurities and from all sins, for the *mikvah* draws down extremely lofty awareness and supernal kindness and compassion. [Likutay Moharan 56]

51. Philosophies and intellectual wisdoms are not needed at all. Only pure and simple faith. Sophistication can greatly damage a person. Devotion to G-d is not even with real wisdom, only with pure and simple faith! It is even necessary in the devotion to G-d, to act and do things that appear foolish or silly, as it says in Proverbs (5) "in his love he constantly errs foolishly", even to roll in all types of mud and mire for the service of G-d and His blessed commandments, even just for a nuance of fulfillment of the Divine Will, to bring our Father in Heaven nachas (enjoyment). Through this one merits to understand the most hidden ways of G-d – even why bad things are brought upon the righteous and the wicked enjoy privileges. One is granted to unrestricted access to G-d's treasure houses. [Likutay Moharan vol. 2, 78; also see the Legendary Tale of the Sophisticate and the Simpleton]

52. The greatest wisdom of all wisdoms is not to be wise at all, rather to be pure and honest with simplicity. [Likutay Moharan vol. 2, 44]

53. A person shouldn't take upon himself added stringencies, as our Rabbis taught 'The Torah was not given to angels.' Stringencies can make one fall from the service of Hashem. Rabbi Nachman testified on himself that he himself had no stringencies, not even regarding Passover (where the Code of Law recommends stringencies). [Likutay Moharan vol. 2, 44]

54. It is incumbent upon every single Jew to study Halacha (Jewish law) every day without allowing a single day to pass without it. Even if he is held back for he didn't have time, he should study at least one section of "Shulchan Aruch" no matter which one, even if it is not in the place he is holding during his usual order of studies. For a Jew must learn at least some law in Shulchan Aruch every single day, all the days of his life. If he is not held back due to extraneous circumstances, he should have a set study in Shulchan Aruch each and every day, in order, from the beginning to the end. When he finishes he should go back and do it again. In this way he should accustom himself his entire life. For it is a very very great fixing of the soul. [Words of Rabbi Nachman 29]

55. When there are harsh judgments on the Jewish people G-d forbid, through dancing and clapping ones hands, the judgments are sweetened. [Likutay Moharan 10]

56. When one sings the words of prayer and the song resonates with great clarity and purity, he dresses the Shechina (Divine Presence) with luminous clothing in the colors of the rainbow. This appeases the Divine wrath. [Likutay Moharan 42]

57. When we clap our hands during prayer it awakens the 28 letters that the world was created with, which parallel the 28 joints in the hands. The air that is expelled, dispels and banishes the impure atmosphere of the lands of the nations, and the air that is drawn in, welcomes and ushers in the pure atmosphere of the Land of Israel. [Likutay Moharan 44]

58. It is a great thing to hear music from a holy person playing on an instrument for the sake of Heaven. Because through this, false fantasies are dismissed, the spirit of depression is dispelled, and the person merits happiness. Through this the memory is preserved, that is, the memory of the World to Come, and a person is able to understand the hints that Hashem is constantly hinting to him everyday. Furthermore, through this a person can reach the level of the spirit of prophecy and divine inspiration, and he will be able to pour out his heart like water before Hashem. [Likutay Moharan 54]

59. The Blessed Holy One constantly constricts His G-dliness from utmost infinity to the most finite center point of this physical world, and He sends to each person; thought, speech, and deed, according to the person and according to the time and place. He enclothes within the thought; speech and deed, hints, in order to bring the person close to His service. Therefore a person needs to delve his mind into this and expand his consciousness in order to understand what the hints are in their details which Hashem is sending to him in the thoughts, words, and deeds of this day according to the specific circumstances he finds himself in. In business or work, and in everything that

Hashem sends to him each day, he needs to delve and expand his mind in it, in order to understand the hints of Hashem. [Likutay Moharan 54]

60. When a Jew turns to G-d to speak to Him in a personal fashion, G-d so to speak drops everything to give this Jew His complete attention. Thus if G-d forbid there was a bad decree being enacted, it will be postponed or abolished. [Words of Rabbi Nachman 70, Adir Bamurom 242-3]

61. You need to know that just as evil arrogance is a very bad character trait, so too a person needs to have holy arrogance. Because it is impossible to come to the true tzaddikim or to draw near to holiness without arrogance, as our rabbis taught, "Be bold as a leopard." [Likutay Moharan 22:11]

62. A person needs holy arrogance, holy chutzpah. He should be bold as a leopard against the people who are preventing him and mocking him. He shouldn't subjugate himself before them, and he shouldn't be embarrassed in front of them at all. Even though it seems that they are tzaddikim and they are better than him, and even if it is true that they are better than him, even so, since his intentions are for Heaven, and they want to confuse him, and block him from the path of life, he needs to strengthen himself with holy arrogance against them. And even against one's own Rabbi, a person needs this boldness, in order to be strong to say whatever he needs to and not be embarrassed. On this it is said, "a timid person cannot be a learned person." [Likutay Moharan 271]

63. Anyone who wants to enter into the service of Hashem, the only way possible is to be like Avraham who considered himself to be the only one in the world. That is, he should

not pay attention to anyone who is preventing him from coming close to Hashem, whether it be his father, mother, in-laws, wife, children, etc. or anyone else in the world who mocks him and tries to prevent him from serving Hashem. He should not pay attention to them at all, rather he should follow the verse "Avraham was one" (Yichezkel 32) As if he is the only one in the world. [Likutay Moharan vol. 2, an insert after the introduction]

The Tzadik (Saint)

64. Rebbe Nachman would often tell his students about the great level that he reached in order to get them jealous and inspire them to serve Hashem like he did. One time someone responded to him, "Who can possibly reach the level of the Tzaddkim like yourself, certainly you were all created with really great souls." Rebbe Nachman answered him in a stringent manner; "This is the main problem with you all, that you think the greatness of the Tzaddikim are due to their high level of soul, that is not true, every single person can reach my level and be exactly like me. It all depends on effort and honest work." [Words of Rabbi Nachman 165]

65. The world says that a person doesn't need to seek greatness. I say that you must certainly seek greatness. Investigate and seek out only the greatest Tzaddik. [Words of Rabbi Nachman 51]

66. Conceptions of G-dliness are only possible to grasp through many constrictions. Therefore a person should search very much for a proper teacher who is able to explain   things   and   make   these   lofty   concepts

understandable, for this, a person needs a tremendously great teacher who is able to explain such lofty concepts on a simple level enabling small-minded people to understand. The smaller a person is and the further away from Hashem he is, the greater teacher he must find, just as the sicker a person is the greater the doctor he needs. Much prayer is needed to find a teacher like this, but one must never lose resolve and settle for mediocrity. [Likutay Moharan 30]

67. A Rav must have in him the two powers that there are in the Torah, that is, "a drug of life and a drug of death" (Yoma 72), in order that it will be possible for those who come close to him to receive according to their own will, as in the Torah "the righteous will walk and the wicked will stumble" (Hosea 14). If he yearns for true service of Hashem he can receive from the Rav a straight path to serve Hashem, but if his heart isn't pure, he can also find in the Rav something impure and be led completely astray. There are those who connect to the Tzaddik and become complete apostates. [Likutay Moharan 31]

68. Every Tzaddik needs to be both; well versed in Torah and full of good deeds, for if he is not learned, our sages say, "an unlearned person cannot be a chassid." But a person only learned, isn't anything, for it is possible to be a very educated and studious person and remain completely wicked, for "If he is not worthy it will be a drug of death" (Talmud Yooma 42b). Torah without good deeds is not only insignificant - it is detrimental. [Likutay Moharan 31]

69. Since the evil forces see that the Jewish people are very very close to the end (to the messiah), and there are Jews nowadays who have tremendous yearning and passion for spirituality and G-dliness, such a thing that has never occurred in past generations, so the evil forces insert arguments between the tzaddikim, and they establish in the world many false leaders, and even between true tzaddikim the evil forces cause great arguments, until no one knows where truth can be found. Therefore, a person needs to plead very much from Hashem to merit to recognize and come close to the true Tzaddik. [Likutay Moharan vol. 2, 44]

:Rabbi Nachman said of himself

70. "A *chidoosh* (novelty) like me never existed in the world." [Life of Rabbi Nachman 247]

71. "I am a river that purifies all stains." [Life of Rabbi Nachman 332]

72. "I am a beautiful and wondrous tree with great awesome branches, but below I am set firmly in the ground." [Life of Rabbi Nachman 245]

73. "How could they not oppose me, for I walk a new path, one that no man has ever walked before, nor any creature since the time the Torah was received. Even though it is a very old path, nevertheless it is completely new." [Life of Rabbi Nachman 392]

74. "There are those who are against me yet they don't even know me at all. This is as it says in the Zohar, when the Torah states that Pharaoh said to the Egyptians, "Let's outsmart the Jews." Could it be that he went to each and every citizen to personally relate this message? Rather he inserted it into their hearts." [Life of Rabbi Nachman 394]

75. "You should constantly review my teachings until you know them by heart." [Life of Rabbi Nachman 346]

76. "All my teachings are introductions." [Words of Rabbi Nachman 200] "My teachings are completely ideational aspects." [Life of Rabbi Nachman 350]

77. "My fire will burn until the coming of the Messiah." [Life of Rabbi Nachman 46, 229, 306; The Petek]

78. "The whole world needs me. You (my students) already know how much you need me, however, even all the Tzaddikim need me, for they too need to be benefited. All the nations of the world need me as well." [Life of Rabbi Nachman 250]

79. Rebbe Nachman said that all of his teachings and sayings are not only for us. Rather, "for those who are here standing with us today and for those who are not here with us today" (Devarim 29:14). In other words, it is for the generations that are yet to come. He spoke to us about this many times and he hinted to us in his words to make it known to the future generations... One time when he told us about passing on everything that happened with us and everything we heard from him to our children, he said this verse with great passion like fiery coals, "You should make known to your children and your childrens' children." And he said, "Know and believe, if its possible to take one person out of the garbage dump, anyone who holds on to

that person will come out as well." [Words of Rabbi Nachman 209; Life of Rabbi Nachman 225]

Coming to the holy Tomb of Rabbi Nachman – especially for Rosh Hashana – the Jewish New Years:

80. Our Rabbi of blessed memory already assured us during his lifetime, and designated two kosher witnesses on this, that when he passes away, when [people] come to his grave and give a penny to charity (*) and say these ten Tehilim/Psalms that we have recorded for remedy for nocturnal emission, Heaven spare us, then our Rabbi himself will span the length and width [of the universe], and will surely save this person. And he said, that he will pull him out of Ge'hinom/hell by his peyos/sidelocks, even regardless of how that person be, and even regardless of what happened, only from now on he must accept on himself to not return to his wicked ways Heaven forbid. And the night before he passed away, he said: "What do you have to worry about, since I go before you; and if the souls who did not know me at all, look forward to my tikunim/remedies, all the more so [should] you" etc. (And likewise even those who were not privileged to know our Rabbi of blessed memory during his lifetime, when they come to his holy grave and rely on him and learn his holy books and accustom themselves to walk in his holy ways that are mentioned in his holy books, surely they have on what to rely. Fortunate are they! Fortunate is their portion! "And none of them that take refuge in Him shall be desolate" [Ps. 34:23], for he already revealed his mind in several terms, explicitly and by hint, that all that he is involved in with us is not only for us, but with "those who are here...and with those who are not here" [Deut. 29:14], as explained further below (see Sichos Haran 209).) (*) Printer's comment [Rabbi Natan]: I heard from Rabbi Naftali z"l, who was one of the two witnesses who Rabbeinu z"l designated on this matter, i.e. Morainu Harav Aharon z"l and Harav Rabbi Naftali as mentioned, that Rabeinu z"l said it then in these words: "When they come to my grave and give a penny to charity for my sake (he means, for remembrance of his holy soul, as commonly practiced), ..." and in Yiddish. "in vet gebin apruta tzedaka fun maynit wegin etc"/and will give a penny of charity for me." [Life of Rabbi Nachman 225]

81. Rabbi Nachman said: "My Rosh Hashana is more important than everything. So its wondrous to me, why my followers who do believe in me, so why don't they warn all those that are drawn to me, that they should all be by me for Rosh Hashana, no one is exempt. For my entire matter is just Rosh Hashana. And he (Rabbi Nachman) warned that an announcement should be broadcasted that whom so ever that is inclined to his directives and is close to him, should be by him for Rosh Hashana, no one should be missing. And whomever merits to be by him for Rosh Hashana is befitting to be very very happy. [Life of Rabbi Nachman 403]

82. Eat or don't eat, sleep or don't sleep, pray or don't pray; just make sure to be by me for Rosh Hashana! [Life of Rabbi Nachman 404]

83. My Rosh Hashana is a great novelty. The Blessed G-d knows that this matter isn't an inheritance from my fathers, just the Blessed G-d gave me this as a present, that I know what Rosh Hashana is. Not only all of you are completely contingent on my Rosh Hashana, even the whole entire world is contingent on my Rosh Hashana. [Life of Rabbi Nachman 405]

84. What can I tell you, there is nothing greater than this [to be by Rabbi Nachman's tomb for Rosh Hashana], and if other tzadikim didn't say this, so that's another question (i.e. people have had all types of questions and problems with Rabbi Nachman, so just mark this up as another...). [Life of Rabbi Nachman 126, 220, 406]

Na Nach Nachma Nachman MeUman

Rabbi Nachman of Breslov

By means of great mercy G-d created the most divine and the utter sublime. G-d shines His light into the souls of Israel and in the reflection of His light we experience and understand Him in every way conceivable [this is the greatest gift, for anything else is secondary]. G-d does this with infinite wisdom granting free choice to the recipients of His goodness to determine that it is in fact G-d's light they are experiencing that is sustaining them. Based on the position of your soul you testify and acclaim G d.

There is a Master of all the souls, this is the Tzadik (righteous one), the Ambassador of G-d (so to speak). Thus our relationship with G-d and our every experience is completely pivoted on the Tzadik. The Tzadik is responsible for building the Kingdom of G-d in the light of G-d as it reflects from all the souls of Israel. The Tzadik guides and uplifts all creation. An individual soul or group of souls can not pay tribute to G-d without acknowledging His Tzadik. We must follow the ways of the Tzadik. When we pay homage to the Tzadik we honor G-d. That is the way G-d chose to create the world for our benefit.

Rabbi Nachman of Breslov lived approximately 245 years ago. Rabbi Nachman was born in the house of his great grandfather the Baal Shem Tov (father of Chasidism). Aside from the purity and holiness of his soul which enabled him to have special perception of the divine, his genius allowed him to learn a book by just perusing it in a few moments. Despite these gifts, Rabbi Nachman did not choose to spend his time and energy in kabalistic meditation or the pursuit of wisdom, rather he desired to seek G-d in the most simple and meaningful fashion. He was particularly fired by stories of devotion of the early Chasidim. At a very young age Rabbi Nachman purged his body of all desire, subjugating it to the holy desires of his soul. He delighted in doing abundant common mitzvot. Most important, Rabbi Nachman mastered the prime service of G-d, prayer, especially *hisbodidus* ['to be alone with G-d', that is to speak to G-d personally, in your own words, knowing that He is paying great attention]. Rabbi Nachman teaches that everything that there is to achieve can be achieved through prayer (more over anything that was achieved without prayer, is lacking). Many Rabbis had previously taught the importance of prayer, Rabbi Nachman established and instilled the ways of prayer in the world. Just as we have now 4 established prayers (shacharis, mincha, mariv, tikun chatzos) when Messiah comes everyone will be praying a 5th prayer, in his own words, known as *hisbodidus*, as established by Rabbi Nachman. Fortunate are those who begin this practice now.

As a result of his great self sacrifice and devotion to G-d, Rabbi Nachman became the Master of all the souls of Israel. Rabbi Nachman saw every soul, from Adam till the coming of the Messiah, and every rectification necessary for every soul, and he addresses each and everyone, without exception, in the holy books which he authored.

Anyone who desires to have mercy on himself should study and practice Rabbi Nachman's teachings. The rectification of the world and the final redemption are completely reliant on this.

In 1922, a Breslover Hasid, Rabbi Yisroel Dov Odesser o.b.m., known as the Saba, received a Petek (note) from Rabbi Nachman:

"Very hard it was for me to descend to you\ my precious student to tell you that I enjoyed\ greatly your service and upon you I said\ my fire will burn until the\ mashiach will come be strong and courageous\ in your service\ **Na NaCh NaChMu NaChMuN MEyUMaN**\ and with this I shall reveal to you a secret and it is\ full and heaped up from end to end (PTzPTzYH)\ and with strengthening of service you will understand it and a sign\ the 17th of Tamuz they will say that you are not fasting."

Rabbi Nachman signed his name in this unique fashion [1,2,3,4]! The Petek says that the continuation of Rabbi Nachman is through Saba Yisroel. Saba Yisroel's name is not mentioned, because the Petek is for everyone to consider personal.

60 years later, the Saba began to publicize the Petek. Saba said: 'If I were to reveal just two words about the Petek, I would annul the free will of the whole world.', 'This is a novelty and wonder, the likes of which have never before been seen in this world. The song Na Nach Nachmu Nachmun MayUman fixes everything and heals everything!', 'This is only from Rabainu, only a miracle. A signature such as this, no Tzadik ever signed a signature like this: the "simple, doubled, tripled, quadrupled." And Rabainu in his lifetime also never signed this way. Only in this Petek — we didn't know — this is found in Likutay Moharan, that the holy Rabainu

317

talks about this Song. He is this Song. But here, he reveals to all the world Na Nach Nachmu Nachmun MayUman. What is now in the world, was never known, we know nothing.' Saba inspired R' Moshe Feinstein zt"l with the Petek, and received from R' Moshe a uniqe letter of approbation and recommendation.

Saba said: 'Na Nach Nachmu Nachmun MayUman is a segula (object, action, or saying with saving and enhancing powers) for every problem and situation.' 'This song is the matter of the redemption.' 'Na Nach Nachmu Nachmun MayUman lifts man from absolute descent to absolute ascent.', 'Just to say this name Na Nach Nachmu Nachmun MayUman, sweetens all the sufferings and all the judgments, all the sins and all the blasphemy – everything! It transforms everything, happy is the one who believes.', 'We have no conception what it is, that we merited, in these generations, to know from this, from a secret like this Na Nach Nachmu Nachmun MayUman. There is a great deal to speak about, but I can not speak!'

What is Na Nach Nachmu Nachman Me-Uman?

'Na Nach Nachmu Nachman Me-Uman' is the name of our holy leader Rabbi Nachman of Breslov. (1772-1811) Through a note he sent (In 1922) in a miraculous manner to Rabbi Israel Dov Odesser (called 'Saba' or 'Saba Israel'), Rabbi Nachman revealed that his name (meaning his soul and teachings) is the Song that is Single (Na - נ), Doubled (NaCh - נח), Tripled (NaChMu - נחמ), and Quadrupled (NaChMaN - נחמן).

Great tzadikim (holy sages) preceding Rabbi Nachman's time spoke of the Song that will be revealed in the future, among them Rabbi Yonason ben Uziel (in his translation of Shir Hashirim – the Song of Songs, in the first verse) and Rabbi Shimon bar Yochai (Master of the Zohar and Tikunay Zohar). These tzadikim explained that before the coming of the Messiah, there will be revealed a song that is Single, Doubled, Tripled, and Quadrupled, and that through this Song the true faith and belief in G-d will be restored in the world as G-d will renew the world in His wondrous ways. All of this will occur before the coming of the Messiah. The Messiah himself will sing this song and redeem the Jewish People and bring the Knowledge of G-d, peace, and compassion to the whole world.

Rabbi Nachman of Breslov taught (Likutay Moharan 64) that every Wisdom and Intellect has it's own specific tune and melody. It is from the melody that the wisdom is produced and extended (as can be discerned in Psalms (47) 'sing enlighten'). Even the wisdom of heresy has it's own specific tune and melody unique to the wisdom of heresy.

[This is what our Sages of the Talmud (Chagiga 15) attributed the deviation of 'Achair' (Elisha, the teacher of Rabbi Meir) stating that it was caused because of Greek melody that was always with him, and that when he would rise from the Torah study hall, books of heresy would fall from his lap, because these two things are dependent on one another. The Greek melody that was always on his mouth was the cause for his having the books of heresy that would fall from his lap, for this particular melody was specific to the heresy that he had.]

Also according to the ascending level of the wisdom so too the tune and melody will be of higher distinction. This is true on every level higher and higher even up to the beginning point of all of creation which is called "the start of Emanation", there is nothing higher than it, nothing that exceeds the wisdom that is there, except the "Light of the No Limit" the wisdom on this level is unfathomable to humans, and so on this exalted level, all wisdoms are a matter of faith.

Faith also has a tune and melody specific to faith. Just as we see that even the mistaken faiths of the Worshipers of the Stars and Constellations, each of their faiths has their own song that they sing and conduct in their houses of prayer. As it is with false faith so it is in holiness, every faith has a tune and melody. This unique melody of the above mentioned faith, which is the faith above all wisdoms and faiths in the world, the faith in the Light of the "No Limit" Himself which encompasses all the worlds, this melody is also higher than all the tunes and melodies of the world which are particular to all wisdom and faith. All the tunes and melodies of all the wisdoms come forth from this melody and tune which is higher than all the tunes and melodies of all the wisdoms, for it is the melody associated to the faith in the "Light of No Limit" Himself, which is higher than everything.

In the future when all the nations will recognize The Name (G-d) (as it says in Tsifanya 3) and everyone will believe in the Blessed G-d, there will be a fulfillment of the verse (Shir Hashirim – Song of Songs) 'come sing from the height of faith', specifically from the 'height of faith', the aspect of the highest faith mentioned above, which is the head (Root or source) of all faith as previously explained. This is why the verse says 'sing' specifically, it is the tune and the melody associated with this height of faith mentioned above.

The aspect of melody of this exalted faith, no one merits except the Tzadik (holy sage) of the generation, who is an aspect of Moshe (Moses), who is on the level of this faith.

With this song of the Tzadik, all the souls that fell into heresy of the Vacated Space (where G-d is hidden) are freed. For his song is an aspect of the 'height of faith' that is the faith which is higher than everything, this song and faith nullifies all the heresy, and all the tunes are included and nullified within this tune, which is above everything, and from which come forth all the tunes, as previously mentioned.

Na Nach Nachmu Nachman Me-Uman is this holy melody that can lift us from our dreary existence to the height of faith and belief in G-d!

More quotes from Rabbi Israel (-Saba) about Na Nach Nachmu Nachman MayUman

Simply by reciting the name of our leader Rabbi Nachman, just as it signed in the signature on this Petek (note) – Na Nach Nachmu Nachman MeUman - this eases all the troubles and sweetens all the harsh judgments, all the sins and all the falls and all of the heresy of the world. This is enough to destroy the Other Side (the Evil Inclination), to dispel all the darkness, everything, it transforms everything. This is a new power like nothing that was ever before in the world.

Na Nach Nachmu Nachman MeUman, this has the power, this opens up all the gates of mercy, all the gates of prayer, all the gates of repentance, all of the Tora.

Na Nach Nachmu Nachman MeUman – this is the main point. This contains all of the Redemption, and all of the salvations are included in this name, for the central point of everything is dependent on Rabbi Nachman.

This is effective for everyone, on both the general and individual levels. Every person should pray and say verbally: "May the merit of Rabbi Nachman protect us and all the Jewish People, the merit of Na Nach Nachmu Nachman MeUman".Our holy leader Rabbi Nachman, this matter is an entirely new secret, yes. Rabbi Nachman revealed that his name is a Song that is Single, Doubled, Tripled, and Quadrupled – Na Nach Nachmu Nachman MeUman.

If one is suffering or there is some sin – immediately say Na Nach Nachmu Nachman MeUman, this already transforms everything. This renews – everything, transforms – to good. Nachman MeUman – this transforms everything.

Na Nach Nachma Nachman

MeUman

Teekoon Haklallee

transliteration

The Comprehensive ("General") Rectification
from Rabbi Nachman of Breslov

Na

NaCh

NaChMa

NaChMaN

Me'Uman

The Teekoon Haklallee is composed of ten chapters from the Psalms, each one representing one of the ten types of melodies which comprise the Psalms. Optimally one should have in mind, throughout the recital, that these melodies of Ti'hilim (-Praises of Psalms) liberate the drops of seed which are under captivity of Lilith (-depressing wailing, antithesis of Ti'heela of Psalms, under the numerical value of 485), with the Divine Kindness and Might invested in the Names, Ai"l (kindness) Elohi"m (might), spelled out (=485:) מם – יוד – הי – למד – אלף, למד – אלף. The root of these melodies are inherent in the ten letters (1,2,3,4 =10) of the name of the tzaddik: Na NaCh NaChMa NaChMaN Me'Uman (=485 & 6 inclusives) – נ נח נחם נחמן מאומן.

Before reciting the Psalms there is a short assertion whereby one binds oneself to Rabbi Nachman for their recital, which can be said in the English presented here.

It is propitious to give charity (or at least set aside), even one penny, for the merit of Rabbi Nachman, before reciting the Tikun.

Transliterator's note: The method used here is not the sophisticated conventional way, rather it is extremely simple and straightforward. There are basically only three rules to keep in mind.

3 rules to reading the phonetics:
1. ch=kh
2. ALL vowels are soft (like: bed, sit, luck. including eh, also at the end of the word) unless they are doubled, like ai, ay, ee, ey, oo, oa, ue, uy
2b. The soft a, is closer to the "a" in "was" and not like in the name "Al."
3. aye=eye

Teekoon Haklalee

Comprehensive "General Rectification"

Hereby, I bind myself, in the recital of these ten chapters of Psalms to all the true tzaddikim of our generation, and to all the true tzaddikim who dwell in the earth, the holy ones whom are in the earth, and specifically to our holy master, the tzaddik foundation of the world, the gushing stream source of wisdom (Nachal Noavaya Mikor Chuchma: acronym Nachman), our Master Na Nach Nachmu Nachmun Me-Oomon may his merit protect us and all of Israel, amen.

16 (Bracha)

1. Michtum liDuveed shumrainee Ail key chusseessee buch.
2. Umart lAdoanuy Adoanuy uttu toavussee bal ullechu.
3. Likidoashim ashehr bu-uretz haimu vi-adeeray kul cheftzee vum.
4. Yeerboo atzvoasum achair mu-huroo bal aseech neeskai'hem meedum ooval essu es shimoasum al sifusuy.
5. Adoanuy mi-nus chelkee vichoasee attu toameech goarulee.
6. Chavuleem nufiloo lee bani-eemeem af nachalus shufiru ulluy.
7. Avuraich es Adoanuy ashehr yi-utzunee af lailoas yisiroonee cheelyoasuy.

8. Sheeveesee Adoanuy linnegdee summeed key meemeenee bal emoat.

9. Luchain summach leebee va-yuggel kivoadee af bisuree yishkoan luvetach.

10. Key low sa-azoav nafshee lishoal low seetain chaseedichu leeroas shuchas.

11. Toadee-ainee oarach cha-yim soava simuchoas es punechu ni-eemoas beemeenichu netzach.

32 (Ashray)

1. LiDuveed maskeel ashray nissoy pesha kissoy chatu-uh.

2. Ashray udum low yachshoav Adoanuy low uvoan vi-ain biroochoa rimeeyu.

3. Key heche'rashtee buloo atzumuy bishaagussee kul ha-yoam.

4. Key yoamum vullayelu teechbad ullaye yudechu nehpach lishaddee bicharvoanay ka-yitz sellu.

5. Chattussee oadee-achu vaavoanee low cheesseessee umartee oadeh allay fishu-aye Ladoanuy vi-attu nussussu avoan chattussee sellu.

6. Al zoas yeespalail kul chusseed ailechu li-ais mitzoa rak lishaitef ma-yeem rabeem ailuv low yaggee-oo.

7. Attu saisehr lee meetzar teetzirainee runnay falait tisoavivainee sellu.

8. Askeelichu vi-ohrichu bidderrech zoo sailaich ee-atzu ullechu ainee.

9. Al tee-hi-yoo ki-soos ki-fe-red ain huvveen bimmesseg vu-ressen edyoa leevloam bal ki-roav ailechu.

10. Rabbeem machoaveem lurushu vi-haboatai-ach bAdoanuy chessed yisoavivvenoo.

11. Seemchoo vAdoanuy vi-geeloo tzaddeekeem vi-harneenoo kul yeeshray laiv.

41 (Maskeel)

1. Lamnatzai-ach mizmohr liDuvveed.

2. Ashray maskeel el dul bi-yoam ru-uh yimallitaihoo Adoanuy.

3. Adoanuy yeeshmiraihoo veeycha-yaihoo vi-ooshar bu-uretz vi-al teetinnaihoo binneffesh oyivvuv.

4. Adoanuy yeesuddennoo all eres divvuy kul meeshkuvvoa huffachtu vichulyoa.

5. Annee umartee Adoanuy chunnainee riffu-uh nafshee key chuttussee luch.

6. Oyivaye yoamiroo ra lee mussaye yumoos vi-uvad shimoa.

7. Vi-eem bu leeroas shuv yidabair leeboa yeekbutz uven low yaitzai lachootz yidabair.

8. Yachad ullaye yislachashoo kul soanuy ullaye yachshivoo ru-uh lee.

9. Divar bileeya-al yutzook boa va-ashehr shuchav low yoaseef lukoom.

10. Gam eesh shiloamee ashehr butachtee voa oachail lachmee heegdeel ullaye ukaiv.

11. Vi-attu Adoanuy chunainee va'hakeemainee vaashallimu luhem.

12. Bizoas yudattee key chuffatztu bee key low yuree-a oyivee ulluy.

13. Vaannee bisoomee tumachtu bee vatatzeevainee lifunechu li-oalum.

14. Burooch Adoanuy Eloahay Yisru-el maihu-oalum vi-ad hu-oalum umain vi-umain.

42 (Sheer)

1. Lamnatzai-ach maskeel leevnay Koarach.

2. Ki-a-yul taaroag al afeekay muyeem kain nafshee saaroag aillechu Eloaheem.

3. Tzumi-uh nafshee lAiloaheem li-Ail chuy mussaye uvoa vi-airu-eh pinai Eloaheem.

4. Hu-yisu lee deemussee lechem yoamum vuluylu be-emohr aillaye kul ha-yoam a-yai Eloahechu.

5. Ailleh ezkirru vi-eshpichu ullaye nafshee key e-evohr basuch edadaim ad bais Eloaheem bikoal reenu visoadu humoan choagaig.

6. Ma teeshtoachachee nafshee va'tehemee ulluy hoacheelee lAiloaheem key oad oadennoo yishoo-oas punnuv.

7. Elloa'haye ullaye nafshee seeshtoachuch al kain ezkurchu mai-eretz yardain vichehrmoaneem mai'har meetzur.

8. Tihoam el tihoam koarai likoal tzeenoarechu kul meeshburechu vi'gallechu ullaye u'vuroo.

9. Yoamum yitzaveh Adoanuy chasdoa oovalaylu sheeroa eemee ti'feelu li-Ail chayuy.

10. Oamiru li-Ail, sa'lee lumu shichachtunee lumu koadair ailaich bilachatz oyaiv.

11. Biretzach bi-atzmoasaye chairifoonee tzoariruy bi-umrum aillaye kul ha-yoam a-yai Eloahechu.

12. Ma teeshtoachachee nafshee ooma te'hemee ulluy hoacheelee lailoaheem key oad oadenoo yishoo-oas punnaye vAiloahuy.

59 (Neetzoo-ach)

1. Lamnatzai-ach al tashchais liDuveed meechtum beeshloa-ach Shu-ool va-yeeshmiroo es haba-yees la'ha'meesoa.

2. Hatzeylainee mai-oyivaye Eloahuy meemeeskoamimaye ti'sagvainee.

3. Hatzeylainee meepoa-alay uven oomai-anshay dumeem hoasheyainee.

4. Key heenai urivoo linafshee yugooroo ullaye azeem low feeshee vilow chatusee Adoanuy.

5. Bilee uvoan yirootzoon vi-yeekoanunoo ooru leekrussee ooray.

6. Vi-attu Adoanuy Eloaheem Tzivu-oas Eloahay Yisru-ail hukeetzu leefkoad kul hagoyeem al tuchoan kul boagday uven sellu.

7. Yushoovoo lu-erev ye'hemoo cha'kullev veesoavivoo eer.

8. Heenay yabee-oon bifeehem charuvoas biseefsoasaihem key mee shoamai-a.

9. Vi-attu Adoanuy teeschak lumoa teelag lichul goyeem.

10. Oozoa ailechu eshmoaru key Eloaheem meesgabee.

11. Eloahay chasdee yikadimainee Eloaheem yarainee vishoariruy.

12. Al ta'hargaim pen yeeshkichoo amee haneyaimoa vichailichu vihoareedaimoa mugeenainoo Adoanuy.

13. Chatas peymoa divar sifusaymoa vi-yeeluchidoo veegoanum oomai-ullu oomeekachash yisapairoo.

14. Kalay vichaimu kalay vi-aynaimoa vi-yaidoo key Eloaheem moashail bi'Yaakoav li-afsay hu-uretz sellu.

15. Vi-yushoovoo lu-erev yehemoo chakulev veysoavivoo eer.

16. Haimu yinee-oon le-echoal eem low yeesbi-oo va-yuleenoo.

17. Va'annee usheer oozechu va'aranain laboakehr chasdechu key hu-yeessu meesguv lee oomunoas bi-yoam tzar lee.

18. Oozee aillechu azamairu key Eloaheem meesgabee Eloahay chasdee.

77 (Neeggoon)

1. Lamnatzai-ach al yidoosoon li-Ussuf meezmohr.

2. Koalee el Eloa'heem vi-etzuku koalee el Eloa'heem vi'haazeen ailluy.

3. Bi-yoam tzurusee Adoanuy durushtee yudee layelu neegiru vilow sufoog mai-anu heenuchaim nafshee.

4. Ezkiru Eloa'heem vi-ehemu-yu useechu vi'sees'ataif roochee sellu.

5. Uchaztu shimooroas ainuy neefamtee vilow adabair.

6. Cheeshavtee yumeem mee'kedem shinoas oalumeem.

7. Ezkiru nigeynusee baluylu eem livuvee useechu va-yichapais roochee.

8. Hali-oalumeem yeeznach Adoanuy viloa yoaseef leertzoas oad.

9. He-ufais lunetzach chasdoa gumar oamehr lidohr vudohr.

10. Hashuchach chanoas Ail eem kufatz bi-af rachamuv sellu.

11. Vu-oamar chaloasee hee shinoas yimeen elyoan.

12. Ezkohr ma-alilay Yu key ezkiru mee'kedem pee'lechu.

13. Vi'hu'geesee vichul pu-ulechu oovaaleeloasechu useechu.

14. Eloaheem ba'koadesh darkechu mee Ail gudoal kAiloaheem.

15. Attu hu-Ail oasay felle hoadaatu vu-ameem oozechu.

16. Gu-altu beezroa-a amechu binay yaakoav vi-yoasaif sellu.

17. Ru-oochu ma-yeem Eloaheem ru-oochu ma-yeem yucheeloo af yeergizoo sihoamoas.

18. Zohrmoo ma-yeem uvoas koal nussinoo shichukeem af chatzutzechu yees-haluchoo.

19. Koal ra-amchu bagalgal hai-eeroo virukeem taivail rugizu vateerash hu-uretz.

20. Ba-yum darkechu ooshveelichu bima-yeem rabeem vi-eekivoasechu low noadu-oo.

21. Nucheesu chatzoan amechu bi-yad Moashe Vi-aharoan.

90 (Tfeela)

1. Ti'feelu liMoashe eesh hu-Eloaheem, Adoanuy mu-oan attu hu-yeesu lunoo bidohr vudohr.

2. Bi'terem hureem yooludoo vatichoalail eretz visaivail oomai-oalum ad oalum attu ail.

3. Tushaiv enoash ad daku vatoamehr shoovoo vinay udum.

4. Key elef shuneem bi-ainechu ki-yoam esmoal key yaavor vi-ashmooru valuylu.

5. Ziramtum shainu yee'hi-yoo baboakehr ke'chutzeer yachaloaf.

6. Baboakehr yutzeetz vichuluf lu-erev yimoalail vi-yuvaish.

7. Key chuleenoo vi-apechu oovachamusichu neevhulnoo.

8. Shattu avoanoasaynoo linegdechu aloomainoo leemi-ohr punechu.

9. Key chul yumaynoo punoo vi-evrusechu keeleynoo shunaynoo chimoa hegge.

10. Yimay shinoasaynoo vu-hem sheeveem shunu vi-eem beegvooroas shimoaneem shunu viruhbum umul vu-uven key guz cheesh vanu-oofu.

11. Mee yoadai-a oaz apechu oochyeerusichu evrusechu.

12. Leemnoas yumainoo kain hoada vinuvee livav chuchmu.

13. Shoovu Adoanuy ad mussuy viheenuchaim al avudechu.

14. Sabainoo vaboakehr chasdechu ooniraninu vineesmichu bichul yumainoo.

15. Samichainoo keemoas eeneesunoo shinoas ru-eenoo ru-uh.

16. Yairu-eh el avudechu fu-ulechu vahadurichu al binaihem.

17. Veehee noa-am Adoanuy Eloahainoo ulainoo oomaasay yudainoo koaninu ulainoo oomaasay yudaynoo koaninaihoo.

105 (Hoadu-uh)

1. Hoadoo lAdoanuy keeroo veeshmoa hoadee-oo vu-ameem aleeloasuv.

2. Sheeroo low zamroo low seechoo bichul neefli-oasuv.

3. Hees-haliloo bishaim kudshoa yeesmach laiv mivakshay Adoanuy.

4. Deershoo Adoanuy vi-oozoa bakishoo funuv tumeed.

5. Zeechroo neefli-oasuv ashehr ussu moafsuv oomeeshpitay feev.

6. Zera Avruhum avdoa binay Yaakoav bicheeruv.

7. Hoo Adoanuy Eloahainoo bichul hu-uretz meeshputuv.

8. Zuchar li-oalum bireesoa duvur tzeevu li-elef dohr.

9. Ashehr kuras es Avruhum ooshvoo-usoa liYischuk.

10. Va-yameede'hu li'Yaakoav lichoak li'Yisru-ail birees oalum.

11. Laimohr lichu etain es Eretz Kinu-an chevel nachalaschem.

12. Beehi-yoasum misay meespur keemat vigureem bu.

13. Va-yees-halichoo meegoy el goy meemamluchu el am achair.

14. Low heenee-ach udum li-ushkum va-yoachach alaihem milucheem.

15. Al teegi-oo vee'misheechuy vi'leenivee-aye al turai-oo.

16. Va-yeekru ru-uv al hu-uretz kul matay lechem shuvur.

17. Shulach leefnai'hem eesh li-eved neemkar Yoasaif.

18. Eenoo vakevel ragloa barzel bu-uh nafshoa.

19. Ad ais boa divuroa eemras Adoanuy tzi'rufus-hoo.

20. Shulach melech va-yateerai'hoo moashail ameem va-yifatichaihoo.

21. Sumoa udoan livaisoa oomoashail bichul keenyunoa.

22. Lesohr suruv binafshoa oozkainuv yichakaim.

23. Va-yuvoa Yeesru-ail Meetzru-yeem viYaakoav gur bi-eretz Chum.

24. Va-yefehr es amoa mi-oad va-yaatzeemaihoo meetzuruv.

25. Hufach leebum leesnoa amoa liheesnakail baavuduv.

26. Shulach Moashe avdoa Aharoan ashehr buchar boa.

27. Sumoo vum deevray oasoasuv oomoafseem bi-eretz Chum.

28. Shulach choashech va-yachsheech viloa muroo es divuroa.

29. Hufach es maimaihem lidum va-yumes es digusum.

30. Shuratz artzum tzifardi-eem bichadray malchai'hem.

31. Umar va-yuvoa uroav keeneem bichul givoolum.

32. Nussan geeshmaihem burud aish le-huvoas bi-artzum.

33. Va-yach gafnum oosainusum va-yishabair aitz givoolum.

34. Umar va-yuvoa arbeh vi-yelek vi-ain mispur.

35. Va-yoachal kul aisev bi-artzum va-yoachal piree admusum.

36. Va-yach kul bichohr bi-artzum raishees lichul oanum.

37. Va-yoatzee-aim bikesef vizu-huv, vi-ain beeshvutuv koashail.

38. Sumach Meetzra-yeem bitzaisum, key nufal pachdum alai'hem.

39. Puras unun limusuch, vi-aish li-hu-eer luylu.

40. Shu-al va-yuvai siluv, vilechem shuma-yeem yasbee-aim.

41. Pusach tzoor va-yuzoovoo mu-yeem, hulichoo batzee-oas nuhur.

42. Key zuchar es divar kudshoa, es Avruhum avdoa.

43. Va-yoatzee amoa visusoan, bireenu es bicheeruv.

44. Va-yeetain lu-hem artzoas goy-eem, vaamal li-oomeem yeerushoo.

45. Baavoor yeeshmiroo chookuv visoaroasuv yeentzoaroo halliloo-Yu.

137 (Mizmor)

1. Al na'haroas Buvel shum yushavnoo gam bucheenoo, bizuchrainoo es Tzey-oan.
2. Al aruveem bisoachu, tuleenoo keenoaroasainoo.
3. Key shum shi-ailoonoo shoavainoo deevray sheer visoalulainoo seemchu, sheeroo lunoo meesheer Tzey-oan.
4. Aich nusheer es sheer Adoanuy, al admas naichur.
5. Eem eshkuchaich Yirooshulu-yeem teeshkach yimeenee.
6. Teedbak lishoanee licheekee eem low ezkiraichee eem low aaleh es Yirooshula-yeem, al roash seemchussee.
7. Zichohr Adoanuy leevnay Edoam ais yoam Yirooshulu-yeem hu-oamreem uroo uroo, ad ha-yisoad bu.
8. Bas Buvel hashidoodu ashray she-yishalem luch, es gimoolaich shegumalt lunoo.
9. Ashray she-yoachaiz vineepaitz es oalula-yeech el hasula.

150 (Haliloo-Ya)

1. Halliloo-Yu halliloo Ail bikudshoa, halliloohoo beerkey-a oozoa.
2. Halliloohoo veegvooroasuv, halliloohoo kiroav guedlow.
3. Halliloohoo bisaika shoafuhr, halliloohoo binaivel vicheenohr.
4. Halliloohoo bisoaf oomuchoal, halliloohoo bimeeneem vi-ooguv.
5. Halliloohoo vitzeeltzilay shuma, halliloohoo bitzeeltzilay siroo-uh.
6. Kohl hanishumu ti-halail Yuh, halliloo-Yuh.

Na Nach Nachma Nachman MeUman

The effectiveness of saying these 10 Psalms is to arouse the ten types of song which are included in the Song of the Future, the song that is single, double, triple, and quadruple, which unites with the name of G-d, and has now been revealed to be the holy name of the Rebbe, Head of the People of Israel: Na NaCh NaChMu NaChMuN Me'Uman. Therefore by pronouncing this name, and especially by singing it, as it is a wondrous song, one invokes colossal rectification for one's soul and effects the faithful and supernatural renewal of the entire world! Many people have experienced awesome miracles, for example sick people without any cure, they received healing and full recovery by saying this holy awesome name!

Na Nach Nachma Nachman MeUman!

Short Prayer

Many say this prayer every day after Tikun Haklalli

This prayer we found in our files, it is short and powerful

Master of the World, Effector of effectors, and the Causer of all the causes, You are above, higher than all, and there is nothing higher than You, for no thought can grasp You at all, and silence is befitting praise for You (Psalms 65:2), and [You] are loftier than all blessing and praise. You, I turn to, You, I beseech to bore a tunnel in a hidden (/established) way from You, by way of all the worlds until my evolution in the place where I stand, in accordance with what is apparent to You, Knower of the hidden, and in this way and path shine upon me Your light, to return me in truly complete repentance before You, as is Your true desire, as is the desire of the choice of creation: Na Nach Nachma Nachman MeUman, that I should not think in my thoughts any foreign thought or any thought or confusion which is against Your Will, just, to bind to pure, pristine and holy thoughts of Your service, in truth, in perception of You and Your Torah. "Incline my heart to Your testimony (Psalms 119:36)," and give me a pure heart to serve You truly. And from the depth of the ocean take me out to great light, extremely quickly and soon, the salvation of Hashem in the blink of the eye, to bask in the light of life all the days I am on the face of the earth. And I should merit to renew my youth, the days that transpired in darkness, to return them to holiness, and my departure from the world should be as my entry – without sin. And I should merit to see the pleasantness of Hashem and visit His chamber (which) entirely resonates glory: amen, netzach (eternally/victorious), selah, vu-ed (forever).

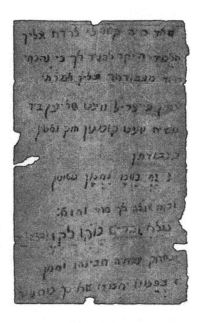

The holy *Petek* Saba Yisroel received from Rabbi Nachman
in 1922, signed Na Nach Nachma Nachman Me'Uman.

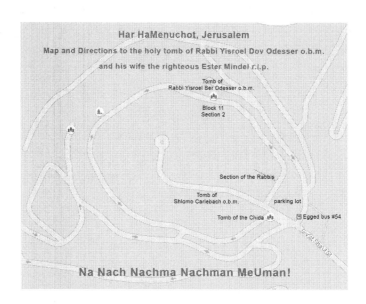

Na Nach Nachma Nachman MeUman! Na Nach Nachma
Nachman MeUman! Na Nach Nachma Nachman
MeUman! Na Nach Nachma Nachman MeUman! Na
Nach Nachma Nachman MeUman! Na Nach Nachma
Nachman MeUman! **Na Nach Nachma Nachman
MeUman!** Na Nach Nachma Nachman MeUman! Na Nach
Nachma Nachman MeUman! Na Nach Nachma
Nachman MeUman! Na Nach Nachma Nachman

MeUman! Na Nach Nachma Nachman MeUman! Na

Nach Nachma Nachman MeUman! Na Nach Nachma
Nachman MeUman! Na Nach Nachma Nachman
MeUman! Na Nach Nachma Nachman MeUman! Na
Nach Nachma Nachman MeUman!
Na Nach Nachma Nachman MeUman!
Na Nach Nachma Nachman MeUman! Na Nach
Nachma Nachman MeUman! Na Nach Nachma
Nachman MeUman! Na Nach Nachma Nachman MeUman!
Na Nach Nachma Nachman MeUman! Na Nach Nachma

Nachman MeUman! Na Nach Nachma Nachman
MeUman! Na Nach Nachma Nachman MeUman! **Na
Nach Nachma Nachman MeUman!** Na Nach Nachma
Nachman MeUman! Na Nach Nachma Nachman
MeUman! **Na Nach Nachma Nachman MeUman!** Na
Nach Nachma Nachman MeUman! Na Nach Nachma
Nachman MeUman! Na Nach Nachma Nachman MeUman!
Na Nach Nachma Nachman MeUman!

339

Na

NaCh

NaChMa

NaChMaN

MeUman

Made in the USA
Middletown, DE
20 August 2021